When the Heavyweight
Title Mattered

ALSO BY JOHN G. ROBERTSON

*Too Many Men on the Ice:
The 1978–1979 Boston Bruins
and the Most Famous Penalty
in Hockey History* (2018)

*The Babe Chases 60:
That Fabulous 1927 Season, Home Run
by Home Run* (1999; softcover 2014)

*Baseball's Greatest Controversies:
Rhubarbs, Hoaxes, Blown Calls, Ruthian Myths,
Managers' Miscues and Front-Office Flops*
(1995; softcover 2014)

BY JOHN G. ROBERTSON AND
ANDY SAUNDERS

*The Games That Changed Baseball:
Milestones in Major League History* (2016)

*A's Bad as It Gets: Connie Mack's
Pathetic Athletics of 1916* (2014)

ALL FROM MCFARLAND

When the Heavyweight Title Mattered

Five Championship Fights That Captivated the World, 1910–1971

JOHN G. ROBERTSON

McFarland & Company, Inc., Publishers
Jefferson, North Carolina

All photographs and illustrations are from the Library of Congress

Library of Congress Cataloguing-in-Publication Data

Names: Robertson, John G., 1964– author.
Title: When the heavyweight title mattered : five championship fights that captivated the world, 1910–1971 / John G. Robertson.
Description: Jefferson, North Carolina : McFarland & Company, Inc., Publishers, 2019 | Includes bibliographical references and index.
Identifiers: LCCN 2019018269 | ISBN 9781476678573 (paperback: acid free paper) ∞
Subjects: LCSH: Boxing matches—History—20th century. | Boxing—History—20th century. | Boxers (Sports)—Biography.
Classification: LCC GV1121 .R63 2019 | DDC 796.83—dc23
LC record available at https://lccn.loc.gov/2019018269

British Library Cataloguing Data are Available

ISBN (print) 978-1-4766-7857-3
ISBN (ebook) 978-1-4766-3731-0

© 2019 John G. Robertson. All rights reserved

No part of this book may be reproduced or transmitted in any form or by any means, electronic or mechanical, including photocopying or recording, or by any information storage and retrieval system, without permission in writing from the publisher.

Front cover: Publicity photographs of Jersey Joe Walcott (left) and Rocky Marciano

Printed in the United States of America

McFarland & Company, Inc., Publishers
  Box 611, Jefferson, North Carolina 28640

To all those talented sports reporters
from yesteryear who covered these
five championship bouts
with passion and panache.
Your work—which lives on forever—
was, and remains, a true joy to read.

Acknowledgments

Thanks go to the following people for their special assistance in this project.

- Carl Madden for his proofreading efforts of this book's first draft and the many excellent general suggestions he made. Perhaps this project made a boxing fan out of him.
- My father, Grant Robertson, for creating systems to help me better access individual issues of my formerly unwieldy magazine collections of both *The Ring* and *Sports Illustrated*.
- Christopher Sykes for saving me with his technical assistance.
- The good people who run the excellent website BoxRec.com, which was frequently an invaluable research source.
- Those anonymous people who posted the five featured bouts (and numerous others) on YouTube. Kudos for keeping 20th-century boxing history alive in the cyber age.
- The folks responsible for creating Google's newspaper archives. Its existence saved me a great deal of travel time and expense. It also provided a wide variety of fascinating perspectives.
- Dr. Terry Aitken for providing a medical explanation for the unusual skeletal injuries suffered by Max Schmeling on June 22, 1938.

Table of Contents

Acknowledgments   vi

Introduction   1

July 4, 1910—James J. Jeffries vs. Jack Johnson:
   Reckoning Time in Reno   5

July 2, 1921—Georges Carpentier vs. Jack Dempsey:
   Gallic Flair and American Fury   52

June 22, 1938—Max Schmeling vs. Joe Louis:
   Nazi Germany Faces America's Champ   100

September 23, 1952—Rocky Marciano vs. Jersey Joe
   Walcott: One Devastating Punch   135

March 8, 1971—Muhammad Ali vs. Joe Frazier:
   The Fight of the Century   165

Afterword   201

Chapter Notes   203

Bibliography   209

Index   211

Introduction

"When the heavyweight champion of the world comes to town, bands should play, fight fans should cheer, and flashlight pictures should be taken in all directions."[1]—John Kieran, *New York Times* sports journalist, 1927

Professional boxing once transcended the world of sports. There was a time, not so long ago, when the man who held the coveted title of "world's heavyweight champion" was indeed a household name. As far back as the 1880s and the wild, rollicking era of John L. Sullivan, the man who ruled the roost in pugilism's heavyweight division was a genuine celebrity. He was often as well known as the president of the United States—sometimes even more so.

That is no longer the case. Since 1995 the following fighters have held at least some share of the "world heavyweight title"—at least according to one of the sport's numerous governing bodies: Corrie Sanders, John Ruiz, Oleg Maskaev, Siarhei Liakhovich, Shannon Briggs, Samuel Peter, David Haye, Deontay Wilder, Lucas Browne, and Bermane Stiverne, to name but a few. It is likely not an exaggeration to say that only die-hard boxing fans would recognize even half of the ten aforementioned names, despite a few of them claiming the title on more than one occasion. Bert Sugar, the colorful late former editor of *The Ring* magazine and *Boxing Illustrated*, once humorously lamented about the proliferation of anonymous boxing titleholders: "They're not even household names in their own households."

The major problem, of course, is that there are now multiple claimants for every professional title—an absurd reality that makes boxing a very difficult sport for casual fans to follow. (Multiple "world champions" in the same weight class is patently ridiculous. Think about it. Can you imagine two, three or four male tennis players each claiming to be the defending Wimbledon champion? How about multiple NFL teams claiming to be Super Bowl titlists? Of course not!) Sadly, nowadays it is rare for any boxer to hold the undisputed championship of any weight classification.

The growth of multiple title claimants began in the 1970s with the World Boxing Association (WBA) and the World Boxing Council (WBC) routinely disagreeing over who held the championship of every division. One could hardly mention a fight for the world featherweight title, for example, without the necessary qualifier that it was for only the WBA or WBC version of the title. It was seldom for both. By the end of the 1980s, the International Boxing Federation (IBF) and the World Boxing Organization (WBO) had joined the alphabet soup of boxing's sanctioning bodies to further water down and inevitably cheapen the term "world champion."

At one time, though, a fight for the world heavyweight championship would routinely inspire widespread interest. Newspaper stories leading up to a fight would sometimes appear weeks before the event actually took place and continue steadily until the day of the bout and beyond. As late as 1982 a closed-circuit screening of the Gerry Cooney-Larry Holmes title bout drew more than 60,000 enthusiastic spectators to a horse-racing venue in New York State. Times have changed rapidly. Sadly, the world heavyweight championship has largely been rendered inconsequential because of multiple title claimants and the general decline of boxing as a mainstream sport. During the 1970s just about every heavyweight title fight was either available via a closed-circuit telecast or on free network television. In 2018 some heavyweight title fights were only available via special internet hookups.

Being world heavyweight champion used to mean international fame for the possessor for his life and beyond. Muhammad Ali's passing in 2016 was a major news story because of the former champ's status as a cultural icon. Nevertheless, three decades earlier, when ex-champions Jack Dempsey and Gene Tunney both died as octogenarians half a century removed from their last ring battles, each man's death was a significant news story. In contrast, when the aforementioned Corrie Sanders was gunned down by thugs at age 46 in 2012 during a robbery at a Pretoria restaurant, his untimely demise was barely acknowledged beyond South Africa's borders. Sanders' last bout occurred less than five years before his tragic death.

Professional boxing is in a sorry state today, but this book will take the reader back to five thrilling occasions from the previous century when the world heavyweight boxing title actually meant something to the sporting and general public. The championship of boxing's top division represented prestige. It was the pinnacle of individual sporting achievement. It was a priceless accomplishment. People were drawn in large numbers to the human drama that surrounded the titleholder and his various challengers. Mike Tyson, who appreciates and cherishes boxing history, was correct in asserting that the heavyweight champion was often regarded as "the baddest man on the planet."

This book will focus on five different world heavyweight title fights—the undisputed variety, of course—and ten different fighters spanning a period of 61 years in the 20th century: James J. Jeffries vs. Jack Johnson (1910); Georges Carpentier vs. Jack Dempsey (1921); Max Schmeling vs. Joe Louis (1938); Rocky Marciano vs. Jersey Joe Walcott (1952); and Muhammad Ali vs. Joe Frazier (1971). All five clashes were contested somewhere in the United States where boxing ballyhoo reigned supreme.

The bouts are listed in chronological order, not by any level of importance—although at least three of them clearly had social implications that extended well beyond the small confines of the prize ring. The narrative will examine each of these championship fights in detail along with the general excitement—hype, if you will—that preceded each one and made it a major news event in its day. Interestingly, only in one of the five bouts did the title change hands, proving that a historic boxing match does not have to feature the ascension of a new champion. Three of them featured boxers who were trying to regain the world championship. All three failed in their attempts.

Five of the ten men featured here were ranked in the top nine fighters of the 20th century by *The 2000 Boxing Almanac and Book of Facts* published by *The Ring* magazine. Two of the five fights in this book were among the best heavyweight title contests ever fought. It is, however, interesting to note that the other three bouts turned out to be not especially competitive—in fact, two were decidedly one-sided—but that is not the point. The fact that they were merely occurring was enough to capture the attention of not just boxing followers, but the general public as well.

Those halcyon days of boxing's heavyweight division may be gone, perhaps forever. None of the ten fighters featured in this book is still alive. Nevertheless, with the accounts of five of boxing's most memorable encounters contained on these pages, the actions of those stalwart men who squared off when the stakes were at their highest can always be revisited—and the excitement surrounding their bouts can be summarily rekindled.

July 4, 1910

James J. Jeffries vs. Jack Johnson
Reckoning Time in Reno

"Ever since Jack Johnson, the negro pugilist, defeated Tommy Burns, the white titleholder … on December 26, 1908, the sporting world has been anxiously awaiting the appearance of a David who will conquer this ebony-hued Goliath and redeem the world's championship to the white race. There was only one man to whom the world could turn at this time with the prospects of success, a giant, James J. Jeffries…"—*Newark (NJ) Sunday Call*, July 3, 1910

"Of course, I think the fight's going to be one of the greatest spectacles ever pulled off in the United States or anywhere else, for that matter. You expect me to say that and it sounds perfunctory or obvious that I should. But really, way down in my heart, I know that the Jeffries-Johnson fight will be talked about long after we're all dead."—James Gleason, co-promoter of the July 4, 1910 heavyweight title fight

"The greatest marathon race of the ages is about to begin between the white race and the darkest races of mankind. What Jack Johnson seeks to do to Jeffries in the roped arena will be the ambition of negroes in every domain of human endeavor." —Reverdy C. Ransom, black civil rights activist and "Christian socialist"

Nat Fleischer founded *The Ring* magazine in 1922 and served as the editor-in-chief of "the Bible of Boxing" until his death at age 84 in 1972. Throughout his long life as boxing journalism's elder statesman, his educated and objective opinions on all aspects of the sport were often sought by fans because Fleischer had witnessed just about every notable professional fighter from the first seven decades of the 20th century. There was one point on which Fleischer never wavered: Until the day he died, Fleischer maintained that Jack Johnson was the greatest heavyweight fighter who ever lived.

John Arthur (Jack) Johnson was born in Galveston, TX, on March 31, 1878. He was the son of emancipated slaves, the third child of nine in the family of Henry and Tina Johnson. Five of the Johnson children survived to adulthood. Both of Johnson's parents were devout Methodists and each worked long hours at blue-collar jobs to put bread on the family table. Jack was the first boy born to Tina (who was nicknamed "Tiny"). During the Civil War, Henry Johnson had been a civilian teamster in the 38th Colored Infantry Regiment. He stood only about 5'5" tall, but he was a strong man for his small stature. His son would grow to be at least seven inches taller than Henry and mature into a truly imposing physical specimen.

Being a black person in the American South during the last two decades of the 19th century provided no social advantages for young Jack Johnson, but he did not feel that he was particularly disadvantaged, either. In Galveston, everyone seemed to be equally poor and race was not nearly the enormous factor it was in other parts of Dixie. Jack recalled his childhood in which he grew up among mostly white youths. "As I grew up, the white boys were my friends and my pals," he noted. "I ate with them, played with them and slept at their homes. Their mothers gave me cookies, and I ate at their tables. No one ever taught me that white men were superior to me."[1] Showing an independent spirit even as a teen, young Jack was expelled from his family's Methodist church for openly doubting the existence of God and proclaiming that religion dominated people's lives in a negative way.

In school Johnson was an inquisitive student, seemingly always in good spirits and eager to learn. Although his formal schooling in Galveston lasted

World heavyweight champion Jack Johnson, circa 1912.

only about five years, Johnson managed to learn how to speak French. But attending school was a luxury and not a requirement. With many mouths to feed in the Johnson home, Jack was expected to work to help make ends meet. He quickly found the best way for him to do so was through boxing. By age 16 Johnson was fighting in private clubs and earning far more money than either of his parents. Johnson learned the science of the sport at a time when it was evolving from old-time prize fighting to modern boxing. The biggest break Johnson experienced was a defeat he suffered a month shy of his 23rd birthday. It was actually a blessing in disguise. On February 25, 1901, in Galveston, Johnson was knocked out in three rounds by a veteran Jewish pugilist named Joe Choynski. Both men were imprisoned for 23 days for violating a Texas law that outlawed prize fighting. Choynski passed the time by teaching Johnson the finer points of the sweet science. Johnson learned that he did not have to be hit. Moreover, by waiting for his foe to go on the offensive, he could exploit an aggressive opponent's mistakes with his quick hand speed. In a very short time, Choynski's pupil developed into a superb defensive fighter and a clever and effective counterpuncher.

According to his biography the *New World Encyclopedia*, Johnson had a very distinct fighting style for his era. He developed a more patient approach than was customary in that day. He favored adopting a defensive strategy, waiting for an opponent's mistake to appear, and then capitalizing on it for maximum effect. Johnson typically began his bouts cautiously. He would slowly tire his opponent by thwarting his aggression and responding with effective counter blows. Over time Johnson would become more assertive as his opponent became wearier with each passing round. He often fought to punish his adversary rather than knock him out, endlessly and deftly avoiding his blows and striking back with swift counterattacks. Johnson often gave the impression of having much more to offer and, if pushed, he could punch quite powerfully. When James J. Corbett lifted the heavyweight title from John L. Sullivan's clutch in 1892 with his brainy approach to the sport, he was lauded by sports journalists for bringing science to the crude world of prize fighting. Yet when Johnson copied and later surpassed Corbett's clever ring techniques, the press often labeled his tactics as cowardly. Late in his life Johnson said, "I made a lot of mistakes out of the ring, but I never made any in it."[2] According to many boxing followers and journalists, Johnson was said to possess a "yellow streak" because of his refusal to simply try to outslug an opponent. How Johnson won seemed to be the most infuriating thing about him if you did not admire his obvious ring skills.

In a preview piece published in the *Milwaukee Sentinel* on the day of the Johnson-Jeffries fight in 1910, an Associated Press writer described what made Johnson stand out among his boxing peers—his imperturbable disposition in the ring: "Tempermentally, Johnson is an interesting study. His chief characteristic is his unfailing good nature, a curious constant sort of even temper that nothing seems to ruffle. His golden smile is seldom out of evidence, and not even the coarse and insulting jibes that frequently greet him from fight spectators seem to have the power to disturb him. Even when ducking a storm of blows and showing wonderful skill in evading the onslaughts of his opponent, Johnson never loses his poise nor his power of observation."

One of the fighters whom Johnson defeated in his ascension to the title was Jack Jeffries—the brother of the reigning world heavyweight champion, James J. Jeffries. Jack, two years younger than James, was far from being in his sibling's pugilistic class. He failed to survive past the fifth round against Johnson in their May 1902 matchup in Los Angeles. Jack reconsidered his career options and never fought professionally again, although he did regularly serve as sparring partner for his champion brother. James J. was in his brother's corner that day. After the bout, Johnson strode directly to the reigning champ and bluntly informed him, "I can whip you, too."[3]

By 1903 Johnson had won the unofficial title as World Colored Heavyweight Champion and was considered a highly dangerous foe for any fighter—white, black, or otherwise. Still, there was little hope that he would get a shot at the bona fide world title held by James J. Jeffries. Giving a black fighter such an opportunity would be unprecedented. While the championships of professional boxing's lighter weight divisions had occasionally been held by black fighters such as Joe Gans and George Dixon without society convulsing, the prestige of the heavyweight crown was too great to risk it falling in the hands of a black man. That had been the precedent set by John L. Sullivan—America's first great sports hero. He was the man who bridged the bare-knuckle era of prize fighting to the modern era of gloves and the Marquis of Queensberry Rules of boxing. He had also drawn heavyweight boxing's "color line."

A robust James J. Jeffries is shown in this photograph circa 1904 when he was undefeated world heavyweight champion. It was said at the time that Jeffries never hit an opponent with his full power for fear of killing him.

James Jackson Jeffries was born in Carroll, Ohio on August 15, 1875, but he grew up as a California boy when his father, a minister, moved his family to Los Angeles. The young man who would enter the 20th century as the world's heavyweight champion was strong, athletic, and speedy in his prime. Standing 6'1½" and typically tipping the scales at 220 pounds—a giant of a man by 19th-century standards—Jeffries was said to have once run the 100-yard dash in 11 seconds flat. Before he took up prize fighting for a lucrative vocation, Jeffries worked as a boilermaker in East Los Angeles—thus forever acquiring "the Boilermaker" as his fighting nickname. His natural strength was abundant. According to one well-circulated tale, Jeffries reputedly saved a stranger from certain death one afternoon by single-handedly lifting several large timbers off him after several other men, working together, had failed to even budge them.

Jeffries began building his boxing résumé as an amateur, but his entire professional career was comprised of just 21 fights. Only one other modern heavyweight champion—James J. Corbett—had fewer total bouts. Blessed with good stamina, a sturdy chin, and above-average punching power, Jeffries was perceived as an unstoppable force both before and during his title reign. As Jeffries rose through the heavyweight ranks, a popular rumor circulated that he was hesitant to unleash his full power against an opponent for fear of killing him with one of his mighty smashes. (Indeed, at least three of Jeffries' vanquished opponents suffered broken ribs from absorbing hard body shots from the Boilermaker.) In retrospect, however, when one objectively examines his record, Jeffries' career was mostly defined by victories over renowned fighters who were a just bit past their primes. Nevertheless, Jeffries' heyday in the ring was an era when the heavyweight champion was perceived as superhuman. As boxing historian Bert Sugar noted, "In the world of the early 1900s, still awash with Victorian gentility and doily-type embroidery on everything from manners and modes to conversation and conventional heroes, the name of the heavyweight champion stood out in stark relief, a man of swaggering virility who epitomized the turbulent yet proud surety of the populace of a nation destined for greatness."[4]

A smiling James J. Jeffries, circa 1903. "The Boilermaker" was considered the epitome of American masculinity and manhood during his five-year reign as undefeated world heavyweight champion.

On June 9, 1899, at the Coney Island Athletic Club in Brooklyn, 24-year-old James J. Jeffries knocked out titleholder Bob Fitzsimmons in the 11th round to become the fourth world heavyweight boxing champion of the gloved era. Jeffries defended his crown nine times. Twice he defeated former champion James J. Corbett. One badly overmatched challenger, Jack Finnegan, was dispatched in a mere 55 seconds with only a left-handed punch to the stomach. (More than a century later it is still the record for the shortest world heavyweight title fight.) Jeffries had beaten at least one black fighter in his ascension to the championship (Hank Griffin), but he did not choose to defend the title versus one. John L. Sullivan had drawn the "color line" for heavyweight champions in the 1880s. Each champion who had followed him had strictly adhered to it until Tommy Burns chose to put his crown on the line versus Jack Johnson in 1908. By early 1905,

James J. Jeffries in a fighting pose in 1909-five years after his last title defense and a year before his ill-advised comeback fight versus Jack Johnson.

with no worthy Caucasian challengers left to crush, Jeffries, not quite 30 years old, retired from the ring to lead the life of a gentleman farmer at a spacious ranch in Burbank, CA. There he happily raised cattle and alfalfa and stayed out of the limelight for more than four years until circumstances beyond his control drew him back to the cutthroat world of professional boxing.

Jeffries hand-picked two leading white heavyweights—Marvin Hart and Jack Root—to battle for his vacated crown. The most noteworthy achievement on Hart's résumé was a highly debatable 20-round decision victory over Jack Johnson on March 28, 1905, in San Francisco. The referee had been the sole arbiter. It was a verdict that was widely acknowledged as both disgraceful and racially motivated. The Hart-Root championship fight took place at the Amphitheater in Reno, NV, on July 3, 1905. To add a special touch to the festivities, Jeffries acted as the bout's referee. Hart knocked out Root in the 12th round to claim the title. Jeffries raised Hart's right fist in the traditional gesture

James Jeffries gives an exhibition of rope-skipping circa 1903. The Boilermaker's popularity made him a beloved sporting figure during the first decade of the 20th century.

of victory and, in a sense, symbolically handed the winner his scepter as world heavyweight champion. At the time it was the most noteworthy sports event to have ever been held in Reno. Seven months later, on February 23, 1906, Canada's Tommy Burns took the crown from Hart via a 20-round decision in Los Angeles in a mild upset. Sometimes called "the Hanover Giant" because his birthplace in Canada was Hanover, ON, Burns was actually only 5'7". Still, he packed a wallop in his small frame. In his reign as world heavyweight champion, Burns strung together eight consecutive successful title defenses that ended with knockouts—a record not equaled until the era of Larry Holmes more than 70 years later.

Burns was certainly a mobile champion, commendably taking the term "world champion" very literally. He defended his title at venues in the United States, England, Ireland, France and Australia. Most of Burns' challengers were fairly easy pickings. One opponent, an Australian named Bill Squires, was defeated three different times in three different countries. Burns was constantly on the move—largely because Jack Johnson was pursuing him for a shot at the title. Eventually Johnson's doggedness won him public sympathy from boxing followers around the world. Even Great Britain's King Edward VII, an avid fight fan, privately labeled Burns as a bluffer and said Johnson

A bill advertising a screening of James J. Jeffries' successful title defense against Tom Sharkey in 1901.

certainly deserved a crack at the world heavyweight championship as the outstanding contender. In the hype leading up to his fight with Jeffries in 1910, Johnson told the Associated Press, "It was not my fights themselves, but my fight to get those fights that proved the hardest part of the struggle. It was my color."[5] One British boxing publication unequivocally stated that Johnson would be Burns' master if the two ever faced each other in the ring.

Burns did not strictly draw the color line on Johnson, but he did draw a money line. Burns insisted he would not consider putting his title on the line versus Johnson unless he was guaranteed a whopping $30,000 purse. When a flamboyant Australian promoter named Hugh McIntosh raised the enormous sum late in 1908, Burns finally acquiesced. Jack Johnson would be paid $5,000—only one-sixth of what Burns would get—but Johnson finally got what he had sought for years: a coveted chance to win the world heavyweight championship. When 50-year-old John L. Sullivan heard the news on the other side of the globe, he was furious. Sullivan claimed Burns had violated "good American precedent"[6] by giving Johnson a crack at the title.

While most Americans were heading to their beds on Christmas night 1908, Johnson and Burns were stepping into the ring at a place called Rushcutter's Bay on the outskirts of Sydney, Australia. It was already the day after Christmas in the land Down Under. Fittingly, in the British Empire, December 26 is Boxing Day. (The holiday has nothing whatsoever to do with pugilism; it is an observance that dates back to at least the 1830s when postmen, errand boys, and other servants could expect to receive Christmas boxes from their regular customers or employers.) The bout was scheduled for 20 three-minute rounds with the understanding that the police would enter the ring and stop the fight if it became too one-sided.

What the 20,000 ticketholders witnessed was more of a public flogging than a world championship fight. The overwhelmingly pro–Burns crowd had literally nothing to cheer about. Burns did not help his chances by overtraining and coming into the fight at a mere 168 pounds. Johnson, who outweighed the defending the champion by 24 pounds, dropped Burns to the canvas just seconds after the opening bell, shortly after 11 a.m., with the first punch he threw—and a second time before the first round ended. In the subsequent rounds Johnson toyed with Burns, even graciously suggesting and offering targets on his body for Burns to hit. When the champion moved within striking range, however, Johnson smacked him sharply with terrific counterpunches. Johnson battered the overmatched Canadian almost at will, sometimes holding Burns up so he could hit him further. By the sixth round Johnson almost became bored with the contest and began chatting with spectators during the action! During clinches Johnson also delighted in taunting the champion he had chased around the globe. Boxing historian Bert Sugar wrote, "Burns never could get to his ... tormentor who spent much of the afternoon ridiculing the champion, his pitiable efforts, and his followers."[7]

"Who taught you how to punch, Tommy?" Johnson asked Burns facetiously, flashing his gold-capped front teeth. "Was it your mother? You hit like a girl. Come on, Tommy, show me $30,000 worth of fight!"[8] On one occasion Johnson mockingly waved to the discouraged Burns as he sadly trudged back to his corner at the end of another overwhelmingly dominant round for the challenger. Between rounds Johnson launched prodigious spit wads into press row, infuriating the white scribes covering the fight. He was having the time of his life.

By the end of the 13th round, Burns was a spent fighter. The policemen went into a huddle, obviously pondering how much longer they should permit the fight to go on. Promoter Hugh McIntosh—who was serving as the fight's referee too—was reluctant to stop the fight on his own. Few champions at the time relinquished their crowns without being counted out; it was considered less than manly to simply quit or to have the referee save you. Nevertheless, McIntosh went to Burns' corner to inquire about the champion's fitness to continue. McIntosh was satisfied and allowed Burns to answer the bell for round 14—and he asked the police not to interfere. With Burns possessing no tools to thwart Johnson's aggression, the challenger came out for the 14th round and attacked in a fury without letting up. Burns was surely about to be knocked out when the local police intervened as promised. They also shut off the motion picture cameras, thus depriving the world of seeing the actual moment that 30-year-old Jack Johnson became the first black man in boxing history to capture the world heavyweight championship. Burns was so thoroughly beaten that more than 15 months elapsed before he stepped into the ring again.

"I never doubted the issue from the beginning," Johnson cockily crowed in a post-fight interview. "I knew I was too good for Burns. I have forgotten more about boxing than Burns ever knew. I was sure I would win from the start. The referee was fair and I have no complaints to make."[9] Later, when Johnson stopped off in Canada en route home, the new titleholder was more conciliatory. He gave Burns credit for letting him fight for the world championship and even applauded the gameness he displayed in the horribly lopsided fight.

The *Duluth (MN) Daily Star* reported the startling news on its December 26, 1908, sports page:

> Jack Johnson, the gigantic negro pugilist, is today the heavyweight champion of the world. He decisively defeated Tommy Burns, the holder of the title, here [in Sydney] in 14 rounds

Jack Johnson, flashing his famous golden smile, shortly after returning to America from Australia in 1909.

of their 20-round battle. He pounded the white man so badly that the police stopped the contest when Burns was swaying about and getting an unmerciful punching.

Johnson appeared fresh after the fight while Burns' eyes were badly puffed and his mouth was swollen to twice its normal size. The Canadian fought a game battle and showed indomitable pluck, but he was no match for the big Texas black.

Johnson's easy victory over Burns horrified a large segment of America and beyond. Bert Sugar wrote nearly 75 years later, "[The fight's result] unleashed a tide of hatred. It was unthinkable that the white man's burden had become his master, that the so-called inferior race was superior to the white man in this, the most supreme contests between two men. Suddenly, the man who represented the strongest, most powerful, and most visible figure in the word was now black."[10] The *Detroit Free Press* wondered, "Is the Caucasian played out? Are the races that we've been calling inferior about to demand that we draw the color line in everything if we are to avoid being whipped individually and collectively?" Similarly, Jack London, the novelist who penned *Call of the Wild*, covered the Johnson-Burns bout as a journalist. Although London was an avid socialist who often publicly espoused leftist causes, he absolutely drew his own line when it came to embracing racial equality. While he was honest enough to state that "not one second of any round could be legitimately scored for Burns"[11] and that the fight resembled a large man cuffing a small child, London could not stomach the fact that a black fighter now held the world's most prestigious sporting title. He had a ready solution, however: London pleadingly and desperately wrote, "[James] Jeffries must emerge from his alfalfa farm and remove the golden smile from Jack Johnson's face. Jeff, it's up to you. The white man must be rescued."[12] Thus, boxing's White Hope Era began simultaneously with the championship reign of Jack Johnson.

When informed of the fight result from Australia, Jeffries evinced no surprise. "I thought Johnson would win unless they had his legs and his hands both tied," he said. "Burns had no right to fight Johnson for the heavyweight championship. I never looked for any other result, but I did not expect the fight to go so far."[13] John L. Sullivan, interviewed in Minnesota, concurred. He too expected a Johnson victory. "The fight came out very much as I had predicted," he declared bitterly. "I am of the opinion that the American public is fast losing interest in the manly art of self-defense."[14]

In 1909 Johnson arrived back in the United States to considerably less than a hero's welcome. The white sporting public was generally hostile to the new heavyweight kingpin because of his race and his brazenly hedonistic lifestyle. Johnson liked fast cars, fancy clothes, high living, and the company of white women—and he was not afraid to openly flaunt any of his preferences. (In studying the troubled career of his predecessor, Muhammad Ali was utterly amazed when he found out about Johnson's preferred female com-

Jack Johnson loved fast cars. His speeding often got him into trouble with the police. Here he is pictured behind the wheel of his Thomas Flyer in 1909.

panions. Ali said, "Jack Johnson was sleeping with white women in 1909! That cat had to be crazy!"[15]) Johnson also opened an opulent saloon, the Café de Champion, at a time when prohibitionist sentiments in America's heartland were growing rapidly. Johnson even alienated a few prominent black Americans who thought his behavior was both disgraceful and certainly harmful to overall race relations. The new champion earned this broad rebuke from Booker T. Washington: "[Johnson's] actions do not meet my personal approval, and I am sure they do not meet with the approval of the colored race."[16] Perhaps, perhaps not. What was indisputable was that the reigning world heavyweight champion was the most polarizing figure in America in 1910. In his terrific book, *100 Years of Boxing*, Bert Sugar suggested, "Had there been a Nobel Prize for dividing the races, Jack Johnson would have won it, gloves down."

In a 2010 article published in the *New York University Journal of Law & Liberty*, Barak Y. Orbach stated why Jack Johnson was so despised by most of white America:

> [Johnson] ignored many social conventions, defeated whites in the ring, had claims for and gained a prime manhood symbol—the boxing heavyweight championship—and had public relationships with white women. Johnson was widely regarded as a "bad nigger," a status that came with many traits, most of which were related to lack

of conformity with social order and norms. Johnson perfected the qualities of the "bad nigger" and, worst of all, disregarded dangerous and interracial taboos. To add insult to injury, Johnson was intelligent, strategic, undefeated [sic], good looking, articulate, and sent his white rivals bleeding to the floor. In the racist United States of the turn of the [20th] century, Johnson was the ultimate "bad nigger."

Apart from a handful of exhibition matches—one of which was against future Oscar-winning actor Victor McLaughlin in Vancouver—Johnson defended his title just once in 1909. In Colma, California on October 16, Johnson knocked out world middleweight champion Stanley Ketchel in the 12th round. To this day, boxing fans debate whether the Johnson-Ketchel fight was completely on the level. The scuttlebutt persists that Ketchel, who was dwarfed by Johnson, had conspired with the champion to let the bout go the full 20-round distance to make the fight films more appealing to moviegoers. In the fateful 12th round, Ketchel ignored the script, so the story goes, and scored a legitimate knockdown against the champion. Thoroughly enraged, Johnson rose from the canvas and flattened Ketchel with a perfectly timed right hand. Ketchel was knocked senseless. Several of Ketchel's broken teeth were found deeply embedded in Johnson's boxing glove. "It was too fast to watch; and in an instant's time Ketchel was on his back and being counted out," recalled an Associated Press correspondent months later. He [Ketchel] did not seem to realize what had struck him, and Johnson himself seemed astonished at the result of his sudden exhibition of strength and speed."[17]

By the time Ketchel had regained consciousness, the hue and cry for James Jeffries to unretire and put the uppity Jack Johnson in his place was renewed with even greater vigor. Some fans illogically claimed that Jeffries was still the legitimate titleholder as he had never lost his crown in the ring. (Few boxing followers seemed to hold that interesting opinion during the 34 months that Tommy Burns was touring the globe as heavyweight titlist.) Johnson scoffed at the notion that Jeffries was still somehow the titleholder, likening Jeffries to a mayor who had stepped down from office. A mayor who no longer holds the office is an ex-mayor, not the present mayor. Similarly, Jeffries was voluntarily the ex-champion, not the present champ, Johnson logically insisted.

At first Jeffries was not especially interested in leaving his serene, bucolic existence to return to the dangerous glory of the prize ring and the scrutiny of millions of Americans. First, his weight had ballooned to over 300 pounds since he had last thrown a punch for pay in 1904. Second, Jeffries was still a keen follower of the fight game. He knew about Johnson's skills. Jeffries must have harbored doubts about his ability to dethrone Jack Johnson—a man who was already being labeled by knowledgeable, unbiased boxing fans and writers as one of the sport's all-time greats. Johnson may not have possessed the devastating wallop of a John L. Sullivan or even Jeffries, but he was certainly the best defensive heavyweight and ring general any objective boxing observer had ever seen in the modern prize ring. Few fighters ever managed to land a meaningful blow against the champion.

But the prospect of sharing a $101,000 purse, plus a $10,000 signing bonus and a cut of motion picture revenues, and the incessant emotionally charged pleas from his legions of admirers finally persuaded Jeffries to pick up the gauntlet for white America. On December 1, 1909, Jeffries announced he would return for one more ring battle. He told the press, "I am going into this fight for the sole purpose of proving that a white man is better than a negro."[18] The bout was scheduled to be held on the Fourth of July 1910 somewhere in the San Francisco area.

The *Milwaukee Journal* was impressed by the huge amount of money that various promoters bid to gain the rights to stage the epic bout. It succinctly explained in its December 2, 1909, edition why this particular ring battle would be the most lucrative in the history of boxing: "A fortune—$125,000—was bid yesterday for a prize ring battle for the heavyweight championship of the world because the title is held by a black man; because the public wants James J. Jeffries to knock Jack Johnson out of the prized position; and because the promoters see hundreds of thousands of dollars profit in what promises to be the biggest fight in modern ring history." The *Toledo Blade* saw twisted priorities in all the dollars connected with the bout. It cyn-

James J. Jeffries, on the right, is pictured with his trainer Sam Berger, 1909 or 1910.

ically wondered why the financing of a prize fight could be done so quickly and efficiently while the financing of an orphanage seemingly took forever.

Jack London was thrilled by the news of Jeffries' comeback and saw his hero's opportunity to dethrone Johnson as wholly fitting the grand narrative of the Caucasian domination of modern civilization's achievements. The novelist giddily declared, "[The white man] has 30 centuries of traditions behind him—all the supreme efforts, the inventions and the conquests, and, whether he knows it or not, Bunker Hill, Thermopylae and Hastings and Agincourt."[19] On some level, most of America's mainstream daily newspapers echoed London's views. The *New York Herald*, for example, which would carry London's coverage of the Johnson-Jeffries fight, continued to portray Johnson in cartoon form resembling a gigantic simian more than a human being. The racial aspect of the fight was clearly going to be its major focal point. Interestingly, in a story that appeared in the May 6 edition of the *Calgary Herald*, Johnson said he did not want the fight to be perceived as a clash between races. At least that was what the champion said publicly. "I have whipped as many negroes as whites while working my way to the front," the champion said. "In the matter of encouragement and support, I have received more material assistance from my white friends than from negroes."

Forty-year-old George Lewis (Tex) Rickard, a colorful character, outbid everyone else to stage the fight—including Hugh McIntosh of Australia. Rickard married a doctor's daughter in 1894, but by 1895 he was a widower. His infant son had died too. Rickard had an eye-catching, eclectic resumé: He had prospected for gold in Alaska and diamonds in South Africa. He had also been a hotelier, a saloon keeper, a croupier, a faro dealer, and a U.S. marshal. Rickard had made a couple of fortunes before his

Jack Johnson, circa 1910.

fortieth birthday but had gambled them away. Despite his nickname, Rickard did not hail from Texas. He was born in Missouri—or perhaps Kansas. From a young age Rickard was afflicted with wanderlust; he liked to be wherever the action was and wherever money could be made.

As was his style, Rickard had entered the boxing business in a big way: He successfully promoted the grueling 42-round Joe Gans-Battling Nelson world lightweight title fight in Goldfield, NV, on Labor Day 1906. He turned a profit in excess of $13,000—and found his true calling. Paul Gallico, the superb New York sports journalists from the *Daily News*, believed Rickard's most lucrative promotions all featured some type of a good-versus-evil element. In Goldfield, Gans was portrayed as the righteous champion while Nelson was advertised as a despicable challenger who would stop at nothing to win. The fight lived up to its billing. In a foul-filled affair, Nelson was eventually disqualified for a flagrant low blow. Interestingly, Gans was a black man; Nelson was white.

Rickard secured the promotional rights for the Johnson-Jeffries contest by paying not only $120,000 for it, but with the added panache of doing so in gold. James Gleason, a onetime actor and playwright who knew Jeffries personally, worked closely with Rickard and was listed as the bout's co-promoter. Rickard was a man full of big ideas. He intended to build a special new stadium solely for this single sports event—that was a boxing first. Everything was moving along nicely in San Francisco, including advance ticket sales. On March 28, Rickard broke neutrality in stating he believed Johnson would win the fight if he

Promoter Tex Rickard was largely responsible for making boxing a mainstream sport in the first three decades of the 20th century. A onetime faro dealer and cattle rancher, Rickard ushered in the era of enormous boxing spectacles, often by playing up the angle of good versus evil. Photograph dated 1924.

came in to the ring in good condition because of Jeffries' long layoff from boxing. Then a stunning announcement came from California governor James Gillett's office in Sacramento on June 15.

California had been the site of some of boxing's most memorable and important bouts in the first decade of the 20th century; in fact, Johnson had fought Stanley Ketchel in Colma, CA, the previous October without any legal problems arising. Likewise, Tommy Burns had won the title from Marvin Hart in Los Angeles in 1906. Just four months earlier, the world lightweight championship had changed hands in Point Richmond—just outside of San Francisco—when Ad Wolgast outlasted Battling Nelson in a memorable and bloody 40-round fight before 18,000 peaceable spectators in an open-air arena.

However, the significance of the Johnson-Jeffries fight was exponentially greater than any of those contests and its racial angle raised the prospects of big trouble. It put California's government under severe scrutiny because, according to a much-ignored 1850 statute—one of the oldest on the state's books—prize fighting was technically a felony. (An 1899 amendment, however, did legalize "sparring exhibitions." What exactly constituted a "prize fight" in California was never clearly defined.) Nevertheless, just 19 days before the fight was to be held, governor Gillett—who had already decided not to run for re-election that fall—caved in to the pressure of anti-boxing crusaders, religious groups, moralists, social reformers, and other factions opposed to the fight. Gillett surprisingly announced that he was refusing to allow the championship fight take place anywhere within California despite the obvious lucrative benefits to be reaped as its host. If the fight went on, its organizers, the two participants, their handlers, and anyone with any other sundry connection to the bout would surely face prosecution.

Gillett explained his decision in a letter to his attorney general that was made public, "Many complaints [have been] made at this office by prominent citizens of this state protesting against this so-called fight."[20] Among those who backed the governor's anti-boxing stance was 74-year-old steel magnate Andrew Carnegie, who sent the following telegram from Scotland where he heard the news while vacationing: "Cordial congratulations upon saving your lovely state from disgrace," wired Carnegie. "Our country is your debtor."[21] Another noteworthy heavyweight bout between contenders Sam Langford and Al Kaufman, scheduled for June 18, was also summarily booted from the Golden State. Langford was black; Kaufman was white. That fight never did take place anywhere. According to the *Toledo Blade*, Gillett's decision "has given boxing on the coast a blow from which it will never recover."

Jeffries was described as "crestfallen" after being informed of the adverse development in his home state. "I can't believe it," the challenger stated. "I did not think [governor Gillett] would do that after he repeatedly stated there would be no interference. I will keep on with my training schedule until I hear that the fight has been cancelled."[22]

Jeffries was quoted in the *Milwaukee Sentinel* as saying, "I think that the action of the governor, taken at this late time, is not at all fair to either the principles or the promoters. It makes no difference to me, as I told Rickard I would fight any place for him."

Jeffries also got in a dig at the religious lobby that was one of the groups pushing for the fight to be moved out of California. The former champion asked rhetorically, "Do they call it religion to allow a man to risk his every penny on a business proposition only to grab his game at the eleventh hour? If they do, I'm afraid the definition of the word has changed considerably since my father [a minister] used to teach it to me."

Johnson took the development completely in stride. "There is only one request I have to make," he said on June 18. "That is to have the fight take place on the Fourth of July. Where, I don't care, just as long as we fight."[23] Johnson said he would be prepared to move his training camp to the new location with just 24 hours' notice.

The mere suggestion of cancelling the Johnson-Jeffries fight was out of the question, of course. Too much momentum had built up and too much was at stake. California's indignation was just a small setback for Rickard et al. On very short notice, Rickard and the two parties had to find a new venue. El Paso, TX, was discussed as a possible relocation site. So was a 30,000-seat bull ring just across the international border in Juarez, Mexico.

Nevada governor Denver S. Dickerson was much more open-minded and obliging. Boxing was completely legal in his state. He

Jack Johnson as he appeared shortly before he was to face ex-champion James J. Jeffries on July 4, 1910, in Reno. Even during Johnson's seven-year reign as world heavyweight champion, many boxing experts rated the highly skilled Johnson as the greatest defensive fighter of all time.

was eager to reap the influx of tourist dollars the fight would generate. Accordingly, Dickerson had no qualms whatsoever with Nevada hosting the most eagerly awaited boxing match in history—"as long as it is on the level,"[24] he cautioned. (One persistent rumor had Johnson being paid handsomely to drop the title to Jeffries by taking a dive.) Rickard assured Dickerson the bout would be contested honestly. On June 17 news reports declared the fight was now likely to be held at Goldfield, NV, but Rickard had his partially completed wooden stadium disassembled and moved 186 miles eastward across the state line to Reno when the Goldfield arrangements fell through. It would be reassembled on the same piece of real estate where Jack Root had been knocked out by Marvin Hart five years earlier when Hart won Jeffries' vacated title.

Johnson and Jeffries quickly uprooted their training camps and found new venues in the vicinity of Reno. They were joined by journalists and various hangers-on. By June 22 Jeffries had set up his training headquarters at Moano Springs, three miles south of Reno. Although Dickerson was not a boxing fan whatsoever—he said he had only ever attended one professional bout in his life—the governor enthusiastically attended sparring sessions at both fighters' training camps and was properly treated as a guest of honor at each of them. Dickerson tactfully declined to make a prediction on the fight's outcome. "I would not care to venture a definite opinion about the result of the fight because I really know nothing of these contestants,"[25] he stated. It was a refreshing tidbit of honesty and straight-talk from a politician. With the state of Nevada's blessing, the imperiled "Fight of the Century" was back on schedule, albeit in a much smaller locale.

Still, Reno, NV—population 15,000—was a geographically favorable location despite its size. It had reliable railroad service for both eastbound and westbound passenger trains. Anyone who wanted to get to Reno could do so without encountering too much difficulty. San Francisco's loss was Reno's financial windfall. By the morning of July 4, some 12,000 visitors would be in the Nevada town for the Johnson-Jeffries showdown. A large portion of them arrived days in advance of the fight to soak in the atmosphere surrounding the big event. And what an atmosphere it was! The excitement was palpable. Reno's hotels were filled to overflowing and the supply simply could not keep up with the demand as people slept in bathtubs and on billiard tables. On July 2 the *Arizona Journal-Miner* reported, "Accommodations are almost impossible to secure. It is understood that most of the special train parties will sleep in their cars parked in the Reno yards." Predictably, the town's few restaurants did a fantastic business. One eatery with a 40-seat capacity reputedly served 3,600 meals in a single day.

However, not every individual who descended upon Reno in the fortnight leading up to the "Fight of the Century" could be classified as an upstanding citizen. Far from it, in fact. Pickpockets were plentiful and had a field day on the crowded streets, in taverns, and anywhere else where people stood in close quarters—which was just about everywhere in Reno. Dozens of ladies of the evening trolled for customers and had plenty of takers. As one journalist frankly commented, "Pugs, gamblers, newspaper reporters, scrubs, whores, and sons of bitches in plenty"[26] dominated the landscape and activities in Reno until fight time. The *Milwaukee Sentinel* reported, "There are 120 members of the rogues' gallery in town and more are coming every hour. The police think they plan to make a 'cleanup' of Reno' while the citizens are at ringside. The street will be patrolled and the banks will be guarded by special watchmen armed with revolvers and rifles."

The same day that Jeffries encamped at Moano Springs, Jack Johnson's love of fast automobiles got him into legal trouble in San Francisco where he was still training. He was fined $50 for speeding and allegedly told the policeman who issued the ticket that the officer could only arrest his "dead body." Johnson was eventually persuaded to pay the penalty so his relocation to Reno would not be delayed. The train carrying Johnson arrived in Reno early in the morning of June 24. According to one reporter, even though it was a little bit past 1 a.m., "Reno gave the champion a hearty reception, there being a big crowd at the station, and no one had anything but the friendliest greetings for the big black man."[27] Tom Flanagan, Johnson's latest business manager, wasted no time in whisking his client to his new training location. Johnson's camp was set up at a roadhouse located three miles southwest of Reno. Johnson was said to be "well pleased" with the venue. Johnson arrived without his former manager, George Little, however. The two men had had a falling out. Little was so miffed over the breakup that he traveled to Reno to place a wager on Jeffries.

Both fighters' training facilities were magnets for curious tourists. Both were exceedingly gracious hosts and shook many hands of well-wishers far beyond the call of duty. Johnson's manner was more insouciant than the serious-minded Jeffries; the champ often put on impromptu concerts with his bull fiddle as a means of relaxing during the lulls in his training. On the day before the fight, more than 1,000 fans flocked to see Jeffries spar with Joe Choynski—the same crafty veteran who had beaten an unpolished Johnson in Galveston in 1901. Choynski, 41, was hired to be a slippery opponent. He did his job too well; Jeffries had trouble landing a telling blow on him, which should have alarmed Jeffries' supporters. The two men were familiar with one another. Choynski and Jeffries had met in a real fight more than a few years previously. As a 17-year-old in November 1892, Jeffries, who had a considerable weight advantage over Choynski, could only manage a 20-round draw against the very skillful older man.

"The contest has become more than a prize fight," declared a writer from

July 4, 1910—James J. Jeffries vs. Jack Johnson

Jack Johnson (white coat) stands with manager George Little, circa 1911. The man at right is not identified.

the *Newark (NJ) Sunday Call* on July 3. "It is a struggle for supremacy between the white race and the black. Thousands are interested [in the bout] who have never before paid the slightest attention to a pugilistic event."

Right up to the day of the fight, the mainstream press lauded Jeffries as a godlike fighter who was going to reclaim his birthright by defeating Johnson. In anticipation of an easy win by the ex-champion, the *Milwaukee Sentinel* gushed on July 4, "When James J. Jeffries was born 35 years ago ... a first-class lightning man was created. He was endowed with everything that goes to make up a fighter, right from the start. He did not need to train or school himself to any great extent. He had both the brain and the brawn, and all he lacked was the ambition to win fame as a fighter. When that ambition did come to him it required but two years to vanquish every fighter worthy of consideration and make the championship title one of his personal assets. Once he secured it, the only way he could find of ridding himself of the burdens it imposed was to give it away."

Everything about the fight was newsworthy. Promoter Tex Rickard, it was announced, would referee the fight himself. (The president of the United States, William Howard Taft, politely declined the offer.) A second referee,

Charles White of New York, was recruited to serve as the alternate third man in the ring if Rickard was indisposed for some reason on July 4. White was actually a substitute for the fighters' preferred backup arbiter, Francis Nelson of Toronto. Nelson was unable to make the trip to Reno due to other engagements close to home and sent his regrets. With alternate officials getting national newspaper coverage, it was not surprising that the press let nothing escape their attention in covering the two fighters' preparations. Every tidbit of information pertaining to the fight, no matter how trivial or minuscule, was eagerly telegraphed around the rule by the 500 journalists who were stationed in Reno to report on the daily goings-on. One dispatch that appeared in the June 30 newspapers gave the following picayune details regarding Jeffries' progress to his hopeful legions of supporters: "Beginning today Jeffries will drink nothing but distilled water. This will aid the drying-out process which is the last step in his training. Also, it was feared that minerals in the water at the springs might cause him some trouble. Jeffries recently ordered his big sunshade to protect him in the ring between rounds. It was delivered today and proved highly satisfactory to the fighter."[28]

The vast interest in the Johnson-Jeffries bout led to several curious peripheral news stories. It was reported that the prisoners residing at Chicago's city jail would be given a special privilege on the Fourth of July: They would be kept abreast of the round-by-round descriptions from Reno courtesy of telegraphed reports. An inmate, who was also a skilled telegrapher, was assigned to monitor the wire. In Hutchinson, KS, the Negro Holiest Church arranged for special services to be held just before the hour of the fight so its parishioners could gather and pray together for a Johnson victory. In contrast, a minister at an Omaha, NE, church told his Sunday congregation the day before the fight that "every man with red blood in his veins"[29] should see Jeffries regain the championship in Reno.

On July 3, Johnson issued the following statement from his training camp: "When I go into the ring on the Fourth of July to fight Mr. Jeffries, I will do so with full confidence that I am able to defeat him at the game of give and take. I honestly believe that in pugilism I am Jeffries' master, and it is my purpose to demonstrate this in the most decisive way possible. I think I know Jeffries thoroughly as a fighter, and, with this knowledge reassuring me, I am most willing to defend the title of champion against him."[30]

Jeffries too had a statement for the press the day before the great contest: "When the gloves are knotted on my hands tomorrow afternoon and I stand ready to defend what is really my title, it will be at the request of the public who forced me out of retirement. I realize full well just what depends on me, and I am not going to disappoint the public. I want those who fancy my chances to know this much: If I had as much as a slight pain, a sore finger, or the most trivial thing imaginable that might annoy me, I would immediately insist on a postponement. Fortunately, I'm as sound as a dollar. I think I will surely beat Johnson. I would not have signed to fight at all unless I was reasonably certain of victory."[31]

That same day, Mrs. Freida Jeffries was asked to make a prediction regarding how her spouse's upcoming fight would end. She declined any specifics. "I'd prefer not to say anything about it," she told a reporter. "I am not interested in prize fighting, but I am interested in my husband's welfare. I believe that he will win, of course, but I do hope this will be his last fight."[32] That night, Freida awoke and found her husband not in bed but staring pensively out the window into the dark Reno night. Undoubtedly the invincible James J. Jeffries was pondering the great challenge facing him the next afternoon and, despite his public proclamations of confidence, he had to be silently wondering if he still had the mettle and skill it would take to do the difficult job most of white America was certain he could do and would do.

A thoughtful-looking James J. Jeffries relaxes during his preparation for his ill-fated 1910 challenge of Jack Johnson.

At a prominent Reno pool room, proprietor Tom Corbett—the brother of ex-heavyweight champion James J. Corbett—was accepting wagers on the fight. (Gambling laws in Reno were so liberal in 1910 that virtually anyone could set up a legal betting parlor.) The day before the bout, the odds at Corbett's establishment were set at 20:17 in the challenger's favor. One could get even money by betting that Jeffries would win by a knockout inside of 25 rounds. Corbett the bookmaker held $5,000 in bets on Jeffries from various San Francisco area "sports" waiting to be matched by Johnson backers. Among the frenzied Jeffries backers clogging the streets of Reno, Johnson money was difficult to find. Still the bookmaker admitted, "This is not a big betting fight, strange to say. We are handling plenty of money, but nothing like the amount we expected to come in. We handled more money in San Francisco before we moved to Reno than we have taken in here."[33] Of the

123 wagering slips Corbett had written 24 hours before the fight, 88 were bets placed on Jeffries. One interesting wagering trend emerged: Based on the payouts one could get on picking the round in which the bout would end, the longer the fight lasted, the more the odds shifted to Johnson's favor. Apparently, the legendary Jeffries stamina was no longer considered to be indisputable now that he was 35 years old.

Jeffries himself was plotting a fight strategy that aimed for a quick knockout. "I will lick Jack Johnson and I will lick him quick," Jeffries predicted the day before the fight. "I don't intend to stall when I meet the negro in the ring. Johnson never saw the day he could beat me. He may be a fairly good fighter. I admit that. He may have been able to beat some good men who were 20 to 40 pounds lighter than he, but just wait until he gets into the ring with a man 20 pounds heavier than he is and a man who has beaten better men than Johnson has ever dreamed of being."[34] Jeffries would enter the ring 19 pounds heavier than Johnson.

With emotions running high and the number of tourists nearly equaling the number of Reno's residents, public safety became a major concern. Quite sensibly, no one was allowed to bring a firearm into the open-air stadium. (One persistent rumor circulating was that if Jeffries were to lose on July 4, an assassin would ensure Johnson would not leave the ring alive.) The sale of alcohol was also prohibited at the venue. Similarly, anyone smuggling their own intoxicating spirits onto the grounds would be subject to arrest. As this was Reno's moment to shine, local law enforcement personnel did their best to assure visitors who were considering traveling to Reno to see the fight that law and order would absolutely prevail. "No one need be afraid to come here," said sheriff C.P. Ferrell. "Everyone will be as safe here as in his home city. Anyone who comes to Reno with the idea that it is a frontier town and that anything goes will find out his mistake before any length of time."[35] One hundred plain-clothes officers had been sworn in by the local chief of police as a precautionary measure.

On the morning of the fight, anyone who bought a copy of that day's *New York Times* could read the following confident statement issued by James J. Jeffries: "That portion of the white race which has been looking to me to defend its athletic supremacy may feel assured that I am fit to do my very best." The newspaper also carried a cautionary warning from Frank Hall, who once managed John L. Sullivan. "Johnson is in his prime," Hall noted. "Jeffries has been out of the game for five years. No athlete in the history of sport has ever come back." Middleweight champion Stanley Ketchel agreed. He said the smart money was backing Johnson to win and he was happy to explain why Johnson would win easily to anyone who was willing to listen to him. Ex-champ Tommy Burns took a contrary view to Ketchel's. He parroted popular sentiment by declaring, "Jeffries will defeat Johnson for the simple reason that in every way he is the champion's physical and mental superior." An editorial in the *San Francisco Chronicle* explained its support of Jeffries and its anticipation of his success more succinctly: "It's a matter of breeding."

Monday, July 4 saw Reno become America's biggest tourist destination that Independence Day. Indeed, the Associated Press reported on July 2, "The Desert City is taking on the appearance of a national convention. Delegates from the world's sporting centers are arriving on every train."[36] Indeed, beginning days before the fight and continuing early in the morning on July 4, one train after another steadily chugged into the small depot, unloading carloads of fans eager to witness history being made. The fact that the fight had been kicked out of San Francisco did not stop residents of that city from attending the fight in great numbers. One train arrived in Reno with 14 Pullman cars carrying some of San Francisco's most prominent people. A significant number of black railroad employees detrained and made beelines to bookmakers to eagerly place bets on Johnson. With most of the wagered money falling on Jeffries' side, anyone wagering on Johnson the day of the fight could get attractive 5:2 odds with a bit of negotiating—and certainly no worse than 5:3.

With Reno's population almost doubling, tickets for the fight were precious commodities. The bowl-shaped wooden stadium's capacity had seats for 16,250 paying customers—not nearly enough room to hold everyone who hoped to see the historic fight. Rickard could have easily sold twice or thrice as many tickets had his arena been twice or thrice as large. (It was a costly lesson, but Rickard would learn it well and make amends for his short-sightedness in 1910 several times in the 1920s with venues that would dwarf the stadium he erected in Reno.) Excitement and anticipation permeated the air—as did the ragtime song "All Coons Look Alike to Me," which was enthusiastically performed by a brass band outside the stadium. Choice ringside seats had a $50 face value, but they were being scalped for $125. (A dollar in 1910 had the purchasing power of about $25 in 2018.) The cheapest seats sold for $10. Four hours before the first bell, Rickard's arena was full—and then some. Another 1,500 people, ticketless but unwilling to miss the great battle, gained access to the stadium by illegally climbing over fences. Promoter Tex Rickard simply accounted for the gate-crashers in his financial books by conveniently categorizing them as "complimentaries." Afterward Rickard announced the total attendance was 18,020—including those who got inside the stadium without paying a nickel. The gate receipts were $270,775, an utterly fantastic sum which shattered all previous records for a prize fight. The fans—whether they held tickets or not—had no preliminary matches to entertain them or whet their appetites. It mattered little. The lone fight on the program was the one the world was waiting to witness: Jack Johnson versus James J. Jeffries for the undisputed heavyweight championship of the world.

As the largely male, largely white crowd settled into their seats in the oppressive July heat—the temperature in Reno reached 110 degrees that afternoon—various boxing celebrities were brought, one by one, into the 24-foot ring to take bows and receive warm receptions: world featherweight champion Abe Attell; dapper world light heavyweight champion Philadelphia Jack O'Brien (who carried a stylish custom-made walking stick); Sam Langford, a longtime outstanding black heavyweight who was seeking a title shot; and Jake Kilrain, the man who had been beaten in the last bare-knuckle heavyweight championship fight by John L. Sullivan in 1889. Kilrain was reported to have gotten the loudest cheer from the overflow crowd.

Sullivan, still a revered boxing icon nearly 18 years after his last bout, was present in Reno too. He was there on official business. With white hair and a spectacular handlebar mustache of the same color above his lip, he looked far older than his 51 years. Sullivan had been hired as a special correspondent for the *New York Times* which would widely syndicate the great John L.'s views on the event. Despite his well-known aversion to black fighters, Sullivan was knowledgeable and unbiased enough to initially have picked Johnson to win, knowing first-hand how a long layoff can reduce a once-formidable boxing champion into a has-been. During a 1910 springtime tour of Great Britain, Sullivan had frankly told the *Irish Independent*, "I cannot see that [Jeffries] can win with a man such as Johnson before him." Sullivan also questioned the wisdom of the syndicate that had paid $200,000 for the rights to film the great contest, believing it to be a highly risky investment. "The cinematograph pictures would be worthless if Johnson would win, for nobody would go to see a nigger beat a white man," he declared. Sullivan's sentiments were echoed in the June 18 edition of the trade publication *Moving Picture World*, albeit with less volatile terminologies: "It is no exaggeration to say that the entire world will await a pictorial of the fight. [With] the unmistakable victory of Jeffries, these pictures should prove in the current locution, a 'gold mine.' This is the wish that is father of the thoughts of hundreds of millions of white people throughout the world. [But] if Johnson wins? It is commonly believed that the pictures [will] then be of comparatively little value, especially among the white section of the community."

However, when Sullivan was hired in April by the *New York Times* to provide his analysis of the contest—along with daily updates from Reno beginning in the middle of June—he was apparently forced to change his tune. Sullivan explained his about-face this way: "Lots of stuff has been written as coming from me about the fight, but it's all bosh. I am saying nothing about who will win." More than two months before the fight, Sullivan colorfully opined that if Jeffries was in proper condition, the ex-champ would not only "whip" Johnson, he would "take that coon and bite his ears off."[37]

At the appointed hour Johnson entered the ring first, as he always did;

it was a superstition of his. He took it so seriously that he had it included in all his fight contracts. His carefree gait exuded confidence. Few people cheered the champion's arrival as he stepped between the two ring ropes wearing a long robe over his tan boxing trunks. Johnson weighed 208 pounds—16 more than when he won the title from Tommy Burns a year-and-a-half earlier. On the other hand, Jeffries' appearance was greeted with a thunderous roar as he slowly moved up the aisle toward the ring. He was wearing a coat and a pair of long trousers. Jeffries removed the pants to reveal light blue trunks symbolically decorated with an American flag as a belt. Though his hair had thinned since his last title defense against Jack Munroe in August 1904, at 227 pounds Jeffries had returned to something akin to what he looked like when he had last stepped into a prize ring. To his admirers he appeared to be the Jeff of old, not the portly gentleman farmer he had been in 1909. Jeffries was chewing gum—and he would keep chewing it throughout the fight! He gazed for a moment at his opponent's corner, and then turned his attention elsewhere. By mutual agreement, there was no pre-fight handshake between Johnson and Jeffries. It would have been a disingenuous gesture. The crowd began to chant, "Jeff, it's up to you!"[38]

By 2:40 p.m. local time the two fighters were equipped with their five-ounce gloves and had been introduced by the stentorian Billy Jordan of San Francisco, who, as usual, performed his task without the assistance of a megaphone. The "Fight of the Century" was just moments away from starting when an absurd delay occurred: Former contender Tom Sharkey, age 39, climbed upon the ring apron to challenge whomever happened to be the winner that day. Sharkey had twice lost competitive bouts to Jef-

Ex-champion James J. Jeffries (center) poses with Minnesota governor Adolph Eberhardt circa 1910.

fries—including Jeffries' first title defense on November 3, 1899. Like Jeffries, though, Sharkey had last fought in 1904 and he had not recorded a victory over anyone since 1901. Sharkey's bluster was quickly ignored and he returned to his seat. At 2:44 p.m. (or a half minute past 2:46 p.m. depending upon which newspaper account one reads), Tex Rickard, who had switched roles from promoter to referee, signaled for the timekeeper's bell. George F. Harting, another San Franciscan, clanged it and clicked his stopwatch. The fight began and the world held its collective breath. Johnson and Jeffries advanced from their respective corners to begin their much-anticipated battle. Much of the world's attention was now focused on a boxing ring in Reno. Newspaper offices around the world were overrun by excited and anxious crowds waiting for round-by-round reports to trickle in. In some cities the crowds numbered several thousand people and their sheer size completely shut down all traffic.

The fight began very cautiously. Johnson was unsure of what the 35-year-old former champion was capable of doing to him. As expected, Jeffries took the initiative, albeit tentatively. Johnson happily allowed him to do so. Jeffries instigating the action played nicely into the champion's hands. Johnson went into a defensive shell, as he had promised to do, stifling Jeffries' attacks and relying on his skillfully timed counter blows. Johnson wanted to test Jeffries' stamina and abilities to see if the ex-champ was anywhere near the fighter he had been a decade earlier. Jeffries fought out of a slight crouch with his left arm extended, as was his style. He twice feinted left-handed blows. Johnson landed the first punch of the contest—a clean left to Jeffries' right eye. Jeffries instigated a clinch—the first of several in the round. Jeffries smiled at Johnson, but Johnson appeared to be the stronger fighter in the clinches—a revelation to many at ringside who were under the false belief that Jeffries was too strong for anyone to tie him up successfully. Johnson also tended to push Jeffries' arms behind his torso to make the challenger work harder to free himself. During the in-fighting, Johnson was far quicker with his hands, landing body blows and occasional uppercuts. Still, Jeffries managed to land one good left to the champion's head and deftly evaded a volley of Johnson's counterpunches. An optimistic pro–Jeffries telegrapher relayed the news that Johnson looked worried.

There was some doubt among the newspapermen over which man had the better outing during the opening frame, but round two was clearly Johnson's. Johnson landed a good left hook to Jeffries' rib cage and managed to target the ex-champ's right eye with solid jabs. When hurt, Jeffries clinched. Johnson began taunting him for holding him. "Love me so, Jim!"[39]

Round three featured some spirited exchanges between the two proud warriors. Jeffries had the most success with body shots while Johnson's jab was scoring well on Jeffries' face. One reporter called it "anybody's round." Yet Jeffries seemed to be laboring after just nine minutes of boxing while

Johnson seemed unruffled and untired. The winner of individual rounds did not concern Johnson very much. Neither he nor Jeffries figured the fight would last the full 45 rounds.

In the fourth round Jeffries managed to open a small cut above Johnson's lip. It was an old wound—suffered during Johnson's training regimen—that Jeffries had reopened. Upon seeing the small trickle of claret, fans seated at ringside excitedly shouted, "First blood for Jeffries!"—as that was one development on which gamblers had wagered. The imperturbable Johnson hardly noticed. Jeffries continued to pursue the champion, but he was generally ineffective. Johnson's almost impregnable defense was both weighing on Jeffries' confidence and sapping the challenger's energy—just as Johnson's strategy dictated. Nevertheless, Jeffries did land some good body blows and was generally thought to have won the round. Johnson was merely biding his time, though.

Johnson opened a cut on Jeffries in the fifth round with one of his slicing left uppercuts. Jeffries began to bleed from his mouth. Jeffries responded with two glancing lefts to Johnson's face, but the champion returned fire and caused more blood to flow from the ex-champ's fresh gashes. Johnson started taunting his opponent in earnest. "Are you having fun yet, Mr. Jeff?"[40] he asked Jeffries. All the while James J. Corbett, acting as one of Jeffries' seconds, was unleashing a torrent of racially charged insults towards the champion. If Corbett hoped to rattle Johnson, he failed. Johnson only smiled at the verbal abuse and kept effectively battering Jeffries with counterpunches. At one point Corbett was reduced to the childish act of making faces at Johnson.

Between the fifth and sixth rounds, Johnson decided to have a friendly chat with John L. Sullivan who had a ringside vantage point near the champion's corner.

"John," said the confident Johnson, "I thought this fellow could hit."

"I never said so," Sullivan insisted, "but I believe he could have six years ago."[41]

Sullivan also informed his journalistic colleagues that the fight was already as good as over. "Take it from me," the experienced old battler said, "Jeff will never win—and he will never be able to fight again."[42]

The sixth round was fought mostly in clinches for the first 90 seconds. Johnson did manage to score some hard lefts on the inside, all the while talking to Jeffries. The fight opened up in the latter half of the round and Johnson scored decisively. Jeffries' right eye was close to closing from the accumulation of Johnson's left-handed blows. His nose was also bleeding. After the round, Jeffries reported to his cornermen that he was feeling the negative effects of his six-year layoff. "My arms aren't working like they should," he informed them. "But I'll be alright, though."[43] His cornermen worked on Jeffries' eye, as the challenger defiantly insisted he was okay.

In the seventh round Jeffries walked directly at Johnson without feinting or bobbing and provided an easy target for the champion. Jeffries pawed at his badly swollen right eye which was clearly bothering him. Jeffries wanted to engage Johnson at close quarters, but Johnson kept his distance and preferred to box the onrushing challenger, which he did masterfully. At one point in the round Jeffries landed a left hook that drew only laughter from the champion. Johnson's overall boxing skill was dominating the fight. His accurate counterpunching was taking its toll on Jeffries who had no answer for it.

Johnson continued to dictate the action in round eight. After connecting with an especially hard blow, Johnson asked his opponent, "Did you see that one, Jim?"[44] Jeffries tried to maul Johnson and shoved him around the ring, but he was generally ineffective in landing any telling blows. Meanwhile, Johnson regularly scored with strong counterpunches. The round ended with both fighters locked in a clinch. In his telegraphed dispatches, the *Milwaukee Journal's* correspondent declared Johnson's blows to be "snappier and cleaner" than those thrown by Jeffries.

In the ninth round, Johnson continued with his counterpunching strategy, a tactic that irked James J. Corbett in Jeffries' corner. "Make, him fight, Jim!" Corbett shouted. Johnson replied to Corbett, "Never mind, just wait."[45] Johnson scored well with defensive jabs as Jeffries futilely attempted to launch an attack. Jeffries did conclude the round with a good body shot to Johnson's ribs, but the round belonged to the champion. Jeffries reputedly told Corbett to cease the insults directed toward Johnson. Jeffries figured Johnson was excessively punishing him for Corbett's unkind remarks.

Round ten offered a glimmer of hope to Jeffries' supporters. It was fought at a quick pace. Jeffries blocked a Johnson left and countered with a left of his own to Johnson's body. Jeffries scored with four left hooks after breaking from clinches. Johnson landed the final punch of the round—a good body shot as the gong sounded. Johnson was not happy with his performance in that three minutes and noticeably frowned as he walked back to his corner.

The 11th round began cautiously. Jeffries threw the first punch, a left that Johnson parried easily. Johnson responded with three quick lefts to Jeffries' head. Whenever Jeffries advanced forward he bobbed his head to avoid being struck by Johnson's stinging uppercuts. Johnson was too accurate, though. A strong left hook by the champion bloodied Jeffries' nose and lips. Jeffries was clearly laboring, but he managed to connect with two body shots that did not faze Johnson who was backpedaling at the time. "Decidedly Johnson's round," reported the *Milwaukee Journal*.

Round 12 saw a continuation of the strength-sapping punishment that Johnson was liberally doling out to the game but overmatched challenger. Whenever Jeffries advanced, Johnson beat him back. At one point in the round Jeffries rested his head on Johnson's shoulder and attempted to attack the champion with body shots. Johnson adroitly blocked them all in a terrific display of defensive boxing skill that drew applause even from the pro–Jeffries crowd. Johnson concluded the round with more hard blows to Jeffries' head. Jeffries spat out a large amount of blood when he got back to his corner. The *Milwaukee Journal*, in its round-by-round coverage, incredibly reported that Jeffries "was apparently not worried and looked fresh."

In round 13, Jeffries again tried to get through Johnson's defenses and work inside. He did not succeed. He forced a clinch without throwing a punch, but Johnson forced him to back away with a swift volley of sharp blows, a right uppercut being the most damaging. Johnson held Jeffries with his right hand and belted him with three left hooks in succession, punctuating them with another painful right uppercut. Still Jeffries resolutely advanced forward, but each time Johnson met him with a fusillade of blows. The round was overwhelmingly Johnson's who coolly and methodically administered punishment. Jeffries was now visibly tired and his right eye was nearly closed.

Round 14 was Johnson's most dominant frame yet. Jeffries immediately walked straight into a stiff left hand and fell into a clinch. Shortly thereafter, Johnson connected with two more lefts to Jeffries' face. Jeffries plodded forward and was smashed with three successive lefts from the champion. Johnson gleefully taunted the rapidly fading ex-champ. "How do you feel, Jim?' How do you like it?"[46] Three more Johnson lefts found their mark. "They don't hurt,"[47] Jeffries mumbled through split lips, clearly lying. At the end of the 14th round, Jeffries was a mess. His face was smeared with his own blood as were his chest and shoulders. His face was puffy and both eyes were close to closing. The outcome of the bout was now obvious, but Jeffries resolutely continued. There was no quit in him.

By the 15th round Johnson had determined the fight had gone on long enough for his liking and the fans had gotten their money's worth of action. At the bell Johnson took the offensive and attacked the wearying Jeffries. About halfway through the stanza, a short Johnson right uppercut and a series of left hooks to the jaw dropped Jeffries to the canvas for the first time in the Boilermaker's professional career. Jeffries' back was resting against the ropes and his right glove clutched the bottom strand. Jeffries was a beaten man and a pitiful sight; his face, bloodied and swollen, showed the pain of a severe thrashing.

But like the gallant champion he had once been, Jeffries rose to face more of Johnson's punches. The was no neutral-corner rule in 1910 so Johnson was allowed to hover over his fallen foe. Rickard pushed Johnson back slightly, though, to give Jeffries an opportunity to rise. Immediately Johnson belted him with a left hook that sent him over the bottom ring rope near his corner. Jeffries almost came to rest in the first row. The unprecedented sight of Jeffries being knocked to the canvas caused emotion to overtake Jeffries' seconds. They rushed to help him up as did a first-row spectator. Jeffries should have been immediately disqualified for receiving such assistance, but Rickard appeared to be not diligently enforcing the rules. It did not matter, though. Once Jeffries had regained his feet, Johnson was on top of him again. A series of blows punctuated by a sizzling straight right knocked Jeffries down for a third time. As the timekeeper's count reached seven, Jeffries' chief second, Sam Berger, entered the ring to save Jeffries from further punishment and the humiliation of a kayo defeat. The official time of the fight's conclusion was 2:20 of round 15. Said the *Milwaukee Journal*, "While Jeffries was not counted out, this was a merely technical evasion. It was evident that he never could have got up inside ten seconds."

Covering the fight for the *Seattle Post-Intelligencer*, reporter Portus Baxter sent the following succinct lead to his editor: "The black wins!"

In an Associated Press story that ran the following day in the *Arizona Journal-Miner*, Rickard tried to sort out the confusion that engulfed the fight towards its end. Rickard explained the fight had officially ended after the second knockdown when Jeffries had been driven through the ropes. "As Jeffries lay there, his seconds caught hold of him and helped him to his feet. Under the rules of the game, this disqualifies him. I thought his seconds were going to carry him to his corner. Instead they pushed him into the ring to be further beaten. I was doing all I could during the confusion to stop the fight." [Author's note: An examination of the fight film shows that Rickard's body language indicated he was somewhat startled that Jeffries was sent back into the ring to continue. However, he did not signal the fight was over, nor did he assertively try to stop the fight when he realized this was the case.] In an unrelated postscript, Rickard added a hearty note of congratulations to the winner. "Johnson is the most wonderful fighter who ever pulled on gloves. He won as he pleased."

After being assisted back to his stool, Jeffries sadly apologized to his cornermen through his blood-covered face. "I am not a good fighter any longer," he muttered. "I could not come back, boys. I could not come back."[48] Strangely Jeffries requested a souvenir of the beating he absorbed. "Ask Johnson if he will give me his gloves,"[49] he added. Jeffries was badly dazed by Johnson's final onslaught and sat sadly on his stool for several minutes before leaving the ring in an exhausted state on unsteady feet. The *Boston Evening Transcript* declared, "Soothing liquids were applied to the [former] champion's bruised face, but his heart was something that could not be reached. He groaned, 'I was too old to come back.'"

In Johnson's corner, the winner and still champion was not even breathing hard. He received warm congratulations from a small group of well-wishers. One suggested the champion go to Jeffries' corner and shake hands with his vanquished foe. At first, Johnson declined. "No, I don't owe him anything now,"[50] he retorted. Eventually Johnson did try to make the sportsmanlike gesture but he was brusquely waved away by both James J. Corbett and light heavyweight champ Philadelphia Jack O'Brien, a friend of Jeffries.

The large glum crowd exited the wooden bowl and dispersed without incident—and with hardly a sound being uttered. Johnson's decisive victory had silenced even his most vocal detractors. The Associated Press reported, "Hope had lived in thousands of breasts until the last minute, and now their idol had crumbled. The black man stood peerless. They [the spectators] could not help but admire him."[51] A tiny portion of the crowd did patiently wait in their seats until Johnson left the ring. They gave him a warm round of applause in recognition of his excellent performance as he headed to his dressing room.

Most of the disappointed tourists left town quickly. Reno returned to normal within a day or two. Reporter Max Balthasar noted, "Sunday night Reno was the wildest, liveliest town in America. Monday night it was almost like a city of the dead because of the punches of big, black Jack Johnson. Save for the desultory explosion of fireworks of small boys, the streets in the heart of the city were as perfectly proper as a New England village. Reno has seen her best day, for the time being at least."[52] Although Balthasar hinted that another major fight would be held in Reno in September, no world championship fight would be held there again until Sugar Ray Leonard defended his welterweight title versus Bruce Finch in 1982. In a nifty publicity gimmick, three elderly gentlemen who produced ticket stubs from Johnson-Jeffries fight in 1910 were given complimentary VIP tickets to the Leonard-Finch fight 72 years later.

"I did not have the snap of youth I used to have," Jeffries accurately admitted to the press in a prepared post-fight statement. "I believed in my own heart that all the old-time dash was there, but when I started to execute, the speed and youthful stamina were lacking. The things I used to do were impossible."

Jeffries continued: "I guess it's all my own fault. I was getting along nicely and living peacefully on my alfalfa farm, but when they started calling for me and mentioning me as 'the white man's hope,' I guess my pride got the better of my good judgment. I worked long and hard to condition myself, and I was fit as far as strength goes, but the old necessary snap and dash, the willingness to tear in and crush, were not with me. I guess the public will let me alone after this."[53]

The *Milwaukee Journal* reported on its front page, "It was one of the most one-sided battles ever staged between two champions. To appreciate the complete mastery of the black man, it would have been necessary to have been on the ground. Johnson was all that was claimed for him. He was cool at all times and his work was very clever all through the bout. [Johnson] was so much faster than Jeff there was no comparison. Jeffries never had the ghost of a chance."[54]

The *Weekly Republican Press* of Cambridge, OH, reported the grim details of what it described as a "disheartening scene." Its correspondent wrote, "Jack Johnson, the negro, is still the world's heavyweight champion. He knocked out Jim Jeffries in the fifteenth round here [in Reno] on Monday. The fight was one-sided from the start. The negro blocked the old champion's blows at every stage of the game and punished him severely in the last five rounds of the fight."

The *Boston Evening Transcript* reported that by the night of July 5, more than 24 hours after the bout's conclusion,

> Here and there groups of fight experts still linger. The big battle is, of course, the one topic and it is discussed in the cold calm that has followed previous enthusiasm. There is no animosity against Johnson [in Reno], rather keen admiration of his ability as a fighter and his beautiful sparring. The fight had not gone five rounds before Jeffries' partisans began to doubt, and in the eighth they felt sure they had been deluded. With Johnson the undisputed world's champion, the next question is who

Young newsboys prepare to distribute extras covering the Johnson-Jeffries fight in Reno, NV, on July 4, 1910.

will wrest it from him. Ring followers agree that no man now in the game measures up to the job.

In all the fight talk, one thing stands out sharply—there is no more mention of Johnson's "yellow streak," the thing that has been written and talked about ever since he came into ring prominence. Not once did he give any indication of fear. He was not afraid of the big man who faced him.

In John L. Sullivan's report for the *New York Times* the following day, he reiterated his "well-known antipathy" to Johnson's race, but he did state the obvious: "The fight of the century is over and a black man is the undisputed champion of the world."

"Jeffries Meets His Waterloo" screamed the enormous headline in the July 5 *Arizona Journal-Miner*. Various reports from Reno occupied most of the broadsheet's front page. One story noted, "Ring experts agree it was not even a championship fight [in quality]. The reviled Johnson was like a black panther, beautiful in his alertness and defensive tactics. The youth and science of the black man made Jeffries look like a green man. Jeffries fought by instinct, it seemed, showing his gameness and great fighting heart in every round, but he was only a shell of his old self."

The *Butler (PA) Times* devoted just a single paragraph to the fight, although it did appear on the front page. It declared bluntly, "Early in the fight between Johnson and Jeffries, it was demonstrated that the latter was a has-been and the fight ended in the 15th round...."

Johnson's triumph was front-page news across Canada too. The *Saskatoon (SK) Daily Phoenix* reported in its July 5 edition, "John Arthur Johnson, a Texas Negro, the son of an American slave, is tonight the undisputed heavyweight champion of the world. James J. Jeffries of California ... the man who had never been brought to his knees by a blow, passed into history as a broken idol. He met utter defeat at the hands of the black champion. While Jeffries was not actually counted out, he was saved only from this crowning shame by his friends pleading with Johnson not to hit the fallen man again...." The newspaper's report further stated that Jeffries "was like a green and untried boy in the hands of the panther-like negro."

Jack London—the man largely responsible for luring the old champion out of retirement—covered the Johnson-Jeffries bout too, as a correspondent for the *New York Herald*—a newspaper that had been decidedly anti–Johnson in its coverage leading up to the fight. London's dream of Jeffries regaining the title had been decisively shattered. He sadly penned, "[Once] again Johnson sent down to defeat the chosen representative of the white race, and this time the greatest of them."

James J. Corbett, a man twice defeated by Jeffries in title fights but now his biggest supporter, was philosophical about what had happened. "It was simply the old story of the pitcher and the well—once to often," he claimed.

"It has happened to a whole lot of us. That it must happen to Jeffries was just as sure as fate."[55]

Jeffries was quoted in some quarters as saying, "I would not have beaten Johnson in my prime. I could not have gotten to him in a thousand years."[56] In other reports Jeffries was not quite so harsh on himself. He opined the result may have been different if he had faced Johnson six years earlier.

The Associated Press reported that Jeffries was "invisible to all comers throughout the evening" in the hours following the fight. However, he did order champagne to be supplied to his friends, although few were in the mood for such a celebratory beverage. Jeffries' personal physician, Dr. Porter, said that although Jeffries' right eye was swollen shut, his injuries were not especially serious. Interestingly, the doctor claimed Jeffries had been in far worse conditions after other fights.

Jeffries' father, the Rev. Alexis C. Jeffries, was tracked down for his thoughts following his son's first loss in the prize ring. "It's the Lord's will," he commented. "Let us not be downcast. I thought that Jim would win this fight, as he has always won because he is so stout and strong. This will break his heart, but I am glad in one way that Jim is beaten for now I am sure he will never fight again."[57]

Johnson accurately assessed what happened: "Jeffries never could hit me. He couldn't penetrate my defense. I have always known this; he has just found it out. When he crouched, I made him straighten up. Then I picked him to pieces. I used everything there is in pugilism on Jeffries and he could not stand the strain." In another statement, Johnson happily gloated, "I won because I outclassed Mr. Jeffries in every department of the fighting game. Jeffries' blows had no steam behind them, so how could he hope to defeat me? I do not recall a single punch that caused me any discomfort. I am in shape to battle again tomorrow, if necessary."[58]

Boxing fans in Toledo, OH, had ample reason to be confused: Despite widespread information to the contrary, the *Toledo Blade* published an extra edition on July 4 somehow containing an inaccurate bulletin from Reno proclaiming that Jeffries had won the fight! "Before the largest crowd that ever beheld a prize fight," it began, "James J. Jeffries won the battle for the world's heavyweight championship this afternoon." The egregious error was fully and gleefully reprinted by a rival broadsheet, the *Toledo News-Bee*, the next day to mock the *Blade*. The newspaper business was a highly competitive industry in 1910.

As the overwhelmingly white crowd dispersed at the stadium in Reno without incident, so did most of the large gatherings in front of newspaper and telegraph offices in every corner of the United States. The final result elicited little more than a collective groan or gasp in most locales. (New Orleans and Dayton, OH, were exceptions; violence did erupt in front of newspaper offices at both locales.) However, news of Jeffries' defeat caused racial problems almost immediately elsewhere in numerous American cities and towns large and small. A black passenger on a Houston streetcar had his throat fatally slashed by a white passenger for loudly boasting about Johnson's victory. In Uvaldia, GA, a mob of angry whites opened fire on a black labor camp when their post-fight celebrations became far too boisterous and uppity for the locals to tolerate. Three workers died. In St. Louis, scores of emboldened blacks began harassing white men and women on city streets in broad daylight. Police reinforcements were swiftly summoned to club the rowdy negroes back into order.

In Norfolk, VA, a navy town, rowdy blacks—and many peaceful bystanders—were engaged in prolonged battles with approximately 300 white sailors on shore leave once the result from Reno was known. The *Boston Evening Transcript* reported, "Many Negroes are in the hospital with broken heads and bruised bodies as a result of the conflict." The agitated sailors nearly beat one black man to death against an outer wall of Norfolk's post office building.

Justice was meted out swiftly in Philadelphia following a post-fight race riot there. More than 100 men of both races, some with their heads prominently bandaged and sporting other visible wounds, were hauled before police magistrates on July 5 for disturbing the peace. Most were fined, but some of the more prominent battlers were sent to the county prison to serve short terms.

In New York, a black man named Nelson Turner was nearly lynched in the city's San Juan section. Turner reputedly instigated the trouble by impudently and foolishly shouting at a predominantly Caucasian crowd, "We blacks have gone over you whites and we are going to do more to you." Turner then drew a revolver which misfired. The incensed crowd was upon him in moments. They promptly hoisted Turner up a lamppost with the intent of hanging him for his effrontery when the police happened by and intervened. Their arrival no doubt saved Turner from a certain ignominious death.

Some of the reports of violence teetered towards the absurd. In Pittsburgh, a large group of blacks fought wildly among themselves in a dispute over how their gambling winnings on the fight were to be shared. Police were summoned to restore the peace. In Muskogee, a small town situated 48 miles southeast of Tulsa, OK, an enraged H.B. Clement, who claimed to be the second cousin of John L. Sullivan, drew a knife and assaulted two boisterous negroes. Meanwhile, a race riot began under truly odd circumstances in Schenectady, NY, when a white man was seen pushing a wheelbarrow "in which a burly negro was reclining."[59]

In Chicago, Jack Johnson's mother offered her opinion on the widespread civil unrest. The *Ithaca (NY) Chronicle*, reported, "Mother Tiny Johnson deplored all the riots that have resulted from her son's victory, but said it was all due to an unwillingness on the part of many white persons to let a negro express himself." Said the champ's mom, "The whites don't like for a black man to be on top, but Jack's there and his victory will help the entire negro race."

Various disturbing post-fight incidents were reported almost every place in the United States where the two races had to co-exist uneasily. The incidents were so plentiful that the *Toledo (OH) News-Bee* did its best to acknowledge some of the worst of them in point form in its July 5 edition. Here were just a few listed under the banner headline "Races Riot as Johnson and White Wife Banquet":

- Atlanta—Negro runs amuck with knife. Mob tries to kill him. Rescued by police reserves.
- Roanoke, Virginia—Six Negroes critically beaten. Many whites arrested. Saloons closed.
- Louisville—Negroes attack newsboys selling fight extras. Draw revolvers.
- Mound, Illinois—Negroes shoot up the town, killing Negro policeman.
- New Orleans—Riots in front of newspaper bulletins. Bricks and knives used. Reserves called.
- Tullulah, Louisiana—Negro kills conductor who demanded railroad fare.
- Pueblo, Colorado—Thirty hurt in race riots at Negro picnic. Two whites seriously stabbed.
- Wilmington—Negroes attack white man. Whites attempt to lynch three Negroes.

The newspaper accurately summarized what was happening all across America on Independence Day 1910: "The rioting was in no sense sectional," it pointed out. "It resounded from the north, the south, the east, the west. All over the country the effect is the same. It is though the blow that sent white Jim Jeffries through the ropes and into semi-unconsciousness was a signal for his dusky brothers to leap on the whites and strike a blow for supremacy."

In Milwaukee there were no reports of serious trouble on July 4 or afterwards, but sportswriter George E. Phair wrote in the *Milwaukee Sentinel* the next day, "The sunburned citizen at the lower end of Wells Street [the heart of the city's black community] has his day and he is spending it chuckling at the expense of his poor misguided white brethren who were foolish enough to bet against the remarkable Mistah Johnsing [sic]." A rival daily newspaper, the *Milwaukee Journal*, disparagingly referred to the victorious Johnson as "the dinge" and "the Big Smoke." Johnson had been commonly referred to as "the playful Ethiopian" in newspapers for years.

At least 26 people—both white and black—are known to have died in racially charged violence as a direct result of Johnson's dominant triumph in Reno. The total could indeed be higher. There was also at least one suicide reported in connection to the bout: In Sacramento, a boxing fan named Antonine Rochi decided life was not worth living if Jack Johnson still held the world heavyweight championship. Rochi ended it all by taking a dramatic head-first plunge from a six-foot platform onto a concrete floor, breaking his neck.

Given the high levels of violence that followed the fight, it was not at all surprising that within days of it numerous municipalities had pondered banning all screenings of the Johnson-Jeffries fight films. Cincinnati, Fort Worth, Washington, Milwaukee, Norfolk, Louisville, Lexington, Harrisburg and Baltimore were but a few that took such measures. All the municipalities cited public safety, particularly the desire to prevent race riots, as the reason for the ban. Many other cities followed through with similar plans—thus ensuring the syndicate that had paid $200,000 for the film rights would absorb a huge loss. Mayor A.R. Turnbull of Canton, OH, came up with a unique reason why the films were banned in his community. "I think the fight was a fake," he declared, "and it would be an imposition to foist the pictures upon our citizens."[60] (This bizarre claim was pure delusion; it ran absolutely contrary to what the press had reported. The correspondent for *the Boston Evening Transcript* wrote: "The fight was on the square. Of that there can be no doubt.") Taking a polar opposite view on the fight films was mayor William Jay Gaynor of New York City. He was quite open-minded about the issue. Gaynor was willing to have the Johnson-Jeffries movies shown in America's largest city, saying it would be hypocritical to ban them while allowing the details of the fight to appear in print. Similarly, the sentiment in Paterson, NJ, was heavily in favor of permitting films of the bout to be shown as there had never been any noteworthy racial trouble in that city. However, the *Paterson Press* commented, "It is predicted that crowds will not be as large as would have been the case if the battle had been more hotly contested."

Not long afterward Congress passed federal legislation to ban all boxing films from interstate commerce, thus reducing their potential audience considerably. This development pleased the anti-boxing advocates. Said Victor Berger, a prominent Milwaukee socialist editor and politician who utterly hated the sport, "As far as brutalizing influences are concerned, people might just as well watch two big bloodhounds, the one white and the other black, gnaw at each other's throats as witness a fight such as the one held on July Fourth." The law stayed on the books until 1940. Reformers were quick to cite the widespread post-fight violence as ample evidence why professional boxing ought to be abolished altogether.

Appalled by stories of assertive and aggressive behavior by blacks in the fight's aftermath, the following ominous editorial appeared in the July 5 edition of the *Los Angeles Times*:

A Message to the Black Man

Do not point your nose too high. Do not swell your chest too much. Do not boast too loudly. Do not be puffed up. Let not your ambition be inordinate or take a wrong direction. Remember you have done nothing at all. You are just the same member of society you were last week. You are on no higher plane, deserve no new consideration, and will get none. No man will think a bit higher of you because your complexion is the same as that of the victor at Reno.

In contrast to the violence occurring elsewhere in the United States, Johnson and his party celebrated his triumph in a private railroad car. He arrived in Chicago, his adoptive hometown, in the early afternoon of Thursday, July 7, to a boisterous and joyous welcome—at least from the city's blacks who resided in the area, which, in 1910, was commonly called "Little Africa." Rose petals were tossed at Johnson's special touring car as he was paraded in grand fashion from the train station to the home that he had recently bought for his beloved mother. She was hosting a chicken feast for her famous son. Two bands provided celebratory music. According to the *Ithaca Chronicle*, a squadron of negro national guardsmen was present "to give an official tone to the reception."

The *Milwaukee Sentinel* described the sizable turnout of celebrants as a "vari-colored crowd of 10,000 persons including whites, negroes, and a sprinkling of Japanese and Chinese." It further noted, "The big negro's face was illuminated by his famous display of golden dentistry." It was undoubtedly the absolute apex of the great champion's tumultuous life. Always one who could be counted on to stir the pot, Johnson told reporters that same day he had been offered a $50,000 bribe to deliberately throw the fight to Jeffries. Johnson revealed no specifics about the alleged bribe—and he and Jeffries had clearly fought honestly—so the story justifiably died a quick death.

Jeffries kept his promise about retiring. He returned to his alfalfa farm and never boxed again. He and Johnson never did become friendly once their ring careers ended, as old adversaries sometimes do. They were too unalike. As late as 1930 Jeffries refused to be photographed with Johnson or shake his hand when, by chance, they happened to be attending the same boxing-related social event in Los Angeles.

Tex Rickard's thirst for travel new adventures returned. By the end of 1910 he had bought 325,000 acres of land in Paraguay and 50,000 head of cattle to raise on it. However, the allure and profits of boxing would bring him back to the United States before the end of the decade.

Johnson waited two years before defending his title again, in 1912, against Fireman Jim Flynn. It was another Fourth of July affair. This time the venue

Top: Jack Johnson and Fireman Jim Flynn get their prefight instructions before their title bout in Las Vegas, NM—that's right, New Mexico—on July 4, 1912. The horrible mismatch was stopped by the local sheriff in the ninth round when the outclassed Flynn began deliberately headbutting the champion. *Bottom:* Jack Johnson and his wife Etta Terry Duryea, a Brooklyn socialite. They met in 1909 and were married in January 1911. Etta committed suicide in December 1912.

was Las Vegas—the Las Vegas located in New Mexico. Few fans thought Flynn had a chance to topple the world champion—and the majority was correct. Before just 3,200 spectators, Johnson won easily. Because Johnson had a guaranteed purse of $30,000, promoter Jack Curley lost about $22,000. As was the case in Sydney in 1908, the police halted Johnson's bout versus Jim Flynn at 1:45 of the ninth round. Flynn was covered with blood and had resorted to numerous instances of head butting to try to thwart the champion. Captain Fred Fornoff of the New Mexico Mounted Police stopped the mismatch because, he later said, the bout had ceased to be a contest of boxing skill. The *Milwaukee Journal* reported that fans felt thoroughly cheated, calling the debacle "the poorest excuse for a prize fight they had seen in many a day."

Following the triumph over Flynn, Johnson's biggest adversary was the law. Congress passed the Mann Act, specifically with Johnson in mind, making it a federal crime to cross state borders with a woman for "immoral purposes." In 1912, to avoid prosecution, Johnson skipped the border into Canada with a black baseball team and boarded a ship to Europe. Back home, he was tried in absentia, found guilty of violating the Mann Act, and sentenced to a year in federal prison—a stint to be served if and when he ever re-entered the United States.

Johnson arrived in England and found he was not particularly welcome there. It was nothing personal, he was assured, but his prolonged presence in Great Britain could hurt Anglo-American relations. Johnson then crossed the English Channel to France where he was received more warmly. With his money running short, Johnson made a title defense in Paris on December 19, 1913, versus Battling Jim Johnson, an obscure American pugilist. Johnson versus Johnson was a terribly dull contest—a ten-round draw in which neither man was particularly assertive. The fans booed loudly throughout. Some boxing historians insist it was actually an exhibition match rather than a genuine title fight. Perhaps it was the prevailing perception. There is no known film of the contest and many American newspapers did not bother to

A well-attired Jack Johnson in a posed photograph, circa 1911.

report the result. If one takes the bout at face value, however, it was the first time in boxing history two black men faced each other for the world heavyweight championship.

The following summer Jack Johnson was still residing in the French capital. He made one more title defense, versus another American, Frank Moran, on June 27, 1914, in Paris. The fight's referee was a very youthful, up-and-coming French fighter named Georges Carpentier. This time there was no doubt if the fight was for the world championship. It was, but it was just as listless as the Johnson-Johnson fiasco six months earlier. Johnson won a 20-round decision, but he was clearly on the decline. "Utterly disgusted, the enormous crowd of fight fans who packed the Velodrome d'Hiver to see the alleged mill vented their dissatisfaction with volleys of boos," declared William Phillips Simms of United Press. "It was not a fight. It was not a near fight. Moran showed absolutely nothing. Johnson was never extended. Whether he can still fight a real man is as much as a mystery as ever." In its coverage of the bout, a headline in the *Milwaukee Journal* labeled Johnson "the best bunco artist in the world."

Jack Johnson on his 37th birthday in 1915-a few days before he would lose his world heavyweight crown to Jess Willard in Havana.

The debt-ridden Johnson never saw a franc of the money he was expecting to earn by putting his world championship on the line versus Moran; his purse was seized by creditors before he could collect it. The very next day Austria's Archduke Franz Ferdinand was assassinated in Sarajevo and much of the world descended into war shortly thereafter. Suddenly who possessed the sports world's greatest prize was not so important.

Johnson finally lost his crown on April 5, 1915, in Cuba to Jess Willard, the latest great white hope—and the first successful one. The old champion was knocked out with a powerful, straight right hand in the 26th round of a scheduled 45-round fight at a Havana racetrack. This is how the end of the bout—and Johnson's six-year reign as world heavyweight champion—was described in one telegraphed report to American fight fans: "The negro's knees folded up under him. He sank slowly to the floor and rolled over on his back, party under the ropes. [Referee Jack] Welsh waved Willard back and began his count. Up and down swung the referee's hand, but Johnson never moved. At the count of ten, Welsh turned and held up Willard's hand, and a new champion replaced Johnson...."

The crowd was overwhelmingly made up of American tourists and expats who rejoiced at the welcome sight of portly referee Jack Welsh tolling ten over the prostrate Johnson. The same joyful reaction was commonplace throughout white America. The *Milwaukee Journal* reported, "[The city] went fight mad when the news was flashed that the championship had been brought back to the white race. Men who had buried boxing when Jeffries lost in 1910 suddenly took renewed interest in the game and were all loud in their praise of the new champion." The *Calgary Herald's* correspondent in New York said America's largest city was, by and large, thrilled with the outcome from Havana. "Everywhere the prevailing impression is that Johnson's defeat by the big Kansan will give a stimulus to boxing and make it more popular all over the United States."

Because fight films were barred from interstate commerce after the Johnson-Jeffries fight in 1910, this photograph of referee Jack Welsh counting over the fallen Jack Johnson in round #26 was the only image most Americans saw of Jess Willard's title-winning fight in Havana, Cuba, in 1915.

Johnson was both philosophical and sportsmanlike in defeat. The following morning he told Barry Faris of the *Pittsburgh Press*, "Give me what credit is due. No other heavyweight in the world could have stood off Willard for 26 rounds. I gave Jeffries credit for gamely taking a beating from me at Reno; now give it to me." Faris claimed that nearly a day after the fight, Johnson "was sore in mind and body. His ebony frame was wracked with pain from Willard's pummeling." On the other hand, Faris noted that Willard, "the new world's white champion heavyweight," was practically unmarked. He was already pondering lucrative offers for vaudeville appearances and "was happy, like a schoolboy with a new slate." Willard was mobbed on Havana's streets as he attempted to go for a leisurely morning stroll on April 6. Crowds blocked traffic to greet him. According to Faris, "The temperamental Cubans went into raptures of demonstrations." Jess Willard clearly was the man of the hour.

Jess Willard, a onetime circus strongman, was an imposing physical specimen at 6'7". He certainly was not in Johnson's league as a boxer—who was?—but the younger challenger's stamina in a marathon bout under the hot Cuban sun was entirely the difference. Johnson had turned 37 five days before the fight. He was old for a boxer and no longer the invincible force he had been in Sydney or Reno. Time had eroded his ring skills. The dethroned titlist later claimed he had taken a dive in Havana for an alleged $50,000 payoff, but most boxing historians doubt his claim. New champion Willard (whom the press nicknamed "the Pottawattamie Giant" after his Kansas hometown) scoffed at the notion too. "If Johnson threw the fight, I wish he had throwed it sooner," Willard commented brusquely. "It was hotter than hell out there."[61]

Johnson continued to box abroad after losing the title to Willard. He was no longer much of an attraction, though, as his skills had faded badly. He eventually cut a deal with American authorities and peaceably surrendered at the Mexico-U.S. border in 1920. He served his sentence at Leavenworth Penitentiary in Kansas where he was a model prisoner. For good behavior—imagine that!—Johnson had his one-year sentence reduced to nine months. In 2018, a serious movement was spearheaded by actor Sylvester Stallone for the long-dead Johnson to be posthumously pardoned by President Donald Trump. It occurred on May 24, 2018. "Today I've issued an executive grant of clemency, a full pardon, posthumously, to John Arthur (Jack) Johnson," the chief executive said.

Jack Johnson died in a single-vehicle car crash on June 10, 1946, in Franklinton, NC, a small community not too distant from Raleigh. He was driving too fast—a dangerous lifelong habit that finally caught up with him. Johnson was travelling from Texas to New York making public appearances for pay. According to unconfirmed reports, Johnson was angrily speeding away from a diner that had refused to serve him. He lost control of his vehicle and crashed into a utility pole. A travelling companion, Fred L. Scott, sustained only minor injuries in the mishap. Johnson was 68 years old. Johnson left behind a wife, Irene, who resided in Chicago. He is buried in that city's Graceland Cemetery under a marker that only says "Johnson." For years there was no gravestone at all. The *Milwaukee Journal*, which published a very favorable obituary, simplistically noted in a wonderfully understated fashion that Johnson experienced "a decline in public esteem" about the time he married a white woman and defeated James J. Jeffries.

Into his so-called golden years, Jeffries remained a beloved figure in the boxing world; perhaps he was a living reminder of simpler, more cherished times for nostalgic fight fans. On Saturday, April 15, 1950—the Boilermaker's 75th birthday—Governor Earl Warren issued a proclamation declaring it "Jim Jeffries Day" in the state of California. Numerous celebrities from Hollywood and the boxing world dropped in on the old champ's home to wish him well. By that time in his life, Jeffries' mind was undeniably sharp but his body was failing. The mere act of greeting all his visitors—even while reclining in an easy chair—was a tiring chore for the old champion. A story about Jeffries' milestone birthday bash appeared in the July 1950 issue of *The Ring* magazine. Editor Nat Fleischer traveled across the continent to be there. He wrote, "Great ringmen of the past, champions and near champions, some with cauliflowered ears, others, like the handsome Jack Root, with not a mark on them, mingled with civic leaders, neighbors and athletes in other fields, to make the occasion 'the happiest of my life,' as Jeffries expressed it. It was a memorable day for big Jim, and he enjoyed every minute of it, though he was mighty tired when the speeches and presentations had been completed. He is not in good health."

Indeed, Jeffries was described in news reports as a "semi-invalid" after suffering a stroke in 1945 at age 70. On Tuesday, March 3, 1953, James J. Jeffries, 77, passed away from a heart attack at his home in Burbank, CA. He was a widower with no children; his beloved wife Freida had been struck and killed by an automobile in 1941. His niece, Mrs. Lillian Bull, had been the former champion's housekeeper and caregiver in his final few years.

As he was a celebrated national and world-famous figure, the Boilermaker's death was major news. Sam Levy, the sports editor of the *Milwaukee Journal*, nostalgically recalled that Jeffries was "the idol of every schoolboy" during the first decade of the 20th century. Obituaries focused largely on Jeffries' famous ring victories and his reign as world heavyweight champion from 1899 to 1905 rather than his ill-advised comeback attempt versus Jack Johnson in Reno in 1910. "In his prime, old-time fight fans aver, there was no one like Big Jim for speed and hitting power," said the Associated Press' death notice—which even went as far as to split hairs: It claimed that Jeffries had never been "knocked out," but it did grudgingly acknowledge that Jeff was saved from a certain kayo defeat at the hands of Jack Johnson by his compassionate seconds on the sweltering afternoon of July 4, 1910.

Rickard, Johnson and Jeffries are all long dead. But the legacy of the "Fight of the Century" has not died, especially in the Nevada town that hosted it. On July 4, 2010, a ceremony commemorating the hundredth anniversary of the Johnson-Jeffries contest was held in Reno. It was only a small part of a larger festival weekend that featured a live professional boxing card and panel discussions featuring boxing and social scholars that focused on the famous fight's overall impact on American history. "We were trying to think of another sporting event in modern times that has captivated the American public like this one did, but we can't come up with one," said event organizer Tommy Lane, a Reno resident and boxing history buff who had long been captivated by stories pertaining to the famous Johnson-Jeffries clash. Lane told Tim Smith, a black writer from the *New York Daily News*, "By far this was the biggest event that Reno ever held. There were no race riots anywhere in Nevada after the fight. People were calling [the folks in] Reno radical for holding the fight. But maybe they weren't that radical after all." Smith's centennial story focused on how unfair and disrespectful the mainstream press had been to Jack Johnson back in 1910. Yet, amusingly, Smith disrespected Jeffries by misspelling his surname as "Jefferies" throughout his article.

Even a century after Jeffries was badly defeated in Reno, the bout was still generating controversy. Boxing writer and historian Richard Hoffer opined in a piece for the July 5, 2010, issue of *Sports Illustrated* that the Johnson-Jeffries fight should not be acknowledged with any sort of positive centennial observation or celebration. Hoffer wrote, "[The fight] set off a coast-to-coast spasm of racial unrest that not only confirmed the cruel bigotry of an adolescent nation, but also did as much to stunt integration as any event of the time. It was an anti–Joe Louis moment, a reverse Jackie Robinson, causing damage that would require nearly half a century of social repair. Which is to say this is not a centennial we can very well celebrate...."

One hundred years after the famous championship fight captivated America and much of the western world, Tex Rickard's wooden stadium on East 4th and Toana streets in Reno was long gone. The site is now the property of the Reno Salvage Company, but there is an upright marker on the corner of the property, erected by the state of Nevada, declaring the historical significance of what happened there on Monday, July 4, 1910. As planned, at precisely 2:44 p.m. on Sunday, July 4, 2010, the same bell that had been used in the Johnson-Jeffries fight a century earlier was brought to the location and symbolically clanged ten times.

July 2, 1921

Georges Carpentier vs. Jack Dempsey
Gallic Flair and American Fury

"France as a nation prays as one that Georges will be returned the victor. His success or failure is a matter of national concern. On the result may hinge the elevation of France. His defeat would be regarded as a national calamity."—Part of a French newspaperman's report to his readers back home on July 1, 1921, as quoted by Ring Lardner

"For they were all here—society women and the shop girl, the merchant prince and the $20-a-week clerk who worked for him, the man who lived by his brains, and the fellow without a profession, and sportsmen from five continents."—A correspondent from the *Milwaukee Journal* describing the diversity of classes among the huge crowd in excess of 91,000 spectators at Boyle's Thirty Acres to witness the Carpentier-Dempsey fight on July 2, 1921

"In the great combat staged there in that colossal sterilizer beneath the Jersey sun there was little to entertain the connoisseur of the gladiatorial delicacies. It was simply a brief and hopeless struggle between a man full of romantic courage and one overwhelmingly superior in every way..."—The opening two sentences of H. L. Mencken's coverage of the Carpentier-Dempsey fight

On the afternoon of Saturday, July 2, 1921, more than 91,000 excited boxing fans crammed their way into a rickety, specially constructed outdoor stadium near Jersey City, NJ, to watch a world heavyweight championship fight. They gladly paid more than $1.7 million for the privilege of being there at a time when $50 a month was a typical working man's wages. Precisely, the final gate receipts were $1,789,238. It was a fantastic sight. No one associated with boxing had ever seen anything remotely close to the huge crowd drawn to the spectacle. Folks who could not attend the bout in person could console themselves by listening to the action being described on the radio—a broadcasting first. The attraction was a fight for the world heavyweight championship with an exotic, international flavor. Oddly enough, the French challenger, Georges Carpentier, was the fan favorite among the crowd and in many parts of the United States, even though the title was held by an exciting, colorful American slugger named Jack Dempsey.

William Harrison Dempsey was born on June 24, 1895, in Manassa, a mining and ranching community in the central part of eastern Colorado. Named after former president William Henry Harrison, Dempsey was the 11th of 13 children. Manassa's residents in 1895 were mostly descendants of Mormon pioneers, but there was some Spanish and Mexican blood mixed into the population along with native American. Manassa was hardly a metropolis at the turn of the 20th century; perhaps 750 souls resided there. More than 100 years later, it was still a small dot on the state map. (Its population, according to the 2010 national census, was slightly below 1,000 permanent inhabitants.)

Dempsey was the son of Mary Cilia (Smoot) and Hyrum Dempsey. His father's name is spelled as "Hiram" in some Dempsey biographies. The Dempsey family's lineage was a mix of Irish, Cherokee, and Jewish ancestry. Hiram worked occasionally as a teacher. The Dempseys never had much money to their names, so they constantly sought new opportunities wherever they were rumored to be had. Because his father had difficulty finding work, the family relocated often. At various times, the family lived in Utah and West Virginia. Dempsey's parents became converts to Mormonism in about 1880. As Manassa had a Mormon population, that is how William Harrison Dempsey came to be born there. Dempsey's obscure place of birth eventually provided him with one of the all-time great ring nicknames: "the Manassa Mauler."

Dempsey, who was admittedly never much of a scholar, dropped out of elementary school to go to work before he was 14. In fact, his eighth-grade teacher, Ray Wentz, bluntly told Dempsey he would amount to nothing. He was an occasional miner; sometimes he found work as a cowboy. His older brother, Bernie, boxed for a few extra bucks in quasi-legal saloon fights and taught his younger brother how to skillfully throw punches in bunches. He also advised William to chew on pine resin to strengthen his jaw muscles and to toughen his skin by soaking it with beef brine. By the time Dempsey was 12 he had worked in a sugar refinery, shined shoes, and unloaded cases of beets for the princely sum of ten cents per ton in Provo, UT. William and left home at the age of 16. His independent existence was no bed of roses.

Dempsey led the life of a vagabond, riding on the undersides of trains and sleeping in hobo camps. Pretty soon he was mimicking Bernie. He would walk into a saloon and challenge all comers to fights. The purses were whatever the other customers were willing to toss to the battlers.

From 1911 to 1916, Dempsey became something of a regular fixture at Peter Jackson's saloon in Salt Lake City where an actual ring had been set up. Hardy Downey, a local promoter, arranged his fights. Dempsey—who assumed the ring name of Kid Blackie—could always hit with fearsome power. In his first bout for Downey he rendered his opponent senseless with a single blow. Ironically, the opponent was billed as "One Punch Hancock." Because boxing was far from being strictly regulated in Utah a century ago, the true number of bouts Dempsey had will never be known. Undoubtedly, his official record does not account for all of Dempsey's formative ring encounters. Dempsey acknowledged that fact in an interview years after he retired. "Who knows how many fights I had between 1911 and 1916?" he declared. "The record books don't contain them, and I couldn't name the number or identify all the faces today if my life depended on doing it. I'd guess a hundred."[1]

Long before the future heavyweight champion took his first breath, there had been a world middleweight champion from Ireland named Jack Dempsey—more familiarly known as "the Nonpareil" Jack Dempsey. (The Irish middleweight died five months after William Harrison Dempsey was born.) Bernie Dempsey was boxing under the name of "Jack Dempsey" around 1914, presumably to evoke the memory of the deceased Irish battler. One day when Bernie was ill, his little brother took his place on a fight card and, for the sake of convenience, used his name. William Dempsey/Kid Blackie won the bout easily, defeating George Copelin in seven rounds, despite giving away 20 pounds to his larger opponent. From that point onward, William Harrison Dempsey was Jack Dempsey, and he was ascending in the rugged world of professional boxing.

When one looks at Jack Dempsey's record, the most startling part of it is the vast number of early round knockouts he recorded. At a time when boxers typically thought the best strategy was to pace themselves for a long contest—some important bouts were scheduled for 20 rounds or more—Dempsey paid absolutely no heed to this notion and immediately went on the offensive from the opening bell. If he could blast someone into oblivion inside of the first round he did it—and he did it often. An examination of Dempsey's ring record shows ten first-round knockout victories in 1918 alone. Five of them came in succession in a short span of 59 days. They were sandwiched between a second-round knockout and a fifth-round knockout. Two opponents of some repute failed to last even 20 seconds with the Manassa Mauler. To prove it was no fluke, Dempsey flattened five consecutive opponents in 1919 in the first round too. Thus, anyone who attended a Jack

Dempsey fight could reasonably expect to witness a brief bout. Dempsey was not beating stiffs, either. He was cleaning out most of the top contenders that separated him from world heavyweight champion Jess Willard. Willard, though, was unimpressed. "[Dempsey] is not going to win the championship in 23 seconds. No, not in an hour and 23 seconds,"[2] he confidently stated.

Dempsey was more than a one-dimensional brawler, though; he put science into his aggression. Demspey would advance out of a crouch, bobbing and weaving his way towards his opponent. Demspey did not block a lot of his adversary's punches, but his slippery movement allowed him to evade them all the same. Dempsey put a considerable amount of thought and strategy into his personal mechanics of boxing. The "Dempsey roll" is the best example of this concept. Dempsey used the law of inertia to his advantage. In simple terms, he used an unorthodox tactic of deliberately being off balance to his benefit. Dempsey would lean his weight into his front leg and then quickly lift it up. The maneuver "triggered" his back leg to prevent him from falling, prompting him to lean forward. This technique allowed Dempsey to put his entire weight into every punch as he was essentially falling forward into his opponent as he delivered his blows. If the punch connected—and it often did—its power was greatly increased over a fighter who merely shifted his weight as he threw a punch.

By the summer of 1919, Jack Dempsey was the leading contender for the world heavyweight title. He had gotten there by singlehandedly inflicting a reign of terror on overwhelmed opponents. He had just turned 24 years old, but he was the obvious and logical opponent for reigning champ Jess Willard. Willard was by no means a great boxer—but he was a huge physical specimen. An ex-circus strongman, he stood somewhere between 6'6" and 6'7" and packed a mighty wallop himself. Stamina was his strength. If a fight dragged on, he could be counted on to go the distance and still be fresh in the later rounds. That was one of the key factors that allowed Willard to beat Jack Johnson for the title in 1915. The fight lasted 26 rounds under the broiling midday sun in Havana, Cuba. The conditions sapped the 37-year-old Johnson of his vigor. Willard was the fresher man and disposed of the old champ with a single straight right hand.

Willard did not do much with his title, however. With the First World War raging, he defended it just once, in 1916, versus the veteran Pittsburgh heavyweight Frank Moran in Madison Square Garden. Willard did not especially enjoy boxing—but it paid more handsomely than being a Kansas farmer. Instead of ring battles, Willard preferred to make lucrative stage appearances. He even starred as the lead in a 1919 silent film drama titled *The Challenge of Chance*. By 1919, the war was over, Americans returned to their love of big-time sports, and a heavyweight title fight was necessary. Jack Dempsey would provide the opposition. The fight was set for Toledo, Ohio on the Fourth of

July. The champion was guaranteed a $100,000 purse by promoter Tex Rickard. Dempsey, the challenger, settled for $27,500—the largest purse in his career to date.

In retrospect, the fact that Willard was the betting favorite—even a slight one at 5:4—seems absurd. Willard himself was now 37 years old—the same age Jack Johnson was when he lost the title. The lone advantages Willard possessed over Dempsey were height and weight. Willard was at least five inches taller and 58 pounds heavier than the young challenger. All other aspects of the fight game—power, speed, punching accuracy, mobility, youth—were clearly edges for the challenger. Moreover, rumors had it that

Jack Dempsey pummels champion Jess Willard en route to winning the world heavyweight title on July 4, 1919, in Toledo, OH. Willard was floored seven times in the first round in the horribly one-sided contest.

Willard thought so little of Dempsey that he had shirked his training and had been consuming an abundance of beverages that were slightly more potent than lemonade. Most of the bettors' money was placed on Dempsey, although there were enough Willard backers to match it. One man had a sign attached to his automobile that said, "I will accept a $4,000 bet against this machine." He was backing the challenger. Dempsey's manager, Jack (Doc) Kearns, a roguish character who had latched onto the soon-to-be-champion in 1917, was so certain that Dempsey would speedily demolish Willard that he bet $10,000 at 10:1 odds that his fighter would win by a first-round knockout. Strangely, when a reporter tracked down Dempsey's father in Utah, Hyrum Dempsey predicted his son would lose.

Tex Rickard went into overdrive promoting the Dempsey-Willard fight as a must-see attraction. He had an 80,000-seat stadium built out of green lumber to accommodate the crowd that was sure to come. Come they did to what was called Bay View Park Arena on the shores of Lake Erie's Maumee Bay, but it was not a sellout. Despite 3,000 fans arriving from New York City alone, fewer than 50,000 people bought tickets. It was still a terrific turnout for a boxing match, but Rickard's initial hopes that the gate receipts would exceed $1 million did not happen. Perhaps the high admission cost dissuaded potential ticket buyers. The cheapest seats cost $10 apiece. Even parking spaces were sold for $2—more than a day's wages for the average American laborer in 1919. Scalpers took a beating. It was reported that two $50 tickets could be bought for $70 from speculators. The smart patrons wisely purchased seat cushions too. Friday, July 4 in Toledo was oppressively hot; the temperature was 105 degrees by fight time—and the raw, untreated lumber used to construct the rows of wooden benches was loaded with pine tar. The sticky goo that oozed forth in the afternoon sun ruined more than one pair of pants. The *Milwaukee Sentinel* commented on the blistering heat, "Cracked ice was worth more at the arena than all the diamonds in the neckties worn by the old-time sports."

Shortly before the fight Rickard spoke to Dempsey in his dressing room. It was hardly a pep talk. Rickard was convinced the much larger Willard would crush the ballyhooed challenger. He compassionately told Dempsey that if Willard hurt him badly he should just fall to the canvas and be counted out. There was no need to be unnecessarily brave and get severely injured.

The size difference in the two fighters was obvious when they met in the center of the ring for referee Ollie Pecord's instructions. Willard was clearly the larger man, but Dempsey looked like more of a fighter. He was tanned and rugged looking. He had the hungry look of a man on a mission. In contrast, Willard looked complacent, almost bored with the scene. Timekeeper Warren Barbour (who would later become a United States senator) rang the bell, but the sound was muffled; hardly anyone heard it. Willard, wearing dark trunks, thought it had rung but he was unsure. He looked toward Barbour for confirmation. The bell rang again—and one of the most memorable first rounds in boxing history began.

Dempsey, clad in white trunks, advanced from his corner. To no one's surprise, he went on the offensive. For the first 85 seconds Dempsey pressed the action but did not land a significant blow. He moved laterally, in and out, probing for an opening. Willard tied him up a couple of times and tried to keep the pesky challenger at bay with his jab. The deciding moment came when Dempsey—using his "roll" technique—launched a four-punch combination. The first three blows were directed at Willard's midsection and forced his guard downward. The fourth was perhaps the most beautiful left hook ever witnessed in a heavyweight title fight. It landed flush, with great impact, on the right side of the champion's jaw. Willard dropped to the canvas, knocked down for the first time as a professional boxer, utterly stunned by the power of young Dempsey's crushing punch. The excited crowd rose and roared.

Willard staggered to his feet unsteadily. Under the rules of the day, Dempsey could hit Willard as soon as he rose; there was no neutral-corner rule nor was there a mandatory eight-count. Dempsey pounced on Willard and belted him with a volley of blows—and Willard went down again. The wounded champ rose a second time, and again Dempsey sent him to the canvas a third time. In all, Willard hit the deck seven times. (Some journalists lost count. The Associated Press correspondent reported that Willard had only been floored five times.) More importantly, as the *Milwaukee Journal* reported, "Everybody, including referee Ollie Pecord and Dempsey himself believed Willard had been counted out." Willard's handlers half-escorted and half-carried their bloody giant back to his corner. Jack Kearns had seemingly won $100,000. However, the muted bell became a factor again. Although almost no one had heard its peal, timekeeper Barbour insisted it had sounded when Pecord's count had only reached seven.

Bedlam overtook the ring as a dozen excited Dempsey fans rushed into it to congratulate the new champion. Dempsey wasn't interested in sticking around and headed toward his dressing room. However, Doc Kearns sensed something was clearly wrong. He got the word from timekeeper Barbour and referee Pecord that the fight was not yet over—Willard had been saved by the bell! Kearns screamed at Dempsey to get his attention above all the clamor and waved for him to return immediately. Dempsey returned before he was disqualified. (What a mess that would have been had Dempsey kept walking!) The carnage continued for six more minutes. Over the next two rounds, Dempsey pounded the courageous Willard's face until it looked like raw ground beef, yet Willard did not quit, nor did he go down again—despite having two teeth knocked out of his mouth. The champion's face and torso were splattered with blood. So was Dempsey—but none of the blood was his. Willard even managed to land a couple of insignificant blows on the relentless challenger. Eventually Willard's cornermen conceded defeat. They compassionately decided not to send their man out for the fourth round to take even more of what the *Milwaukee Sentinel* called "a merciless beating." Willard thus became the first world heavyweight champion of the gloved era to relinquish his title while sitting on his stool. (Forty-five years would go by before it would happen again—to Sonny Liston.) The battered Willard reportedly muttered these consoling words to himself through his swollen face: "I have $100,000 and a farm in Kansas…. I have $100,000 and a farm in Kansas." Amazingly, Willard's surrender was criticized by some writers. William H. Rocap of the *Philadelphia Ledger* sadistically denounced the dethroned champion's "lack of courage" and called for a formal investigation into his capitulation. Dempsey, the victor, was completely unmarked.

Years later a wild controversy emerged regarding Dempsey's victory in Toledo on July 4, 1919. Early in 1964, *Sports Illustrated* printed parts of Doc Kearns' yet-to-be-published memoirs. In them he stated that Dempsey's gloves—specifically his hand wraps—had been treated with plaster of Paris when he beat Jess Willard for the title! The 68-year-old Dempsey adamantly denied the charge. There were several problems with Kearns' remarkable accusation. First, Kearns had died in July 1963, so the *SI* story was published posthumously. Dempsey and Kearns had not had a working relationship in nearly 40 years; there had been acrimony between the two men since the mid–1920s. Finally, the physical evidence of wrongdoing simply was not there. The gloves Dempsey wore in Toledo were retrieved from a collector. They were in good condition and contained no traces of the alleged plaster of Paris. Experts further declared that had Dempsey worn loaded gloves, they would have been in tatters and Dempsey would have broken his hands. Moreover, the films of the fight show Willard examining Dempsey's hands inside the ring prior to the first bell. Nothing was amiss. In 1919 it was commonplace for the combatants to be gloved inside the ring—not in their dressing rooms as is the modern routine. That was the case for the Dempsey-Willard fight. Few boxing historians give Kearns' story any credence. Nat Fleisher, the editor of *The Ring* magazine thought Kearns' accusation was preposterous. He stated he had been inside Dempsey's dressing room when the challenger's hands had been taped by one of his seconds—and Kearns was not even present! It was likely that Kearns, a spiteful man, was trying to hurt his most famous client from beyond the grave. It was also a nifty ploy to sell books. Kearns' memoirs were eventually published in 1966 under the title *The Million Dollar Gate*.

Be that as it may, Jack Dempsey was the new heavyweight champion of the world at age 24. Lightweight boxer Richie Mitchell, who covered the fight

Jack Dempsey (left) stands alongside his manager, Jack (Doc) Kearns, in this photo from February 1924. The two men parted ways not long afterward.

for the *Milwaukee Journal*, called Dempsey "the greatest puncher the boxing game has ever turned out." His aggressive style, rags-to-riches past, and spectacular record of quick knockouts certainly made Dempsey the most marketable champion since the days of John L. Sullivan. Dempsey was also personable and ruggedly handsome. (During a visit Dempsey made to Europe in 1924, his hotel in Berlin was besieged by dozens of smitten frauleins who had gathered to gawk at the famed American fighter.) He was always a good interview too. Be that as it may, Dempsey was not yet the beloved sports figure who would be eulogized by Red Smith in 1983 as having more lasting popularity than any other star athlete from the 1920s. Dempsey had a public-relations skeleton in his closet: a lack of a military record during the First World War. Boxing historian Bert Sugar wrote in his book *The Great Fights*, "One thing that could not be tolerated by a proud and victorious America was anyone who had not 'pulled his weight' in the war effort." Indeed, Grantland Rice made a huge point of this Dempsey shortcoming in his report from Toledo:

> If [Dempsey] had been a fighting man he would have been in khaki when at 22 he had no other responsibilities but to protect his own hide. So let us have no illusions

about our new heavyweight champion. He is a marvel in the ring, the greatest boxing or the greatest hitting machine even the old-timers have ever seen.

But he isn't the world's champion fighter. Not by a margin of 50,000 men who either stood or were even ready to stand the test of cold steel and exploding shell for anything from six cents to a dollar a day.[3]

Here is the origin of the controversy: When the United States entered the Great War, Dempsey remained active as a fighter but worked occasionally at a Tacoma, WA, shipyard. One day Doc Kearns thought it would be good for Dempsey's reputation to show him doing his patriotic bit for America, but the plan backfired badly. He arranged for a publicity photograph to be taken of Dempsey at the Sun Shipyard in Philadelphia—where he did not work—holding a jackhammer. It was assumed the photo would be used for recruitment purposes. It wasn't. It appeared in daily newspapers instead. Dempsey was wearing shiny patent-leather shoes instead of work boots, so the photo was obviously staged. Dempsey had tried to enlist in the army but was ruled ineligible because he was married at the time. (It was hardly a fairy-tale romance. Dempsey's spouse at the time was a rough-edged ex-prostitute named Maxine Cates whom he barely saw, but nevertheless the army classified him as 4-F for having a wife as a dependent. He was also the primary supporter of his parents.) For years, Dempsey endured the cries of "slacker"—a pejorative term describing someone who shirked his patriotic duties during the war. He found the label hard to shake—even after he was formally and quickly cleared by jury of evading military service. Thus, when Dempsey was pitted

Jack Dempsey, world heavyweight champion, circa 1920.

against Georges Carpentier—a decorated French aviator—the Frenchman was regarded as a sentimental favorite by a sizable percentage of the American public in 1921.

Georges Carpentier was one of Europe's most accomplished boxers. He was born on January 12, 1894, in Pas-de-Calais, France. He began boxing for pay at the youthful age of 14. Remarkably, Carpentier competed in every possible weight division from flyweight to heavyweight. He would eventually hold the European championships of four weight classes. When he reached physical maturity, Carpentier stood just a half-inch shy of six feet, but seldom weighed more than 175 pounds—the limit for the light heavyweight classification. Boxing observers in France figured Carpentier would be wise not to venture above the welterweight division. Carpentier earned the nickname "the Orchid Man" based on the title of a silent movie in which he appeared. However, it was far from the most terrifying moniker one can bestow on a professional boxer. Be that as it may, Carpentier was armed with terrific boxing skills and a surprisingly heavy punch for his slight stature. He was highly successful in the ring despite often being dwarfed by his opponents. His most cherished victories—ones that made him a heroic figure within France—came against Great Britain's heavyweight champion Bombardier Billy Wells, whom he twice knocked out in short order in 1913 despite the Frenchman being undersized. Carpentier could also take a solid punch—a skill he would desperately need if he had any chance to defeat Jack Dempsey for the world heavyweight championship.

France's Georges Carpentier, slight of stature, hardly looked the part of a man who could upend heavyweight champion Jack Dempsey. Nevertheless, his pro boxing résumé listed victories over Europe's best heavyweights. Photograph dated circa 1920.

Georges Carpentier

July 2, 1921—Georges Carpentier vs. Jack Dempsey

Along with having superlative boxing technique, Georges Carpentier possessed surprising punching power in his undersized frame. In this photograph dated circa 1920, he practices his timing with a speed bag.

also holds two unique distinctions in boxing history: At age 20, on June 27, 1914, Carpentier refereed the Frank Moran-Jack Johnson world heavyweight championship bout in Paris. It made him the youngest person to ever preside over a heavyweight title tilt—and, in retrospect, Carpentier became the first man to referee a world heavyweight title fight before he competed for the same title. Others have done third-man duty after retiring as active boxers— James J. Jeffries and Jersey Joe Walcott are two—but only Carpentier did it beforehand. (After his retirement from the ring, Carpentier would still occasionally referee significant bouts in Europe.)

Carpentier would also win the world light heavyweight championship by easily and impressively knocking out Battling Levinsky at a minor league baseball park in Jersey City, NJ, in four rounds on October 12, 1920. It was Carpentier's first visit to the United States—and it was essentially his dress rehearsal for a heavyweight title match with Dempsey sometime in 1921. It was a spectacular American debut. "Carpentier won as he pleased," reported the *Milwaukee Journal*. "Carpentier feinted, punched, feinted and punched some more. [He] simply punched Levinsky stupid. Levinsky didn't have the ghost of a chance." Referee Dan Morgan was so impressed with Carpentier's punching power that he boldly stated that Carpentier would certainly knock out Dempsey—if the two ever met for the world heavyweight title. The victor was given a huge ovation by the impressed American crowd. The stylish Carpentier was everything the European boxing writers had said he was.

However, the *Milwaukee Journal* was quick to warn, "Most fans here believe it would be well for Georges to let Jack Dempsey very much alone. [Carpentier] is too small, and his stamina, as compared to Dempsey's, is that of a weakling. But there is this: Carpentier can hit like a jolt from the butt of a bridge pile—it's hard and true. He is essentially a hitter." Indeed, Carpentier was a hard-hitting fighter. A film of him in training for his 1919 fight versus Joe Beckett shows an incident where Carpentier broke a speed bag. Carpentier would win his first six postwar bouts by knockout.

France's Georges Carpentier arrives in America in 1920 to face world light heavyweight champion Battling Levinsky. Carpentier's easy victory convinced promoter Tex Rickard that the dashing Frenchman might be a good draw if he were matched against Jack Dempsey.

Doc Kearns made a point of attending the Carpentier-Levinsky fight and apparently left the venue impressed by the new world light heavyweight titlist. "In my opinion [Carpentier] is one of the greatest hitters in the world," declared Dempsey's manager. "Of all the men who walk the earth, he can give the champion [Dempsey] a tussle."[4] The seed had been planted. The hype for the next big Dempsey fight had begun.

After winning the title in 1919, Dempsey took a much-needed hiatus from the ring. He had fought at a breakneck schedule before becoming world heavyweight champion, sometimes contesting three bouts in a calendar month, sometimes more. (He had four fights in July 1918, impressively winning all four by first-round knockout, of course.) Dempsey took more than a full year off before putting his title on the line for the first time. It was not exactly planned for Dempsey to be out of action for such a length of time.

On November 4, 1919, four months after annihilating Jess Willard, Dempsey signed a one-bout contract with promoter Dominick Tortorich. It was an agreement to fight British heavyweight champion Joe Beckett in a 20-round fight in New Orleans on March 17, 1920. However, it was contingent on Beckett defeating Georges Carpentier for the European heavyweight title in London on December 4, 1919. The Dempsey-Beckett fight completely fell apart when Carpentier knocked out the overmatched Beckett in the very first round. (Depending on which newspaper one read, the fight lasted either 70 or 74 seconds.) Beckett had entered the fight as a 5:4 betting favorite. One of the disappointed and stunned spectators at ringside was the Prince of Wales—the future King Edward VIII. Correspondent Joseph W. Grigg opined, "Never in the history of boxing in this country has such a clean-cut blow so precipitately ended the championship hopes of any British boxer in any class."[5] The *Milwaukee Journal*'s

A well-dressed Jack Dempsey in a photograph taken around the time of the 1921 Carpentier bout.

headline unkindly—but accurately—declared, "England's Heavyweights are 1-Round Heroes." The stereotype of Britain's horizontal heavyweights had been reinforced again, but, nevertheless, the sporting British fans who witnessed the massacre gave Carpentier a heartfelt ovation for his convincing win over their man.

"Georges Carpentier is apparently the logical contender to meet Jack Dempsey for the world's heavyweight championship," said Tex Rickard upon hearing the result from England. "Staging such a bout is far from an easy task,"[6] he cautioned when asked if he would try to arrange it.

After a 14-month hiatus, Dempsey finally put his world heavyweight crown on the line. However, the man standing across the ring from him was not Georges Carpentier. The opponent was instead Billy Miske, one of the toughest heavyweights operating in the United States. Miske was defeated rather handily in three rounds at a baseball stadium in Benton Harbor, MI on Labor Day, September 6, 1920. It was certainly a disappointing bout. About 15,000 fans attended the contest. No films of the Dempsey-Miske bout are known to survive, making it the last world heavyweight title fight to exist in memory alone.

Miske was a shell of his former self for good reason: He was quietly suffering from the early stages of Bright's Disease, a kidney disorder. Years later Dempsey realized he had fought a sick version of Miske, not the robust man who had twice gone the distance with him. But Dempsey was vaguely aware that something was not completely right with Miske at Benton Harbor that afternoon. "During the fight," Dempsey told Miske's biographer, "I began to feel that Billy wasn't giving me as tough a battle as I had expected. He did not seem like his old self."[7] Miske's title shot was a significant payday for the challenger—precisely $25,000. Dempsey was only charitable to a point, however. All business once the bell rang, he knocked Miske cold with a sizzling straight right hand about a minute into the fateful third round of a scheduled ten-round fight. It was the only time in Miske's long and impressive career of more than 100 professional bouts that he suffered a knockout defeat. In fact, the St. Paul, MN, heavyweight had never been knocked off his feet before Dempsey dumped him to the canvas in the second round.

Georges Carpentier displays his reach and his physique, circa 1919. Despite being small of stature, Carpentier possessed terrific knockout power.

A headline in the next day's *Milwaukee Journal* referred to the one-sided title fight as a "burlesque." Another correspondent, T.S. Andrews, was more generous in his assessment of the Benton Harbor battle. He lauded Dempsey for fighting smartly and measuring his opponent. Herbert (Hype) Igoe, nationally renowned as a boxing expert and as a superb sports cartoonist, also sang the Manassa Mauler's praises. Igoe noted, "If the [14-month] layoff bothered the champion, we'll never tell it. Dempsey didn't waste a single punch. He fiddled around with Miske until the proper opening presented itself."[8] Less than four years later, Miske would be dead at age 29.

Having hardly broken a sweat versus Billy Miske, Dempsey was back in action against Bill Brennan, a Chicago-based heavyweight, three months later, putting his world championship title on the line for a second time. On paper, Dempsey versus Brennan looked like a mismatch because Dempsey had manhandled Brennan in a 1918 bout in Milwaukee, scoring a one-sided technical-knockout victory. In the 1918 encounter, Brennan was floored five times in the bout, four of the which came in the second round. The final knockdown, in round six, was so powerful that Brennan toppled to the canvas violently, twisting his leg as he fell, breaking an ankle. Brennan gamely tried to rise, but the referee stepped in to wisely stop the bout.

The venue for the Dempsey-Brennan rematch was at Madison Square Garden. The date for the 15-round contest was Tuesday, December 14, 1920. On the day of the fight, newspapermen picked Dempsey to win in a romp. The *Milwaukee Sentinel* declared Dempsey to be "a top-heavy favorite" and opined that the champion "is conceded every fistic advantage over his rival." The general consensus among boxing observers was that Brennan would not even make it halfway through the scheduled 15 rounds. Yet Brennan, who was not regarded as highly as Miske, summoned the skill and fortitude to put up a terrific fight and looked, for a while at least, to be on his way to scoring a tremendous upset. Here is what Henry L. Farrell of United Press said in his report that appeared in the December 15 issue of the *Milwaukee Sentinel*:

> The world's heavyweight crown still rests on the scowling brow of Jack Dempsey.
> But the face under it was somewhat altered today.
> The left ear of the champion was smashed and torn, his lips were puffed out and cut. His jaws were swollen and his eyes were puffy and red.
> He was in bed, tired and worn from going the longest distance in his career and taking his worst beating.
> Billy Brennan ... stayed twelve rounds with the "man killer" last night in Madison Square Garden, and in those twelve rounds he made the champion work the hardest that he has ever worked and take more than he has ever taken.
> Two vicious punches in the stomach and a smashing right on his head in the middle of the twelfth round folded Brennan up and he fell on his head and elbows in a neutral corner, knocked out.

Farrell said he had scored the first five rounds for the challenger—Brennan landed some especially hard shots on Dempsey in the second round—but Dempsey rallied to take control of the bout beginning in round six. In the eighth round Dempsey assumed total command of the action. Nevertheless, Brennan was cheered loudly for his game effort against a vicious fighter who was already being listed as perhaps the best heavyweight champion in boxing history. Brennan took his boxing winnings and invested them in a Prohibition-era saloon in New York City called Club Tia Juana. One day in June 1924, gangsters told Brennan he was buying beer from the wrong distributor. Brennan roughly tossed them out of his establishment. Not long afterward, Brennan was shot to death by two assailants described as "street thugs." He was not quite 31 years old, and he left behind a wife and child. About 5,000 people attended Brennan's memorial service. Oddly, Dempsey's first two title challengers (Brennan and Billy Miske) each died within six months of each other in 1924 as very young men, albeit under very different circumstances.

About seven weeks before the Carpentier fight, Dempsey told journalist Henry L. Farrell that he was not exactly feeling chipper when he fought Brennan, which accounted for his less than dominant performance. "I was sick. That's all," Dempsey claimed. "The Garden was cold that night. With only a towel over my shoulders, I took a chill while they were introducing the celebrities and getting ready for the [pre-fight] pictures. I remember how my legs shook when I was posing for the last picture just before the gong sounded."[9] Dempsey scoffed at accusations that having the luxuries from being the world champion had made him softer than he once was. He added, "I'll be alright on July 2—and you can tell the world!"[10]

Still, the Dempsey-Brennan title fight showed something that boxing followers had not expected from the 25-year-old Jack Dempsey at this point in his career—a bit of vulnerability. The man who had been obliterating the heavyweight division for the better part of four years perhaps could be defeated after all. Maybe, just maybe, a boxer-puncher such as Georges Carpentier might have a legitimate shot at dethroning the Manassa Mauler if given the opportunity sometime during 1921.

The Dempsey-Carpentier matchup was a natural on many levels: boxer versus slugger; cultured European versus a rough-hewn American; war hero versus so-called "slacker." Interest in hosting the bout spanned two continents. On March 28, 1921, it was reported that British interests were willing to put up a $500,000 purse to hold the bout in London. That group was headed by Solly Joel, who was described in American news stories as "a financier and sportsman." The British plan was to hold the bout in the last week of June near Epsom Downs shortly after the annual English Derby horse race when thousands of Europeans would be visiting England. Other offers to host the bout came from Montreal and Spokane, WA.

New York State was definitely out of the running to be the fight's host, because, as the *New York Times* recalled 54 years later, "Governor Nathan L.

Miller prohibited it as a threat to good morals and manners."[11] No matter. The state of New Jersey was quite happy to have this economic windfall land in its lap—and it was just a short jaunt form New York City, so Rickard would be assured of a sizable crowd on the day of the bout.

On April 10, Rickard officially announced with great fanfare that the bout, scheduled for 12 rounds, would be held somewhere in the state of New Jersey on Saturday, July 2—the first day of a three-day holiday weekend. Jersey City, Newark and Atlantic City were thought to be the three frontrunners. "While there has been nothing official upon which to base the report," declared the *Milwaukee Sentinel*, "it appears to be the general opinion among those who have followed the match negotiations is that Jersey City will be the ultimate choice, all things being equal." The newspaper said Jersey City seemed to fit the bill perfectly because it was close enough to New York City to draw spectators from the Big Apple, and that accommodations in Atlantic City would be difficult to obtain over the Fourth of July weekend.

Holding the bout in New Jersey presented an interesting situation. Under the laws regarding boxing contests in that state, no decision could be rendered

The contract is signed for the 1921 Dempsey-Carpentier world heavyweight title bout. Dempsey is seated on the far left. Carpenter is seated second from the right and promoter Tex Rickard third from right. Dempsey's manager, Doc Kearns, is standing at the far left. Others are unidentified.

Manager Doc Kearns (left) and world champion Jack Dempsey near the seashore at Atlantic City prior to the champ's July 2, 1921, contest versus Georges Carpentier.

if both men were on their feet at the end of the fight. If the bout on July 2 went the full 12-round distance, it would go into the books as a "no-decision bout" regardless of how one-sided the fight might be. In other words, the only way Dempsey could lose his title was by disqualification or by Carpentier scoring a knockout. (The no-decision system was thought to keep the sport clean from corrupt judging and help distinguish a legal "boxing match" from an illegal "prize fight." It did not stop the public from betting on fights, however. Journalists often rendered their own decisions in the next day's newspapers. Wagers were often settled based on what came to be known as "newspaper decisions." No-decision endings in world title fights were not unknown. In Jess Willard's only successful defense of the heavyweight championship, he and Frank Moran battled to a ten-round no-decision in New York City's Madison Square Garden on March 25, 1916. Willard was given the newspaper verdict.)

On April 11 it was reported that Dempsey had departed the previous day from Seattle. His final destination was a training site somewhere near Jersey City. The champ had made a few theatrical appearances in the Pacific northwest to pick up a few bucks before he embarked on the serious work of preparing himself to face the threat of Georges Carpentier. (Personal appear-

Doc Kearns, Jack Dempsey's manager, waves from the balcony of the building where Dempsey's 1921 training camp was established.

ances were staggeringly lucrative for Dempsey. The day after he defeated Willard for the championship, Dempsey was paid $25,000 for just showing up at a park in Cincinnati.) Said Dempsey, "I have a little personal business which will take a few days and then I will be ready to open my camp." He further assured his fans, "I will be in the best of shape, of that you may be assured—for Carpentier is a worthy opponent."[12]

As late as mid-April, it was not entirely settled that Jersey City would host the fight. However, promoter Tex Rickard met with various civic official at a Chamber of Commerce luncheon on April 14—where Rickard was feted as the guest of honor—and went over several proposed sites to build a suitable stadium. According to a story in the *Milwaukee Journal*, Rickard seemed "particularly impressed by the police and fire protection Jersey City affords large crowds." A few days earlier, Rickard had met with mayor Frank Hague who was privately assured that the big event would indeed take place in his municipality. Rickard did not have much time to waste. The fight was only 11 weeks away. On April 16 Rickard made it official: Jersey City, NJ, would be the site of the much-awaited Dempsey-Carpentier fight. "There are just a few more obstacles to overcome before I name the exact spot," Rickard stated, "but they will be attended to in a few days. Then we can begin getting things in shape for the big contest."

In mid–May Carpentier boarded a ship for the United States. It was the French liner *La Savoie*. Before embarking for America, the challenger exuded plenty of self-confidence in statements to reporters, although he did refer to Dempsey as "the killer of men." *La Savoie* was scheduled to dock in New York City on Monday, May 16. He was not going to arrive without considerable fanfare. "Indications are that a warm welcome will greet France's war and ring hero," declared the *New York Times*. "Members of various local French societies have been looking forward eagerly to the arrival of their champion, the man in whom they place implicit faith to wrest the championship crown from the brow of Dempsey." Tex Rickard would lead the welcoming party, naturally. Jack Dempsey politely sent Carpentier a telegram, which he received while still aboard *La Savoie*, welcoming him to the United States.

Dapper Georges Carpentier was perceived as an elegant and worldly challenger for Jack Dempsey in 1921. His good looks and polished European style made one newspaper claim that 99 percent of the women in America were rooting for Carpentier to defeat Dempsey. Photograph dated 1920.

As expected, Carpentier was overwhelmed by the favorable reception he was accorded upon arriving in America. A special cutter had sailed out from New York Harbor loaded with journalists and photographers to get images and impressions of the Frenchman before he had even stepped ashore. Henry L. Farrell of the *Pittsburgh Press* wrote, "The pier was crowded with a big delegation from New York's French colony who were waiting to give Georges assurance by a big demonstration that he was not without friends."[13]

When France's favorite son finally disembarked, he was engulfed by mobs of well-wishers everywhere. According to the *Meriden (CT) Morning Record*, "Several thousand persons waited for hours near the entrance of the steamship pier to greet him. Carpentier ... had difficulty making his way to the waiting automobile. Through it all he retained his grip on the leash of the big black Belgian police dog, his constant companion. Included in the crowd were many fellow countrymen of Carpentier who shouted encouragement in their native tongue."[14]

Carpentier had experienced a smaller but very similar welcome to America in 1920 when he arrived to fight Battling Levinsky for the world light heavyweight title, but fully expected this time to be different. He assumed he would be received with some degree of hostility. After all, Carpentier was a foreign interloper who was attempting to take the world heavyweight crown—the biggest prize in pro boxing—to distant Europe. Instead, he was cast in the role of a patriotic hero. Carpentier was also pleasantly surprised by the wide variety of questions that American reporters asked him, and that they were not all related to boxing. In contrast to Dempsey, there was no one questioning what patriotic deeds Carpentier had done during the Great War. As a member of the Service Aéronautique (France's air corps), Carpentier piloted two-seater observation aircraft over the Western Front. He was twice wounded and he had been awarded two of his nation's most prestigious military decorations: the Croix de Guerre and the Médaille Militaire. Promoter Rickard was only too happy to have the championship bout turned into a good guy-versus-bad guy confrontation; it was certainly good for advance ticket sales.

Dempsey was not universally disliked by the military and other patriotic groups in his own country. In fact, many ex-soldiers supported him as America's representative in a major international sporting event. The *New York Times* reported on May 18 that the members of Atlantic City's Willis Gale Post of the Veterans of Foreign Wars—a group whose members were required to have had overseas military during either the Spanish-American War or the Great War—were solidly behind Dempsey. That was in stark contrast to the American Legion members who announced they would be rooting against him on July 2. The *Times* reported, "A special committee from the veterans waited on Dempsey Tuesday afternoon and informed him of the action taken by the Gale Post. The champion, who had been smarting under the actions ... of the American Legion members, appeared deeply impressed."

The acclaimed Frenchman set up his training camp on an estate in the community of Manhasset on Long Island. Visitors aplenty came to watch the European champion work out. They included Vincent Astor and William H. Vanderbilt. Carpentier employed Joe Jeannette (a former top-flight black heavyweight) and Paul Journee as his main sparring partners. Carpentier's presence quickly transcended the sports sections of the major newspapers, especially those on America's east coast. Female society columnists raved about his good looks, worldly ways, Gallic charm, and impressive wardrobe of 75 silk shirts and tailor-made suits. Many newspapers reprinted a recently taken profile photograph of the challenger—in the women's section. Some people thought Carpentier resembled silent screen heartthrob Rudolph Valentino who, in 1921, was setting females' hearts aflutter as a breakthrough star. George Bernard Shaw took to extravagantly calling him The Greek God. The fact that Carpentier was married, had his wife with him, and was the father of a small child was barely mentioned and did not seem to matter to the smitten ladies. The *Milwaukee Journal* estimated that 99 percent of American women would be rooting for the glamorous French challenger to upset Dempsey on July 2. Sportswriters highly doubted that outcome would happen. A blunt article that appeared exactly one week before the fight in the *Pittsburgh Press* was titled "Expert Opinion Solidly in Favor of Jack Dempsey." Penned by journalist Henry L Farrell, it stated, "Outside of a few personal

Carpentier set up his training camp in a rural section of Long Island. Visitors flocked to the training centers of both Jack Dempsey and Georges Carpentier as the excitement about their July 2, 1921, fight reached unprecedented levels. Photograph undated.

friends of Georges Carpentier, no one gives him more than an outside chance against the champion."

Dempsey set up his training facilities at an abandoned airport near Atlantic City and established his headquarters at a nearby cut-rate hotel. Raffish friends of Doc Kearns occasionally made nuisances of themselves there, upsetting the champion. Dempsey began his rigorous physical workouts on May 9 but waited another two weeks before he actually stepped into the ring to shed any rust and to test his boxing skills. Jumping rope accounted for a great part of his training program, the Associated Press reported. That same day Dempsey and his group took a leisurely stroll along the famous Atlantic City boardwalk. He was quickly recognized by hundreds of people who greeted the champion warmly. Dempsey had also been overwhelmed by invitations to attend dozens of local civic events as the guest of honor. Once Dempsey finally donned the padded gloves in his camp, his primary sparring partners were Jack Renault and Larry Williams. Each man was hired to mimic Carpentier's fighting style as best he could. His training regimen would last more than seven weeks. The world heavyweight champion was determined to look considerably better than he had versus Billy Brennan in December.

A young female fan visiting Jack Dempsey's training camp shows the champ her small pet monkey, 1921.

On May 19, a bird's-eye illustration of what Rickard's Oval's seating plan would look like upon its completion appeared in many newspapers. There were to be eight sections, designated by letters A to H, in neat geometric wedges that began at ringside and extended skyward. Rickard was trying to do his best to fill his latest stadium with boxing fans—or at least with thousands of people just wanting to be part of the biggest American social event of 1921. An endless stream of stories about the champion, challenger, and all the tiniest trivialities connected to the fight kept everyone constantly informed on all the latest happenings pertaining to the July 2 international boxing match. No seat would go unsold if Rickard could help it.

Rickard also got plentiful and valuable free publicity from an unexpected source: Bud Fisher's hugely popular "Mutt and Jeff" comic strip. In the weeks preceding the bout, several installments of "Mutt and Jeff" portrayed the "two mismatched tinhorns" as trying to bluster their way into landing jobs as Jack Dempsey's sparring partners. (In the storyline, Mutt and Jeff actually managed to sign up to spar with Dempsey. However, when they were asked to list their next of kin "in case Jack happens to land a wild swing," they abruptly quit.) Cartoonist Fisher had a connection to boxing: He was formerly a sportswriter for the *San Francisco Chronicle*. In 1921 there was hardly a daily newspaper in America that did not carry "Mutt and Jeff." Rickard must have been appreciative of the free plugs his main event was getting. Still, Rickard also paid well for indirect advertising. Some newspaper reporters—a badly underpaid lot—got under-the-table payments of $500 to $1000 for writing plenty of advance stories about the fight. Author Mel Heimer wrote in his 1969 book *The Long Count*, "No one ever claimed Rickard was a saint, but generally his character was considered excellent, at least for a fight promoter."

Dempsey, in his June 25 column for King Features Syndicate, announced that he had celebrated his 26th birthday the day before by "loafing" and entertaining some of his sportswriter buddies at his training camp on a particularly muggy day. (Both Dempsey's and Carpentier's respective opinions about all and sundry pertaining to the upcoming fight were widely circulated under their bylines in many American newspapers. They obviously were heavily assisted by ghostwriters.) A gigantic cake bearing 26 candles was provided by a local caterer. He also received birthday greetings and gifts on June 24 from "intimate friends" and complete strangers. One telegram came from Georges Carpentier and his manager François Descamps—a friendly gesture which delighted the champion. "I certainly do appreciate their thoughtfulness and courtesy,"[15] Dempsey noted, and lauded them as "regular fellows." Dempsey also expressed an eagerness to go for a leisurely dip in the Atlantic to escape the New Jersey summer heat, but apparently any and all swimming was verboten during the champ's preparations for July 2. "My training rules bar the water treatment,"[16] he wrote.

July 2, 1921—Georges Carpentier vs. Jack Dempsey

Most of Dempsey's serious training concluded on Thursday, June 30. The *Milwaukee Sentinel* reported in its July 1 edition that "after a day of loafing and frolicking around the house that has been his home for eight weeks, [Dempsey] went to bed at 9:30 on Thursday night with his mind as peaceful as a five-year-old boy." To avoid being disturbed by zealous fans, Dempsey's group would spend most of Friday and the hours leading up to Saturday's bout at a private home in Jersey City. Only Doc Kearns knew the exact locale. "I haven't told anybody [where the house is]," Kearns stated. "Jack doesn't even know himself. When we arrive in Jersey City, we'll go directly to the house and stay there in seclusion until it's time to go to the arena. I want him to have absolute rest the last 24 hours."[17] Kearns' concerns were legitimate. Dempsey's training camp had become a busy tourist attraction. Quiet times there were rare. At one point on June 30, a group of 300 Chicagoans arrived by special train with the sole purpose of meeting the world heavyweight champion and to wish him well. Despite a heavy rain, Dempsey warmly greeted every one of them with handshakes and pleasant conversation.

Carpentier too wrapped up his heavy training on Thursday, June 30. He proclaimed to reporters that he felt fitter than at any previous time in his boxing career. That day, while doing some light jogging with his handlers, the group was caught in a heavy downpour. They ventured into an abandoned barn to escape the rain. Carpentier shadow boxed there for 30 minutes to pass the

Jack Dempsey trains before a sizeable crowd of onlookers at his training camp. Both Dempsey and Georges Carpentier's training facilities were large tourist attractions in June 1921.

time. His trainer, Gus Wilson, announced to the press that Carpentier was "on edge." The challenger's weight was 172 pounds—the heaviest he had ever tipped the scales at any point in his professional boxing career.

Demand for tickets for the championship fight was expected to be high, but not even Rickard foresaw the enormous financial bonanza his hype had created. Another one of Rickard's newly minted wooden stadiums was specially erected for the fight. He borrowed $250,000 to finance its construction at a location outside of Jersey City, NJ, informally called Boyle's Thirty Acres—which was actually 34 acres of real estate. (John F. Boyle was a manufacturer of paper boxes who owned the vacant lot.) The amphitheater became known as Rickard's Oval—although the finished structure was really an octagon. The project took 500 carpenters and 400 general laborers nine weeks to complete—and it only occupied seven acres. Originally, Rickard's plans called for the venue to hold 50,000 spectators, but the initial design was soon expanded to accommodate 70,000 fans as interest in the international boxing clash grew to unprecedented levels. When even that vast number was thought to be insufficient, the amphitheater stadium, comprised of 2.25 million feet of lumber, was modified to hold a throng of more than 90,000 people. It was not overkill. At a time when a first-class postage stamp cost just two cents, a newspaper could be bought for three cents, and a cake

The numerous moving-picture cameramen assemble to be photographed themselves prior to the Dempsey-Carpentier bout at Boyle's Thirty Acres on July 2, 1921.

of soap could be purchased for six cents, nearly 92,000 people paid an astonishing sum in excess of $1.7 million to watch the must-see battle. It was boxing's first million-dollar gate—and it was nearly double that vast amount. Rickard ended up hiring 1,147 temporary employees to usher in the enormous crowd.

The tickets themselves were works of art. Though engraved on usual cardboard, they were oversized and embossed in gold on the back; they were obviously meant to be kept as cherished souvenirs. Admission prices ranged from $5.50 general-admission tickets to $50 ringside seats and reserved mezzanine boxes. ("Did you ever see so many millionaires?"[18] a pleased Rickard repeatedly asked to all and sundry when he saw who was in attendance.) Those fans in the most distant bleacher seats were perched 312 feet from the center of the ring and 34 feet off the ground. Years later boxing writer and historian Bert Sugar humorously described their vantage point as "somewhere east of Newark."[19] True, they probably did not see much of the action with any degree of clarity, but at least they could happily produce their snazzy ticket stubs and boast to friends and family about being present for the big event. Despite the huge crowd, ticket scalpers did not fare especially well. Apparently, the non-traditional boxing crowd was quite happy to pay the minimum price to gain admission and was not particularly choosy about seat location. The *Meriden (CT) Morning Record* reported that its two reporters were offered $50 premium seats for just $25 per ducat and $30 seats for a mere $15 apiece.

At least 85 telegraphers were on duty to relay the news from Rickard's Oval as it happened. They were among some 778 reporters—both male and female—who were granted credentials to see Tex Rickard's fourth "Fight of the Century" since he had gotten into the lucrative boxing business in 1906. Some journalists had come from as far away as Tokyo and Copenhagen. It was easily the largest paid attendance not just at any boxing match, but also at any sporting event in American history to that point. Rickard, who always rued losing any potential revenue, later lamented that he could have doubled the ticket prices and still would have likely had his desired sellout. Regardless of the fight's outcome, Dempsey would receive $300,000 for his afternoon's labors while Carpentier got a guaranteed $200,000. The combined total of the two pugilists' purses exceeded the amount that any previous fight had ever grossed. Each man also would be entitled to 25 percent of the motion picture earnings. Truly the Golden Age of Sports was underway.

Tex Rickard, of course, continued his unabashed hyperbole to the very last moment. On the day of the fight, his comments graced the pages of numerous newspapers, including the *Lewiston (ME) Morning Tribune*. Rickard, somewhat immodestly, proclaimed, "The bout itself has created greater interest, both nationally and internationally, than any other ring contest at any weight. After the promotion of the [Johnson vs.] Jeffries match in

Reno in 1910, I thought that no future battle could equal that battle in general interest, but a short span of 11 years has produced another heavyweight title bout greater in every respect. I base this statement upon the number of applications for press seats and the fact that every country in the world will be represented … at ringside."

Rickard was also quick to declare that regardless of the result on July 2, he expected none of the "unpleasantness" that followed the Johnson-Jeffries fight in 1910 to recur.

Only July 1, Barry Faris of the *Pittsburgh Press* gushed about the excited fans arriving for the great ring battle:

> From faraway Japan, Australia, France, England, Spain, South America, and from every state in the Union, fight fans have made their way [to Jersey City] to witness the struggle between the champion of Europe and the conqueror of Jess Willard.
>
> Every train that arrived in New York today brought scores more who want to be present at Boyle's Thirty Acres tomorrow. Many of them have their tickets. Many more have not, but hope to get the coveted pasteboards when the cheaper seats are placed on sale early tomorrow.
>
> Every hotel within a radius of 50 miles of Greater New York reports all rooms engaged for tonight. Judging from the steady stream of arrivals, there will be a great many who will have difficulty finding places to sleep tonight.

Even non-boxing-related businesses tried to latch on to the excitement of the impending battle at Rickard's Oval. On July 1, Helfer's Credit Jewelers on Penn Avenue in Pittsburgh bought a sizeable ad in the *Pittsburgh Press*. It ran under the following attention-grabbing headline: "Who's Going to Win Tomorrow? Dempsey or Carpentier?" The text beneath it continued, "The big fight tomorrow is the talk of the whole country. But it will soon be over and forgotten about. Think of this: For less than a price of a seat at the fight you could buy a beautiful diamond, something you will always have and always be proud of. And the easiest credit terms in the city."

Not everyone was as thrilled about the upcoming contest, however. The International Reform Bureau (IRB), whose members were clearly not fans of the sweet science, was trying to stop it on legal grounds. In 1921, prize fighting was illegal in New Jersey—but boxing exhibitions were not. How one differed from the other was not entirely clear and was certainly open to more than one interpretation. The IRB saw the Dempsey-Carpentier contest as an undoubted felony. Dr. Wilbur F. Crafts of the IRB announced on July 1 that his group had sent a letter to New Jersey's governor, Edward Irving Edwards, formally requesting he use the full authority of his office to promptly put a stop to the fight. Governor Edwards claimed he was not aware of any such correspondence—and he had no intention whatsoever of stopping the Dempsey-Carpentier bout. "The fight will go on and will be conducted absolutely within the law,"[20] said Edwards tersely.

Few people paid attention to it at the time, but the Dempsey-Carpentier fight would be the first championship bout to be sanctioned by the newly formed National Boxing Association. The NBA would change its name to the World Boxing Association in 1962.

Dempsey's war record—or lack thereof—continued to be an ongoing story as the fight approached. On July 1 the *Milwaukee Journal* printed a story stating that members of the American Legion had vowed to swarm into the ring to confront Dempsey if the champion dared to appear with an American flag as a belt around his boxing trunks. Dempsey had already announced he would not do that—but he would have an American flag in his corner.

No detail about the much-awaited bout and its participants was too insignificant for the sportswriters to ignore. Based on a special dispatch from the *New York Times*, the *Milwaukee Sentinel* reported in its July 1 edition that Dempsey would be sporting three days' growth of facial hair when he stepped into the ring the next day. "The fighter's face on Thursday was covered with a heavy stubble which added to its grim appearance," the report noted. "By Saturday the whiskers should be a veritable armor about his jaw."

The Dempsey-Carpentier tilt was not the only major sporting event to be held on Saturday, July 2, 1921. Across the Atlantic, it was also the day of the gentlemen's singles final at Wimbledon. By the time the two boxers entered the ring in Jersey City, America's Bill Tilden had successfully defended the singles title he had won in 1920 by defeating Brian Norton of South Africa, but it had not been easy. Tilden dropped the first two sets before rallying to win the final three—and he had to save two match points at 4–5 in the fifth set. A day earlier, France's invincible Suzanne Lenglen had handily trounced Elizabeth Ryan in the women's final to repeat as the ladies' champion. Ryan was an expatriate American who was happily residing in Great Britain. (Lenglen and Ryan teamed up to win the women's doubles, however.) Hopeful French sports fans who were looking for positive omens interpreted Lenglen's 6–2, 6–0 victory over Ryan in the singles final as a sign that Carpentier would beat Dempsey too.

On the afternoon of the fight, everybody who was anybody showed up at Rickard's Oval to see if the titanic clash would live up to its considerable ballyhoo. It was absolutely the place to be. "The arts, sciences, drama, politics, commerce, and bootlegging industry have all sent their pink, their pick, and their perfection to grace the occasion," wrote Irving S. Cobb in the *New York Times*. The notables in attendance included Henry Ford, Charlie Chaplin, John D. Rockefeller, Al Jolson, George M. Cohan, and assorted members of President Warren G. Harding's cabinet. With only a hint of hyperbole, journalist Raymond G. Carroll gushed, "Almost everyone you ever heard about was there."[21]

The atypical fight crowd greatly pleased the promoter. Before the main event, Rickard excitedly barged into Dempsey's dressing room to tell him what was happening. He could not contain himself. "Jack, you've never seen anything like it!" he yelled. "We've taken in $1 million already and it's still coming! And the people, Jack! High-class society folks—you name 'em, they're here! And the dames! I mean classy dames—thousands of them!"[22] Rickard was not exaggerating. According to Barry Faris of the *Pittsburgh Press*, "Never in the history of fistiana has such an assemblage of women graced the ringside of an encounter, either in this country or abroad. It was impossible to estimate with any degree of accuracy the number of women present. Officials guessed the number anywhere from 10,000 to 25,000." It was about as far as Dempsey could possibly get from his days, not all that long before, when he earned pocket change as a roughneck saloon brawler in Utah.

The weather was sticky at the outdoor venue on July 2. Correspondent Faris duly noted, "The sky was overcast by gray, sullen-looking clouds during the fight. The sun had peeped out from behind the clouds for a short time while the preliminary fights were underway, but it disappeared before Dempsey and Carpentier got into the ring." Faris continued, "It seemed as though it were about to rain every minute, but it did not. The humidity was oppressive and the spectators sweltered in their seats, but all seemed cheerful enough." The eager ticketholders were permitted to enter Rickard's Oval at 8 a.m. that Saturday—more than seven hours prior to when the main event was slated to begin. A handful of fans required medical attention at the stadium's first-aid area due to their prolonged exposure to the hot weather. Another chap, clearly displaying signs of mental illness, was arrested for threatening several people during one of the preliminary bouts. After being corralled, he was also escorted to the first-aid station where he bit an attendant and attacked a doctor.

The last preliminary fight before the spotlight was on Dempsey and Carpentier featured a skilled pugilist from New York City named Gene Tunney. He had been the light heavyweight boxing champion of the American Expeditionary Forces during the Great War and had thus far compiled an undefeated record as a professional. Tunney handily defeated Soldier Jones in seven rounds. His methodical win was very efficient but not especially crowd-pleasing. When his hand was raised by the referee in the symbolic token of victory, the number of cheers and boos he received were about even. He was no Dempsey, but the bookish, analytical Tunney would be heard from in the future by both fighters competing in the main event.

Despite the celebratory atmosphere at Boyle's Thirty Acres, there was an obvious lingering danger hovering over the festive gathering, however: Police and fire officials watched with growing concern as the hastily enlarged stadium began to noticeably creak and sway from the weight of the enormous crowd filing in, especially in its upper reaches. A headline in the next day's

July 2, 1921—Georges Carpentier vs. Jack Dempsey

Milwaukee Journal blared, "Spectators Near Tragedy as Vast Stands Tremble." The *Journal*'s accompanying story read,

> Those in the $5 seats got their money's worth.
> ... For many minutes the huge arena swayed perceptibly. It began when Dempsey and Carpentier first entered the ring and was accelerated during the subsequent excitement. There was one rush from the $5 seats at the rear of the arena to the $10, $15, and $20 seats below. Here scores [of fans] were stopped by the police.
> As Dempsey was presented with a huge wreath [by admirers in the center of the ring], a man rushed forward shouting, "Everybody stay down; you're in a dangerous place. The arena is reeling. Everybody down! If you police can't make them sit down, club them down!"
> The swaying was rhythmical. Hundreds standing on the rails in front of the seats accelerated the motion. An engineer who had been with the AEF in France said afterward that he had expected the arena to "fold up." He said the rhythm was the most dangerous part of it.
> "If they had ever gotten to stamping together," he said, "there might have been a tragedy."

One newspaper correspondent completely agreed, writing, "There would have been an awful crash had it come down. Two-thirds of the people would have been crushed."[23] Proving that there are two sides to every coin, however, the construction company that had erected Rickard's Oval would later boast that since the enormous stadium had swayed without collapsing, that was irrefutable proof that it had been built well.

Fearing the structure was in danger of collapsing, the officials in charge of public safety urged Rickard to start the main event as early as possible. Nobody objected—not even pioneer radio announcers Major Andrew White and J.O. Smith, who were trying to broadcast a heavyweight title fight to a major audience for the first time. (The 1920 Dempsey-Miske fight had been broadcast on an experimental station to a limited area in the vicinity of Benton Harbor, MI. Dempsey-Carpentier was a much more ambitious project: It was being broadcast nationally.)

Dempsey was a solid 2:1 betting favorite on the day of the fight despite his unpopularity in some quarters. The odds had become closer in the final few days before the fight, dropping from 3:1 in Dempsey's favor due to an unexpected rush of Carpentier money being wagered. The *New York World* reported that the American occupation forces stationed in Coblenz, Germany on the Rhine River did not seem to mind the "slacker" label that had been affixed to the heavyweight champ. The soldiers had been betting heavily on Dempsey with local bookmakers regardless of the Manassa Mauler having no war record.

As Dempsey calmly awaited the signal to leave his dressing room, he was given one important, impassioned instruction by Rickard before heading for his scheduled appointment in the 20-foot ring: "Give the people out there a good run for their money, Jack. Please don't knock him out in one round! Don't kill him! Don't kill everything! If you kill him, boxing will be dead!"[24] Rickard could afford to be in a generous mood. The following day's *Meriden (CT) Morning Record* estimated that Rickard, after settling all his expenses, stood to make approximately $550,000 on the event. The newspaper also pointed out the federal government was going to do very well from the taxes it would accrue from both the promoter's profit and all the fighters' purses. The state of New Jersey would also reap a boon from the 10 percent tax it collected on each ticket that Rickard had sold. As for scalped tickets, the *Record* stated with apparent seriousness, "Ticket sellers who resold their pasteboards are required and expected to give 50 percent of their profits to the government."[25]

A tanned, fearsome-looking Dempsey with two days' growth of rough whiskers and weighing 188 pounds, entered the 18-foot ring. He was clad in a heavy sweater despite the humid conditions; he liked to stay warm before the opening bell of all his fights. Dempsey received a noticeably mixed reception of cheers and hisses. When Joe Humphreys introduced the reigning world champion first via a Magna-Vox (a primitive microphone system), only a ripple of applause could be heard. "It could not even be designated as a mild greeting," Barry Faris reported with a degree of surprise. On the other hand, Carpentier, at 172 pounds and chalk white under his robe, was greeted with a deafening roar. "What a rousing greeting he received! It could be described as almost wild," wrote Faris. "Men stood up and cheered the Frenchman to the echo; it was fully two minutes before the [noise] subsided." The crowd's enthusiastic response almost embarrassed the challenger. The *Milwaukee Journal* reported, "From the moment [Carpentier] entered the ring, the crowd was with him and he felt it." Said Carpentier after the fight, "I am sensitive to such things. You know, I was honestly a little bit sorry for Jack whose own countrymen were favoring me."[26] Indeed, Dempsey was annoyed. He scowled in his corner during the huge clamor in support of the challenger.

When the two men met in the center of the ring for the referee's final instructions, Dempsey sized up his challenger. He liked what he saw. "He was thinner than I expected," Dempsey wrote of Carpentier years later in his autobiography. "He looked like a graceful statue. I looked like a street fighter."

White was the color of the day at Boyle's Thirty Acres. The ring was encased in three white ropes. Both pugilists wore white trunks; Carpentier's shorts featured a vertical blue stripe on each side to distinguish him from the champion. Referee J. Harry Ertle, age 37, was nattily clad in a fashionable all-white summer ensemble with a dark bow tie adding a slight dash of color to his pristine wardrobe. (The official fight films were shot from a high roost by a crew of 20 cameramen. The distinct lack of contrast between Ertle and the light-colored canvas makes him almost invisible at some points of the battle.) Ertle was a good choice to serve as referee. Small in stature compared to the two combatants, he was a capable, veteran official who would work as the third man in the ring in more than a thousand professional bouts in his career. At the time of his death in 1932 at the young age of 48 from a stomach disorder, Ertle was serving as the secretary of the New Jersey State Boxing Commission.

As was the custom of the day, the eight-ounce gloves were put on the fighters' fists inside the ring. The opening bell rang at exactly 3:16 p.m. Adhering to Rickard's concerned request to extend the fight for at least a couple of rounds, Dempsey did not fiercely attack his opponent in the first frame, as was his usual tactic. The best punch of the opening frame was landed by Carpentier. Dempsey seemed unfazed by it. Carpentier took the offensive in the second stanza and caught Dempsey with two solid blows. The second punch was a perfect right hand to the chin that temporarily stunned the champion. In Dempsey's corner, Doc Kearns turned ashen as Dempsey tottered slightly.

Jack Dempsey and Georges Carpentier clash in the center of the ring at Boyle's Thirty Acres in New Jersey, July 2, 1921. Carpentier is the fighter with the vertical stripe on his trunks. Harry Ertle is the referee.

"No man had ever been hit harder, yet Dempsey did not go down," claimed the *Milwaukee Journal*. The pro–Carpentier crowd rose in the excitement and anticipation of seeing Dempsey hit the canvas. It did not happen. After several hopeful seconds the ringside patrons sat down again—and the color returned to Kearns' cheeks. Unfortunately for the challenger, that punch he staggered Dempsey with had three negative effects: Carpentier had broken his thumb in two places when he struck Dempsey's jaw. He had also sprained his right wrist slightly. Worse still, Dempsey was now angry with the Frenchman. The enraged champion fired volleys of punches at Carpentier in rapid succession. Many found their mark. One journalist later compared Carpentier's blows on Dempsey to slapping an ox in the face. Similarly, W.O. McGeehan of the *New York Herald Tribune* likened Carpentier's blows to artillery shells "bursting against an impenetrable armor plate."[27]

Both tired and fearful of toying with such a potentially dangerous foe, Dempsey took firm control of the fight in the third round. He was clearly the pursuer now, landing several smashing blows to Carpentier's face and a wicked shot to his stomach. "His body blows were the ones that hurt," declared the *Milwaukee Journal*, "and they came deep and hard. At the end of the third round it was plain that Georges was not long for the role of challenger. Dempsey was sinking in his blows, and the world knows that Carpentier isn't stout enough to take a Dempsey smashing." Few fighters in 1921 had that skill. Carpentier's midsection was noticeably a bright shade of red at the end of the third round.

"Jack came out fresh for the third round," Carpentier recalled in an interview years later, "and he hit me with the hardest punches any human ever threw. Nobody could hit like Dempsey that day. And he was shaking off my punches as if I was patting him with an open hand."[28]

Between rounds three and four, Carpentier elevated his legs on one of his second's laps while the others massaged them—an unusual sight in an American boxing ring. Just about one minute into the fourth round, Dempsey tagged the Frenchman with a short, powerful left hook to the jaw followed by a clipping right hand. The left did the greater damage. Carpentier went down on his hands and knees. He looked to be finished, but the courageous challenger suddenly jumped up between referee Ertle's count of eight and nine to continue the battle. In a retrospective *New Yorker* article published decades after the fight, journalist John Lardner wrote that Carpentier, "faithful to [his manager's] code of histrionics ... stayed down for the count of nine and then, jumping up, made an artful rush at Dempsey, which carried his chin headlong into Dempsey's right hand."

In hindsight, Carpentier should have remained on the canvas. Upon rising, he had barely regained his feet when Dempsey was on top of him again in full fury. A volley of stinging punches by Dempsey—punctuated by another vicious, paralyzing blow to the body—terminated the fight. Radio announcer Major Andrew White screamed into his microphone, "The Frenchman is down! Three ... four! Carpentier makes no effort to rise. Six ... seven! He's lying there. Nine ... ten ... he's out! The fight is over! Jack Dempsey remains the heavyweight champion of the world!"

Moments after Ertle counted to ten at the 1:16 mark, Dempsey, in a sportsmanlike gesture, rushed in, along with the referee, to help lift the vanquished Carpentier off the deck and assist him back to his corner.

American telegraphers flashed the final result to boxing fans in France: "Your champion flattened in the fourth." The poetic French reply, which probably lost something in the translation, was, "We shall weep in the small huts."[29] Some Parisians learned the fight's result in a spectacular and unusual way. Tens of thousands of fans had expectantly gathered on the Place de la Concorde to witness a signal from a passing airplane. If the aircraft flashed a blue light, it meant Carpentier had won. A white light meant that Dempsey had retained his world championship. The *Milwaukee Journal* reported, "A sigh seemed to go up from the vast assemblage as the people realized their national hero had been smashed" when a white light was sighted.

Jack Dempsey and Georges Carpentier exchange pleasantries after their July 2, 1921, fight as the 92,000 spectators begin to exit the stadium. There was no animus between the two boxers. Dempsey and Carpentier remained friends for life.

When Dempsey got back to his corner, his gloves were removed while he stood passively. With the issue decided, the heavyweight champion of the world finally allowed himself the luxury of cracking a smile for the first time since he left his dressing room. Dempsey waved with both hands, still wrapped in gauze, to his happy, albeit outnumbered, supporters. Interestingly, many people who had entered Rickard's Oval to unabashedly root for Carpentier suddenly did an about-face and warmly cheered the reigning champ's latest triumph. "And so it is on this mortal coil," said an editorial in the *Meriden (CT) Morning Record*, commenting on the fickle nature of sports fans. "The winner of the plaudits in any line of endeavor is the man who has a million friends, apparently." Similarly, the *Milwaukee Journal* playfully noted in its July 3 sports briefs, "Those 99 women out of 100 who were said to have been betting on Georges are by this time keeping at least 297 men out of 300 busy explaining how it was done. And the one out of 100 who pulled for Dempsey isn't cheating the world out of knowing about it."

Esteemed sports scribe Damon Runyon praised the undeniable pluck of the challenger from start to finish. "Carpentier came out of his corner at the clang of the bell ... like a little gamecock shooting his right at the brown body of the champion as soon as he got within range. He fell as gamely. He fell like a soldier of France, brave to the end."[30]

Sports journalist Joseph J. O'Neill superbly described what the challenger looked like during the bout's final few seconds:

> Flat on the canvas, midway along one edge of a white-roped ring, lay a slender-seeming, pale-appearing body.
> Face downward on the floor it was, with the eyes and nose buried in a pair of wet crossed gloves. The shoulders were heaving slightly upward and slumping down again. The legs were drawing up, perhaps an inch at a time, and then stretching back again.
> That was Georges Carpentier, 13 minutes and 16 seconds after he started from his corner to do battle with Jack Dempsey for the [heavyweight] boxing championship of the world.
> Defeated—yes. Knocked out—yes. But, like the game, gallant thoroughbred he has always been, he was trying to get up, trying to go on. His fighting heart was telling him to rise. The muscles of his superb physical organization were endeavoring to respond, but the vital spark that completes the connection between command and response was flickering, was almost gone. There lay the athletic idol of France, helpless.[31]

Also covering the bout was the acerbic H.L. Mencken, who enjoyed being billed as "America's foremost critic of arts and manners." Despite his outward contempt for all things plebeian, Mencken appreciated the fight game and understood the significance of what he had just seen in the ring. He accurately declared, "The difference in weight was a good deal less than in many another championship battle, and Carpentier's blows seldom failed by falling short. What ailed them is that they were not hard enough to knock out Dempsey or even to do him any serious damage. Whenever they landed, Dempsey simply shook them off and, in the intervals between them, he landed dozens and scores of harder ones. It was a clean fight, if not beautiful. It was swift, clear cut, brilliant and honest."

Mencken further stated that Carpentier was simply in over his head versus a heavyweight champion of Dempsey's quality. To Mencken, the mere notion that the Frenchman had any legitimate chance to attain victory was "apocryphal, bogus, hollow and null, imbecile [and] devoid of substance." Mencken added, "Dempsey was never in any more danger of being knocked out than I was, sitting there in the stands with a pretty gal beside me and five or six just in front."[32]

Based on what he saw Dempsey do to Carpentier, one deluded spectator (and IRB member) absolutely saw it as his civic duty to file an assault complaint against the champion! The *Milwaukee Journal* humorously reported what occurred:

> The technical description of just what Dempsey did to Carpentier was supplied immediately after the fight by Hubert Clark Gilson, counsel to the International Reform Bureau, who attended the fight with a group of Jersey City clergymen.
> As soon as he could make his way through the crush of the departing fight fans, Mr. Gilson hurried to the temporary police station ... and advised Lieutenant Gus Martin, that as a result of his attendance at the fight he had discovered that Jack Dempsey had assaulted Georges Carpentier and that he wished a warrant for Dempsey's arrest.
> When Lieutenant Martin advised him to see a magistrate, Mr. Gilson demanded that a record be made of the fact that he had filed a complaint and said he was going to see the chief of police.

Back in Salt Lake City, the locale that Dempsey still referred to as home, the champion's mother—now estranged from her husband—was delighted with the outcome from Boyle's Thirty Acres when informed of her son's resounding victory over the French challenger. Cilia Dempsey (who was misidentified as "Ciciline Dempsey") proudly told a reporter, "My son told me he was going to win. I am happy now—more happy than I have ever been after one of Jack's bouts. Yet, I'm human, you know. My sincere regards and respects are extended to Mr. Carpentier." The titlist's mom also injected a touch of humor into her interview. "By the way," she noted, "Jack isn't the champion. I hold the championship myself because I licked him once for bringing home too many dogs."[33]

Warren G. Harding was spending his first Fourth of July weekend as U.S. president vacationing in Raritan, NJ, at the home of Senator Joseph S. Frelinghuysen. Harding was as keenly interested in the fight's outcome as anyone. Nevertheless, it did not keep him from enjoying his favorite hobby, though. While the bout was taking place, he was playing 18 holes on a nearby links. As soon as he got back from his golf game, however, Harding was greeted with two words by First Lady Florence Harding: "Dempsey won."

Carpentier received a conciliatory overseas cable from his wife and daughter that was released to the media. It read, "Too bad, dear Georges. But don't worry. All our hearts are with you. Come home to us quickly." Mrs. Georgette Carpentier had been receiving round-by-round reports of the contest at the offices of a Paris newspaper. She "kept up her courage until the fourth round,"[34] according to French journalists.

After the fight, Dempsey retreated to the relative quiet of the private Jersey City house where he had spent the day before the fight trying to relax. Its location was no longer a closely guarded secret, and the media descended upon it to interview the winner and still world heavyweight champion. "[Dempsey] gave no appearance of having just emerged from one of the most serious battles of his life," reported the *Milwaukee Journal*. A reporter who tried to lead Dempsey into admitting that he had totally outclassed Carpentier was met with a modest non-reply from the champion. The story continued, "Jack had the expression of a country schoolboy looking for a knothole into which wiggle a stone-bruised toe. This was the heavyweight champion of the world." With a gentle smile Dempsey said his immediate plans included shaving his unsightly facial stubble and putting on a collar. Like Carpentier, Dempsey too was a gentleman outside the ring.

Dempsey was considerably more forthcoming in his syndicated newspaper column the following day. Here is a portion the Manassa Mauler's views as they appeared in the July 3 edition of the *Pittsburgh Press*:

> The heavyweight championship of the world remains in America. Europe sent into the ring this afternoon the greatest ring battler she has developed in 40 years, but he was a little too light, a little too small—too frail really, to take back to his homeland the fistic crown of the universe.
>
> What a fast fellow Carpentier is, how clever and how he can hit with only 172 pounds backing him up! He crashed the old right-hander to my head in the first [round] and caught me flush on the chin with it in the second. Not once but twice. Those punches shook me up, but they really meant the beginning of the end of Carpentier's dream of pugilistic conquest of the world.
>
> For when he hit me twice in the second with everything he had and I stayed on my feet, I knew I couldn't lose the fight. I abandoned the early caution for I had nothing more to fear and went out to cut him down in a hurry. The end came in the fourth....

Along with being paid for writing his impressions on the fight, Dempsey was also quick to cash in on an endorsement deal. Just one day after the contest, the July 3 edition of the *Milwaukee Sentinel* featured a quarter-page ad showing the champion in a fighting pose and promoting the healthful benefits of something called Nuxated Iron tablets "to increase one's strength vigor and vitality." Dempsey blared, "Nuxated Iron put me in such superb condition as to enable me to whip Carpentier." Doc Kearns, of course, agreed entirely, saying the tablets were a vital part of Dempsey's training regimen before both the Willard and Carpentier fights. "I strongly advise people who are in a weakened, rundown condition to try this wonderful strength and blood builder." Among the other eclectic notables who sang the praises of this trendy cure-all were baseball greats Ty Cobb, Shoeless Joe Jackson—and Pope Benedict XV.

Tex Rickard continued to try to squeeze every last dime he could from the Dempsey-Carpentier rivalry—long after the Frenchman had been counted out at Boyle's Thirty Acres by Harry Ertle. In an article summarizing the enormous money that the fight generated, the *Milwaukee Sentinel* also reported on July 3 that Rickard was seriously trying to arrange a swimming race between Dempsey and Carpentier in Madison Square Garden before Dempsey traveled to his Salt Lake City home and Carpentier headed back to France! There is no record of this aquatic showdown ever having occurred.

On the running board: Jack Dempsey (left) and his manager Doc Kearns pose by their automobile for newsreel photographers.

Carpentier, despite not being able to communicate in English all that well, was also not averse himself to making extra money in the newspaper game. Well before the fight he had regularly penned his thoughts about training, boxing, his personal history and blissful family life, and just about anything else in a syndicated column for United Features Syndicate. (In one segment shortly before July 2, Carpentier said he strongly disapproved of the "American custom" of permitting spectators to smoke at boxing matches, declaring it to be a torture on the fighters—quite an extraordinary statement for 1921.) Even after suffering a knockout defeat, Carpentier's columns continued to appear regularly in American newspapers until he departed for France.

Carpentier was surprisingly spritely following his knockout loss. He seemed unaffected by his defeat when he was approached at his Manhasset headquarters a few hours after the fact. Undoubtedly Carpentier's huge $200,000 purse helped reduce some of the bitter sting of losing to Dempsey. The *Milwaukee Journal*'s correspondent was thoroughly surprised by what he saw: "Out from his farmhouse, where he was supposed to be suffering from the effects of his beating from Jack Dempsey, strolled Georges Carpentier Saturday evening—an apparently unconcerned young man." The newspaper reported that the Frenchman cheerfully played with his police dog Flip, joked with his friends, "and was as cool and smiling as ever." Carpentier had nothing but praise for the victorious Manassa Mauler. He acknowledged Dempsey to be "the greatest champion who ever fought."

French journalists were busily praising both their man and the victorious Dempsey. André Glarner, the sports editor of the *Paris Excelsior*, evenhandedly commented,

> Georges Carpentier will never be world's [heavyweight] champion. He was beaten here by a man whom I do not hesitate to call a better, a greater, and a more rugged fighter than our champion. Let us be sports and acknowledge that.
> But I know there is not an American who saw the fight who will not agree with me that Carpentier put up a fight of which everyone in France should be proud. Our man fought like a lion. Though stopped time and time again in the first round by terrific punches, his face beaten to a pulp, the Frenchman came back for more and in the second round got his chance.
> In that round he caught Dempsey with two beautiful one-two punches to the jaw which would have brought down anyone in the world, barring Dempsey. Terrific force was put into those two blows. I noticed it immediately, and when I saw the force of those punches did not stop the American, I knew that victory was further away than we thought.
> Of course, Dempsey himself will sooner or later be beaten, but never as long as he fights the way he did on Saturday. I have for Dempsey the fighter the greatest admiration. He is worthy of his title. And Carpentier was worthy to challenge him for it.

In writing about the Dempsey-Carpentier bout nearly a century after it occurred, Dempsey biographer Thomas Brennan accurately noted, "And so the 'Battle of the Century' proved instead to be the 'Promotion of the Century.' The entire fight proved to be almost totally one-sided. The fight's build-up turned out to be the most successful aspect of this hugely popular sporting event. If anyone's talents truly shined, it was Tex Rickard's promotional genius."[35]

The day after the contest, Dempsey rode in the backseat of a car, alongside manager Doc Kearns, to a nearby Jersey City movie theater that was already showing the fight film and treated himself to a viewing of his two-fisted handiwork. He was curious to see how close his world title had come to slipping out of his possession. The *Bakersfield Californian* reported, "[Dempsey] saw the punches that in the second round caused the mass of humanity in the great arena to gasp in the belief that the blond French boxer was to make good his threat to carry the title across the sea. Dempsey saw himself totter and sway as the Frenchman sent those punches to his jaw. Perhaps not until he saw the picture did he realize just how near he had been to dropping to the canvas floor, for after the fight Dempsey declared the punches had not bothered him. As Dempsey saw himself on the screen inflicting punishment upon his lighter opponent, his eyes sparkled and he leaned forward eagerly and uttered an exclamation of admiration for the way Carpentier gamely came back."

A few days before the fight, Milwaukee's daily newspapers had ruefully reported that an ascending Jack Dempsey had been approached to fight an unnamed opponent in that city back in 1916, but the Mauler's demand of a $75 purse for a ten-round main event was thought to be outrageously exorbitant. Thus no Dempsey fight ever took place in that city. After the vast amount of money that Dempsey earned on Saturday, July 2, 1921, a reader submitted the following clever poem that appeared in the *Milwaukee Journal's* sports section:

Bums, Take Notice!

Five years ago, a bird called Jack
Was up against it hard;
His stomach leaned against his back,
A bum on any card.

Three-quarters of a hundred, then,
Was all he asked to fight.
Promoters told him, "Guess again,
Your price is outta sight."

But soon he walloped poor old Jess,
Oh boy, it's different now!
For fifteen minutes, more or less,
He cops three hundred thou!

With few exceptions, Jack Dempsey befriended most of the men he faced in the ring. Georges Carpentier was no exception. Carpentier and

Dempsey remained on friendly terms for the rest of their lives, routinely exchanging birthday greetings and other pleasantries. Carpentier even travelled to America in June 1970 to help celebrate Dempsey's 75th birthday and, of course, rehash the old stories from 1921 when a large percentage of the world was fixated on Tex Rickard's rickety oval at Boyle's Thirty Acres. Carpentier died of a heart attack on October 28, 1975, at the age of 81 at the Paris home of his daughter, Jacqueline. The passage of time had seemingly erased his fame on the other side of the Atlantic. The *New York Times* printed a substantial obituary for The Orchid Man, but that was an outlier. Carpentier's death was generally ignored in most American newspapers or reduced to a couple of sentences in the sports notes. The *Pittsburgh Press, Milwaukee Sentinel* and *Milwaukee Journal*—three papers that had each covered Caprentier's unsuccessful heavyweight title quest in minute detail 54 years earlier—made no mention whatsoever of the French boxer's passing.

Jack Dempsey circa 1924. Dempsey always enjoyed being photographed with children who were often awestruck in the presence of the famous boxing champ.

Dempsey outlived Carpentier by nearly eight years. He died of natural

Opposite top: Near the end of his career, Jack Dempsey (left) trains with an unknown sparring partner. Photograph undated. *Opposite bottom:* Jack Dempsey scores with a straight left in his title defense versus Tommy Gibbons on July 4, 1923. Dempsey won a 15-round decision to retain his world heavyweight title. The bout took place in tiny Shelby, MT. The far-flung location dissuaded many fans from attending. Moreover, without Tex Rickard's promotional genius, the bout drew just a few thousand people to a huge 50,000-seat stadium. The gate receipts did not even satisfy Dempsey's guaranteed $300,000 purse. Gibbons did not earn a dime for his noble losing effort-and the small town went bankrupt.

July 2, 1921—Georges Carpentier vs. Jack Dempsey

causes in his New York City apartment on May 31, 1983, less than a month before his 88th birthday. At the time, Dempsey was the oldest living ex-world heavyweight champion, once again besting Jess Willard who formerly had that distinction.

Jack Dempsey reigned as world heavyweight champion for seven years—although he made no title defenses in 1922, 1924 or 1925. He did, however, make two successful appearances in 1923. The first was a lifeless and largely forgettable clash with Tommy Gibbons in tiny Shelby, MT on July 4. The second, on September 14 versus Luis Firpo of Argentina, was arguably the most exciting heavyweight title fight of all time. It featured 11 knockdowns in less than four minutes of fighting. After losing the crown by a lopsided decision to Gene Tunney in 1926 (and the subsequent rematch in 1927), Dempsey's popularity oddly soared as he settled into retirement from boxing. As Red

World heavyweight champion Jack Dempsey is front and center in this photograph taken circa 1924. His manager Jack (Doc) Kearns is to the right in the light-colored coat. Others are unidentified. Dempsey and Kearns would part ways while Dempsey was still champion.

Smith noted in Dempsey's *New York Times* obituary, "From that day on, the gallant loser was a folk hero whose fame never diminished."³⁶

For the 39 years it operated from 1935 to 1974, anyone who ventured into Jack Dempsey's Broadway Restaurant—a longtime magnet for general tourists and especially boxing fans—was warmly greeted with a jovial and ingratiating "Hiya, pal!" from the smiling Manassa Mauler whenever the old champion happened to be present. Dempsey's dining establishment provided New York City's best dessert—and a very genial and beloved celebrity host. "Jack Dempsey's cheesecake has been in existence for almost 40 years. And in New York it is an institution in itself," Dempsey himself wrote in a letter to *New York Magazine* in December 1973. "It is baked on our premises, eaten in our restaurant, as well as airmailed all over the United States and Europe. We have had requests for our cheesecake from tourists who come to New York from faraway places; we've fulfilled requests over the years from France's late President Charles DeGaulle, who had his cheesecakes sent several times a year."

In his second career as a restaurateur, Jack Dempsey autographed tens of thousands of souvenir menus for his adoring customers. Most contained thoughtful personalized inscriptions for the happy recipients. "Mr. Dempsey never knowingly hurt anyone except in the line of business,"³⁷ Smith noted. The scribe was referring to Dempsey's pugilistic exploits—not the restaurant business.

An amusing story Dempsey loved to relate occurred in June 1949 when he was dining with friends in Chicago. Ezzard Charles and Jersey Joe Walcott were set to clash the following

Jack Dempsey playfully carries wife Estelle Taylor as his manager, Jack Kearns, looks on. Kearns was opposed to Dempsey's marriage. That was one of the major reasons why the two men parted ways in 1924.

night for his old title that had recently been vacated by the retirement of Joe Louis. A stranger passing Dempsey's table excitedly recognized the 54-year-old former world champion and approached him.

"Jack Dempsey!" he said, offering his hand, which Dempsey shook. "Oh, boy, Jack! Do I remember how you gave it to Jess Willard back there in Toledo!" Leaning forward towards Jack's ear, the man's voice dropped to a near whisper. "I hope you beat the hell out of that guy tomorrow night," he said and quickly strode away. Speechless for an instant, Dempsey stared at the departing stranger. "Well, I'll be damned," he said. "He thinks I'm still champion!"[38]

Jack Dempsey and wife Estelle Taylor in a 1926, near the end of the champion's title reign.

Red Smith was not surprised by that anecdote at all. He wrote, "To many, Mr. Dempsey always remained the champion, and he always comported himself like one. He was warm and generous, a free spender when he had it and a soft touch for anybody down on his luck."[39] Even as an octogenarian when he was not so spritely and required the use of a cane, he was routinely mobbed by knowledgeable boxing fans who congregated in the neighborhood near his New York City apartment building hoping to get a glimpse of the famed and beloved Manassa Mauler. No one could ever recall Dempsey refusing an autograph request. Lord help anyone who tried to mess with him, however. One summer night not long after Dempsey had turned 70, two punks tried to mug him as he stepped out of a cab near his eatery. Dempsey belted both of them as if it were 1919 instead of 1965. When they woke up they were in police custody. Dempsey only felt pity for the would-be robbers and believed boxing might have steered them away from a life a crime.

Shirley Povich, the esteemed sports writer of the *Washington Post*, agreed with his colleague Red Smith. He wrote that Dempsey, despite his very humble beginnings, "emerged [as] arguably the most famous warrior in all boxing history, the owner of a name that connoted the greatest ferocity ever known to the prize ring. America acclaimed him. In victory he was extolled as the invincible one. In defeat, he gained more stature."[40] In the typically stilted language of the man who succeeded Dempsey as heavyweight titlist, Gene Tunney once described the Manassa Mauler thusly: "He had the most binding cords of association with the public of any man."[41]

When the editors of *The Ring* magazine put together *The 2000 Boxing Almanac and Book of Facts*, they concurred. In discussing the Manassa Mauler, they wrote, "In the 70 years since his last fight ... Dempsey's standing among the great heavyweights has only dropped slightly. Dempsey stood just under 6'1" and never approached 200 pounds in his fighting days, but in any way you care to measure, he is one of the biggest fighters ever."

Dempsey is interred in quiet Southampton Cemetery in Suffolk County, NY. His gravestone acknowledges him as world heavyweight champion from 1919 to 1926 and describes him as "a gentle man and a gentleman."

June 22, 1938

Max Schmeling vs. Joe Louis
Nazi Germany Faces America's Champ

"All Germany—from little Hans and Gretchen to papa and mama Schmidt—is confident that 'Unser Max' Schmeling will take Joe Louis' heavyweight crown."—*Milwaukee Journal*, June 22, 1938

"The world will interrupt its affairs for an hour or so on Wednesday night to watch the primitive spectacle of two men battling to see which is the better. War, politics, and economics will stand still until the people of many nations learn whether Joe Louis is still heavyweight champion or Max Schmeling has become the first man in pugilistic history to regain the crown."—*Milwaukee Journal*, June 22, 1938

"Louis will never be able to outthink the cool, cagey Schmeling, who, like Gene Tunney, has an IQ much, much superior to the colored man from the cotton fields. The Bomber will simply have to outpunch him."—*Milwaukee Sentinel*, June 22, 1938

America and much of the world held its collective breath on the evening of Wednesday, June 22, 1938. Even those who held no particular interest in boxing—or any other sport, for that matter—realized that night's main event (which would take place in a floodlit ring erected over Yankee Stadium's infield) had implications that obviously transcended athletics. The participants were world heavyweight champion Joe Louis, a 24-year-old American light-skinned black man, who was making the fourth defense of his title. The challenger was a former champion, 32-year-old Max Schmeling. He resided in Nazi Germany. With Adolf Hitler flexing his military muscle and war clouds on the horizon, the symbolism surrounding the bout was abundantly clear. In 2005 the *New York Times* labeled the fight "the undercard of World War II."[1]

Joe Louis was the first black fighter to hold the coveted world heavyweight title since 1915 and the stormy days of Jack Johnson—a tumultuous era in boxing which many people desperately longed to forget. Even though Louis had possessed the championship for just a year, he was already projected to be among the greatest champions in boxing history. His place in fistic lore was not as important as what he was fighting for that early summer night in 1938. Joe Louis was representing democracy and the good old USA. His adversary, Max Schmeling, who had held the same title from 1930 to 1932, was being lauded by Adolf Hitler and Nazi Germany's hierarchy as the ideal example of Aryan manhood. A victory by Schmeling would lend credence to the daily inflammatory racial rhetoric emanating from Berlin—and lift the championship from American soil. War clouds were in the air in Europe, and the sense was the hostilities would eventually spread to the United States too. Louis, who received pre-fight words of encouragement from president Franklin Delano Roosevelt, was motivated by more than pure patriotism: He wanted to avenge his only defeat as a professional—a stinging loss that Schmeling had inflicted on him two years before when Louis was thought to be an unbeatable and unstoppable ascending force in the heavyweight boxing ranks.

Joe Louis Barrow was born on May 13, 1914, in Chambers County, a rural part of Alabama about six miles north of Lafayette. The site of his birth was a ramshackle shack. A big baby, Joe weighed 11 pounds at birth. He was the grandson of slaves and the seventh of eight children in his family. His mother, Lillie (Reese) Barrow, was part Cherokee. His father, Munroe Barrow, was sent to a mental institution in 1916 when Joe was two. (As a kindness, Joe had been told that his father had died although he actually lived until 1938. Munroe went to his grave apparently unaware that his son was a world-famous fighter.) Little is known about Joe's formative years in Alabama except for two factoids: he suffered from a speech impediment and did not talk much until the age of six, and he was not much of a scholar. The Barrow family eked out a living as sharecroppers. Lillie eventually remarried. Joe's stepfather was Pat Brooks, a construction contractor. They resided in Alabama until 1926 until a run-in with the Ku Klux Klan caused them to question their collective future prospects in the Deep South. After due deliberation, the Barrows/Brookses joined what became known as the Great Migration to the industrial cities of America's north. They ended up settling in Detroit. Some family members got jobs with the Ford Motor Company. Joe worked briefly there alongside one of his brothers.

Lillie thought Joe should learn to play the violin. She would send him to his scheduled lessons with money in his hand. His musical career did not advance because somewhere along the line he started to spend the money on gym fees. He was learning how to box. The musical world may have lost another Jascha Heifetz but the sports world gained Joe Louis. (The surname Barrow was dropped to prevent his mother from knowing about his ring aspirations, according to one tale.) According to Louis folklore, he hid his boxing gloves in his violin case. His first amateur bout was a loss to Johnny Miler—a tough foe who would represent the United States at the 1932 Los Angeles Olympics. Louis was decked seven times by Miler, but it must have been a wonderful learning experience for him. Louis did not lose much after that. He ended up with a 50–3 amateur record and numerous titles, including the 1934 National AAU light heavyweight championship. Forty-three of Louis' opponents were defeated by knockout.

Louis began trading punches for pay in 1934. He latched onto a Chicago-based black promoting outfit and had ten of his first 12 pro fights in that city. On July 4, 1934, Jack Kracken went into the record books (and trivia books) as Louis' first professional opponent. Kracken crashed inside of one round. Knockout followed knockout. Within a year, Louis was boxing's hottest commodity based on his untarnished record and seemingly flawless ring skills. He was beautiful to observe. There was hardly a wasted motion in Louis' boxing technique. He did everything well—and he could hit with power when the opportunity presented itself. The Brown Bomber, as the press dubbed him, was dispatching both hapless and quality opponents with regularity—and with no setbacks. The "name" fighters Louis thumped included notable ex-champions Primo Carnera and Max Baer. Louis handled them as if they were cadavers.

Race was an unspoken issue in Louis' road up the heavyweight ladder. No one doubted he was a superb fighter—but the men who wielded the power behind the scenes were not especially keen to have another black world heavyweight champion in the aftermath of Jack Johnson's wild title reign from 1908 to 1915. Louis' handlers knew this too. Their prodigy would have to lead an exemplary, non-controversial life if he had any hope of getting a shot at the world heavyweight championship—a title that was being passed from white hand to white hand with dizzying frequency during the early 1930s. Louis had to be the anti–Jack Johnson: He could not grin at an opponent or gloat over a win; it was best to be very businesslike in the ring at all times. He could not unnecessarily punish an opponent, either. Quick knockouts were preferred. And, of course, he had to stay far, far away from the pleasures of white women.

The Max Baer fight took place on September 24, 1935, at Yankee Stadium. Even though no title was at stake, it was scheduled for 15 rounds, which was not uncommon at the time. It probably showed Louis at the height of his talents. (Indeed, years later Louis rated it as his best outing as a professional.) He was certainly confident about the outcome. Louis thought so little of Baer—who had just lost the title to James J. Braddock in his previous fight—that he married the former Marva Trotter a few hours before the fight!

Baer had hoped a victory over Louis would regain his lost stature among the heavyweight field. It was not to be—not by a longshot. After three rounds of ceaseless battering from Louis, Baer returned to his corner where one of his seconds, former champion Jack Dempsey, still outwardly exuded confidence. "You can still win, Max! He's not hurting you!" Baer, who was always ready with a witty reply, remarked, "Well, keep your eye on the referee because somebody's beating the hell out of me!"[2] Baer was mercifully floored and counted out in round four. When reporters wondered about Baer not showing too much desire to rise to his feet and face another barrage of Louis' blows, Baer had a ready answer for them too. He noted, "Sure I quit. He hit me 18 times while I was going down the last time. I got a family to think about, and if anybody wants to see the execution of Max Baer, he's got to pay more than $25 for a ringside seat...."[3]

Along with Baer, the bout's timekeeper did not have a particularly good night either. There were two blatant errors with the stopwatch. The first mistake was when the rest period between rounds three and four somehow was extended to 74 seconds instead of the usual 60 seconds. The second error was when the fourth round ran longer than the regulation three minutes. The time of the knockout was, oddly, 3:09 of the fourth round. Under New York State's boxing rules in 1935, Baer should have been saved by the bell—just as he had been at the end of round three. When told of the timekeeping errors, Baer dismissed them as unimportant to the final result. His frank response was, "What's the difference? I was beaten and beaten in grand fashion."[4] Somehow the Louis-Baer bout was decreed Fight of the Year for 1935 by *The Ring* magazine. Apparently competitiveness was not a major criterion.

Maximillian Adolph Otto Siegfried Schmeling was born on September 28, 1905, in Klein Luckow in what was then the Kingdom of Prussia. In 1921, Schmeling's father took him to see the film of the Dempsey-Carpentier championship fight. Schmeling, who was not yet 16, was immediately hooked by boxing; he wanted to be just like his new hero, Jack Dempsey. He was a quick learner. By 1924, Schmeling was the national amateur boxing champion of Germany in the light heavyweight division. He turned professional shortly thereafter.

Although the brawling, aggressive-minded Dempsey was Schmeling's ring idol, he boxed with a style far more similar to Dempsey's nemesis Gene Tunney. Schmeling was a thinking man's fighter. He was quite content to allow an aggressive-minded opponent make an error and then exploit it with clever counterpunching. When Dempsey toured Europe in 1925, he boxed a few exhibition bouts with various up-and-comers. One of those rising stars was Max Schmeling. Dempsey was apparently impressed with the 20-year-old German's ring savvy. The champ politely wished the youngster well. By the summer of 1926 Schmeling had won the German professional light heavyweight crown. By 1927 he was the 175-pound champion of Europe. (The bout in which he won that title was the first one ever broadcast on German radio. Schmeling moved up in weight and captured the German heavyweight championship in 1928. He was clearly the most famous boxer in Germany; his fans began affectionately calling him "Unser Max" (Our Max). With nothing much left to prove in Germany, Schmeling traveled to the United States—the Mecca of professional pugilism—in hopes of securing both bigger purses and bigger prizes.

As Schmeling was rising through the ranks of the European heavyweights, the world championship was entering a period of uncertainty. On September 23, 1926, Gene Tunney outpointed Jack Dempsey in a ten-round fight in Philadelphia to win the world heavyweight title and end Dempsey's seven-year reign as champion. The following year Tunney topped Dempsey in a rematch in Chicago that featured the famous "long count." On July 26, 1928, Tunney beat New Zealander Tom Heeney at Yankee Stadium in another successful defense. The 30-year-old champion then unexpectedly retired from the ring, the first heavyweight kingpin to do so since James J. Jeffries in 1905. Tunney had recently married socialite and steel heiress Polly Lauder who reputedly insisted he quit the sport that had made him rich and famous. Since his boxing earnings had made Tunney

Max Schmeling in a fighting pose, 1938. Although Schmeling himself had no fondness for the Nazi regime in his country, Adolf Hitler believed the former champion was the ideal Aryan athlete.

extremely wealthy—and he was marrying an even wealthier woman—he agreed with no regrets. Unlike Jeffries, Tunney stayed retired. This created an obvious vacancy at the top of the heavyweight heap that had to be filled.

Upon defeating Paulino Uzcudun on a 15-round decision at Yankee Stadium, Schmeling was chosen as one of the two combatants to battle for Tunney's vacated title. Jack Sharkey—known as the "Boston Gob" for his adopted home town—was the other. At Yankee Stadium—which was quickly becoming the preferred venue for important fights in the United States—the two hopefuls met on Thursday, June 12, 1930. It turned out to be the third of five major controversial bouts that would dominate Sharkey's career. The end of the fight was unsatisfactory as Schmeling became the first man in the modern era to win the world heavyweight championship on a foul. Sharkey seemed to be on his way to the title, having won the first three rounds handily by most reporters' estimation. However, in the fourth round, one of Sharkey's body shots aimed at the German may or may not have drifted below the belt. Schmeling crumpled to the canvas in a heap with a painful expression on his face.

Schmeling's manager, Joe Jacobs, entered the ring in a fury and began lobbying for Sharkey to be disqualified. Under New York State's boxing rules in 1930, a low blow could result in an immediate disqualification. Referee Jimmy Crowley seemed unsure of what to do; he never began a count. Schmeling's cornermen literally dragged him back to his stool. Eventually Crowley ruled Sharkey's punch to have been low and severe enough to merit disqualification. Sharkey broke into tears upon realizing he had lost on a foul. The fight film seems to be slightly inconclusive on the matter, but the New York State Athletic Commission agreed with Crowley's decision as did most boxing writers at ringside. Max Schmeling was the new world heavyweight champion of the world, but the circumstances surrounding his victory were hardly glorious. As British boxing historian Harry Mullan eloquently stated, "Max became the only man to be crowned heavyweight champ while sitting on the floor clutching his privates."[5] Nat Fleischer, the editor of *The Ring* was a little more genteel about the circumstances. He wrote it was the first time in boxing history that "a challenger gained the world heavyweight title while resting on his haunches."[6]

But did Sharkey actually foul Schmeling—and was it serious enough for the fight to be terminated? Opinions differed. Reporter John Durant, who thought Schmeling was faking, wrote, "Schmeling went into a grimacing act that would have drawn applause from the Barrymores."[7] James Dawson of the *New York Times* disagreed. He claimed, "The left hook Sharkey directed for the body landed foul and merited disqualification because of its obvious disabling effect."[8]

The way in which the title passed to Schmeling made some people wonder if Schmeling truly deserved to be recognized as the new heavyweight champion of the world. Ronald McIntyre of the *Milwaukee Sentinel* wrote, "There will only be a few who will recognize the German invader as the titleholder. No one was satisfied with the foul ending, especially because Sharkey was so far ahead and appeared to be headed on the way to a knockout victory when the blow was struck."[9]

Controversial champion or not, Schmeling managed one successful title defense: On July 3, 1931, he stopped Young Stribling on a technical knockout in the 15th round in Cleveland to retain his crown. It was a one-sided and impressive win for "the Black Uhlan," as the American press liked to call Schmeling. Although he is largely forgotten today, Stribling, a hugely popular contender from Georgia, was a busy fighter—to put it mildly. He compiled a truly extraordinary record of 224-13-14 in 251 verifiable professional fights in 13 years from 1920 to 1933. Large as it is, this total may be a conservative number. Some sources credit Stribling as having nearly 300 career bouts. (Boxing historians have long questioned the quality of Stribling's opponents—but they cannot question their sheer quantity.) His loss to Schmeling was the only time he was knocked out! Beloved in his home state, Stribling was a model citizen outside of the ring: a Bible-class teacher who worked with disadvantaged children. He also possessed movie-star good looks; his critics said he should have been an actor rather than a boxer. Following his tragic death from a motorcycle mishap in October 1933 at the young age of 28, some 25,000 mourners filed past his coffin at a public auditorium in Macon, GA. Ten thousand people attended his funeral rites.

"Let it be said that Max Schmeling is no longer a 'cheese' champion," wrote Yale Merrill in the *Pittsburgh Press*. "The smiling, black-haired German removed whatever doubt there may have been to his right to the world title by scoring a dramatic fifteenth-round [technical] knockout over W.L. (Young) Stribling 14 seconds before the scheduled end of their bout at the new Municipal Stadium."[10] Merrill also stated that Schmeling would be taking a vacation in Germany and return to the United States sometime, likely September, to face the enormous, lumbering Italian heavyweight Primo Carnera.

But an all-European matchup for the world heavyweight title would be a tough sell anywhere in the United States—especially with the Great Depression severely hurting sports attendance everywhere. The American boxing public—those who could afford such a luxury during hard economic times—much preferred a Schmeling-Sharkey rematch to settle the score from the 1930 low-blow incident. They would get it in 1932—and since Jack Sharkey was involved, controversy would have to be involved too.

On June 21, 1932, at Madison Square Garden Bowl—an outdoor venue erected specifically on Long Island for boxing events—Jack Sharkey won the world heavyweight championship in a split decision from Max Schmeling.

Former heavyweight contender Ed (Gunboat) Smith was the referee. He scored the fight heavily in favor of Sharkey (seven rounds to three with five rounds even) while Judge Charles F. Mathison had Schmeling comfortably winning ten rounds to five. The remaining judge, George Kelly, had Sharkey ahead eight rounds to seven. Kelly defensively told reporters, "Sharkey fought the best battle of his life. The trouble is few critics around the ringside recognized it."[11]

The *Pittsburgh Press* reported the following day that "a storm of protest broke around the newly occupied world's heavyweight boxing throne as an aftermath of the fight on which Jack Sharkey was awarded the title on points."[12] National partisanship was put aside as the crowd of 70,000 fans viciously booed the verdict. Schmeling's manager, Joe Jacobs, said his man had "been robbed" and claimed he had been warned beforehand that Schmeling would not get a victory if the fight went the distance. Jacobs insinuated that Sharkey had long been the fair-haired boy of the Madison Square Garden Corporation, and that his popularity within that all-powerful promotional group carried far too much weight. New York State's boxing commissioner, William Muldoon, scoffed that there was some sort of conspiracy at work against the German or for Sharkey, although he opined that the bout should have been scored a draw. Even New York City mayor James J. Walker weighed in. He was in attendance and figured Schmeling should have gotten the decision.

In his dressing room Schmeling was utterly mystified by the controversial verdict. "In my corner we thought we had the fight won easily," he said. "The announcement came as a terrible shock to me."[13]

United Press reported that fans listening to the bout on the radio were certainly under the impression that Sharkey was losing badly. An 89-year-old Sharkey fan in Denver named Michael Carey bemoaned how badly the contest was progressing for his man during the 14th round. According to his daughter, he angrily arose from his chair, tottered a few steps, and collapsed to the floor. He was dead by the time it was announced that Sharkey had actually won the fight.

Sharkey did not know what all the uproar was about. "I won the title. I won it fairly," he deadpanned. "Now I will defend it. I will be a fighting champion."[14] Rightly or wrongly, Schmeling, at age 26, was now an ex-champion and was swiftly relegated to has-been status.

For the next five years the glamorous and prestigious heavyweight championship of the world turned into something akin to a hot potato: No one could hold onto it for very long. Sharkey lost the title to Italy's Primo Carnera a year later on June 29, 1933. It was Sharkey's first and only defense of the crown. Carnera was a huge and affable man—he weighed 260 pounds when he faced Sharkey—but his boxing skills were debatable. He was said to have ties to organized crime, so many of his victories have been questioned over the years as to whether they were honest wins or mere setups. Suspicions linger to this day about the legitimacy of the sixth-round knockout that Carnera scored against Sharkey. It came from a single right uppercut in a fight that Sharkey was clearly winning despite being outweighed by 59 pounds. Carnera gleefully repeated the same broken-English phrase over and over in his dressing room after the fight: "Now my mama and papa be happy!" Not surprisingly, boxing fans in Rome went wild upon receiving news of Carnera's victory. The American press, always searching for clever nicknames to bestow upon famous athletes, came up with "the Vast Venetian" for the new champion from Italy.

Like Sharkey, Carnera only held the title for one defense. He was toppled—in every sense of the word—by Max Baer on June 14, 1934, at Madison Square Garden Bowl. Baer, a hard-hitting Californian, had scored his first important win by stopping Max Schmeling in 1933. Three years earlier, in 1930, Baer had killed an opponent in the ring—Frankie Campbell. Given a title shot, the hard-hitting Baer turned Carnera into a human yo-yo, flooring him 11 times in 11 rounds before the referee sensibly stopped the one-sided affair. The fight was absolutely farcical in the middle rounds as Carnera and Baer spent more time wrestling each other than trading punches. Several times they fell to the canvas still locked together in a clinch. (After one such undignified incident, Baer elicited a few laughs from ringside ticketholders by shouting, "Last one up is a sissy!"[15]) The title thus passed from the jolly Italian to the slugger from America's west coast. Although Baer was born in Nebraska, he was dubbed "the Livermore Larruper" by sportswriters because his mailing address for most of the past decade had been that northern California community.

The trend of short-term champs in pro boxing's most important division continued unabated. Three hundred sixty-four days after winning the championship, Baer surprisingly lost it to 10:1 underdog James J. Braddock at the same place he had won the crown—Madison Square Garden Bowl on Long Island. (At one point in its brief history, Madison Square Garden bowl hosted seven consecutive world title fights in which the defending champion lost his crown!) Based on the long odds against a Braddock win that night, it was the biggest upset in a world heavyweight title bout to that time—and would remain so until Buster Douglas shocked Mike Tyson in Tokyo in 1990.

Braddock was a prohibitive underdog for good reason: He had 22 losses on his record when he stepped into the ring that night in pursuit of the ultimate prize in boxing. Nevertheless, Braddock simply outboxed the overconfident Baer and won a well-deserved 15-round decision. The prevailing opinion was that Baer wasted too much time and energy clowning in a fight he thought would be a cinch. Chester L. Smith of the *Pittsburgh Press* could scarcely believe 30-year-old James J. Braddock was the new heavyweight kingpin, referring to the new champ as "a plodding scion of mediocrity" and a "likeable Irishman without either a punch or the faintest shade of color." But even Smith had to concede Braddock's improbable rise from the relief rolls to the world heavyweight championship was a thoroughly compelling narrative. "Horatio Alger should be writing this story,"[16] Smith commented. Indeed, more than 30 years after Braddock died, his life story was made into the 2005 movie *Cinderella Man* with Russell Crowe in the title role and directed by Ron Howard.

So while the world heavyweight boxing title passed from Gene Tunney to Max Schmeling to Jack Sharkey to Primo Carnera to Max Baer to James J. Braddock, the most consistent heavyweight boxer on the horizon was young Joe Louis who was steadily amassing one victory after another from his 1934 pro debut to the summer of 1936. If anyone could bring much-needed stability to a most unstable heavyweight division, it was the Brown Bomber. However, on June 19, 1936, the unthinkable happened to Louis and his nicely choreographed cakewalk to the heavyweight crown: Max Schmeling, considered to be past his prime and a prohibitive underdog, stunned the sports world by

Max Schmeling demonstrates a left jab, 1938. It was not much of a weapon for the onetime champion; Schmeling did possess a powerful right hand, however.

thrashing the Brown Bomber in 12 rounds at Yankee Stadium. Entering the bout, Louis was a perfect 27–0. Schmeling was supposed to be another name added to Louis' victory roll, but he had not read the script. What Schmeling had done was his homework. By closely studying films of Louis in action, Schmeling had detected some subtle but important flaws in his technique— a tendency for Louis to momentarily drop his left guard just after throwing a right cross, and a slow left hook that allowed for a quick counter right. Schmeling exploited these tidbits of knowledge and blasted Louis into submission with deft counterpunches, stunning boxing fans on two continents. Virtually nobody foresaw the shocking outcome. Bookmakers had listed Schmeling as a 12:1 underdog. In some places the odds rose to 20:1—and still very little Schmeling money was wagered.

Eddie Brietz of the Associated Press dutifully reported, "The fight world today acclaimed Max Schmeling, the man who walked alone, for achieving the supposedly impossible—the knockout of Joe Louis. The beetle-browed German, who wasn't given a Chinaman's chance, not only knocked the hitherto invincible 22-year-old negro from the top rungs of the fistic ladder, but he did it in the most convincing manner possible—he stopped Louis cold."[17]

Joe Louis looks for an opening against Max Schmeling in their first bout in 1936. Schmeling, considered past his prime, surprisingly defeated the unbeaten Louis with a knockout in the 12th round.

The defeat was thorough. Louis' mother, watching her son fight for the first time, was escorted away from ringside before the bout's conclusion. She was madly shouting that she did not want to see her child killed.

According to Brietz, Louis was in a daze from the time he was decked in the fourth round until being finished off by Schmeling at 2:39 of the 12th frame. "I was just in a fog out there," Louis bluntly said afterward. Brietz reported, "Until his handlers told him about it, the Brown Bomber hadn't the faintest idea what transpired [in the bout's final eight rounds]."[18] Louis had fought from the fifth round to the 12th purely on boxing instinct. John Roxborough, one of Louis' handlers, expressed surprise that Louis was not knocked out earlier in the fight.

Another AP scribe, Alan Gould, declared Louis' poor outing versus the former champion was nothing less than startling to the 39,878 people in attendance. He wrote, "The collapse of Louis was as complete as it was shocking to those who had all but put him on the pedestal of invincibility. From start to finish, the youthful Negro not only failed to display his accustomed punching power and boxing skill, but his chocolate chin was a target for Schmeling's vicious right-hand thrusts." Gould also referred to Louis as the "bombed bomber."[19] Truly, all glory is fleeting.

"I studied Louis carefully," Schmeling eagerly told the men of the press the following day as he basked in unexpected glory. "I found from [other fight] pictures that he was easy to hit with a right hand. I planned my whole campaign accordingly. Everything was concentrated in my right. I knew I would have to take punishment from his left to have an opening for my right cross, but I won the way I figured."[20] In truth, Schmeling relied on his powerful right hand almost completely. A sportswriter once commented that Schmeling's left hand was "merely something for holding a fork."[21]

In Harlem, things took a nasty turn in response to Louis' surprise defeat. According to a report in the *Montreal Gazette*, mobs of black hoodlums set upon and attacked random white males while vandals stoned automobiles. Six hundred extra police officers and 100 detectives were hastily sent to trouble spots to restore order.

Elsewhere, the German government was certainly pleased with Unser Max's totally unexpected victory. As soon as Nazi Propaganda Minister Josef Goebbels received a bulletin about the upset, he took the liberty of telephoning Max's wife, Anny Ondra, a Czech actress, to pass along his personal congratulations regarding her husband's big win—and Adolf Hitler's best wishes too. Ondra had stayed up until the wee hours of the morning to listen to the radio account of the bout. She declared her husband's win to be the most exciting night of her life. Goebbels also happily cabled Schmeling in New York City. The message said, "To your wonderful victory, my best congratulations. I know you fight for Germany; that it's a German victory. Heil Hitler.

Regards."[22] The *Calgary Daily Herald* reported that "Schmeling will return home to a turbulent reception—far different than his leave-taking for the fight when most German newspapers did not even register his departure."[23] Like it or not, Schmeling was suddenly Nazi Germany's new sports hero and the living embodiment of Aryan supremacy. He was engulfed with congratulatory messages from all over the world, from boxing fans and non-boxing fans alike, who were pro–German, anti-black, anti–American, or who just liked an old-fashioned feel-good story of an underdog defying long odds.

A story on the front page of the *Regina (SK) Leader-Post* said that Madison Square Garden officials were "elated over the unexpected defeat of the erstwhile Brown Bomber"[24] and promoter Mike Jacobs was already trying to arrange a championship bout between James J. Braddock and Schmeling, perhaps for as early as September 1936. (Jacobs had succeeded Tex Rickard as the man in charge of boxing promotions for Madison Square Garden after Rickard's sudden death in early 1929.) A rumor that the fight would be held in Germany was dismissed immediately. Furthermore, Jacobs predicted that "a lot of guys will want to fight Louis now."[25] Schmeling announced he would be flying back to Germany in grand style on the dirigible *Hindenburg*. His only immediate plans, he said, were to rest and attend the upcoming 1936 Berlin Olympic Games as a spectator.

Louis, nevertheless, rebounded from the shattering loss to Schmeling. His brain trust handed him a busy schedule to get him back into the muddled heavyweight title picture. From August 1936 to February 1937, Louis knocked out seven opponents in succession to regain his momentum if not his irretrievable aura of invincibility. The quality of Louis' opposition varied widely. One was former champion Jack Sharkey (who was flattened in three rounds and retired from boxing shortly thereafter). Another was Steve Ketchel, a fighter who was making his professional debut. (The neophyte was counted out in round two.) With negotiation between champion James J. Braddock's camp and Schmeling's people now hopelessly stalled, Louis' new winning streak was enough to earn him a crack at Braddock's title at Chicago's Comiskey Park on Tuesday, June 22, 1937.

Braddock had been inactive in the two years since he had upset Max Baer for the title. Attempts to pit Braddock against Schmeling in a championship bout fell through for a number of reasons. Politics was always at the forefront. Braddock's handlers were Jewish and they did not want to deal with anyone connected with Nazi Germany. There was also the great fear that if Schmeling won the championship that the world title would be locked in Germany for the foreseeable future. Braddock simply bided his time until Joe Louis worked his way back into title contention. When Louis signed to challenge Braddock for the world heavyweight championship, one unique clause in the fight contract provided that if Braddock happened to lose, he would receive a percentage of all Louis' future title-defense purses. No one could have possibly foreseen that Braddock would be getting a share of 25 such paydays.

Louis was supposed to blow out the rusty Braddock without too much trouble. However, in a startling development, Braddock dropped Louis for a flash knockdown in the first round. But it was only a momentary setback. For the Brown Bomber it was not to be a repeat of the disastrous Schmeling loss. After that early surprise, it was a fight thoroughly dominated by the challenger. Within three rounds it was clear to everyone in the ballpark that Louis was the superior fighter. Louis won the bout and the world championship with an eighth-round knockout. "Louis beat an aging fighter in Jimmy Braddock," wrote Ed Baker of the *Ottawa Citizen*, "a fighter of the gamest variety but lacking in skill."[26] Baker also said Braddock's long absence from the ring worked against him as he was missing the same types of punches on Louis that Schmeling had successfully connected with in 1936. Braddock himself told newsmen after the contest, "The two-year layoff beat me. I felt it coming from the fifth round up."[27] One reporter oddly asked Louis if he were planning on retiring! The new champion responded with a chuckle, "No, not now. I'm just starting out again."[28]

With his victory, Louis became the sixth different man to hold the world heavyweight title during the dizzying 1930s—and the decade still had 30 months left in it. (In contrast, only two fighters—Jack Dempsey and Gene Tunney—held the championship in the entire previous decade.) No one was aware of it yet, but after an array of uninspiring, short-term titleholders, the longest reign atop the heavyweight heap by one man had begun.

Nevertheless, Louis was not especially joyful when he lifted the crown from Braddock's head. "I don't want nobody to call me champ until I beat Schmeling,"[29] Louis tersely told his happy handlers in his dressing room after his victory over Braddock. Regardless of the double negative, Louis' meaning was very clear to all: He himself doubted his rightful claim to the world heavyweight title until he defeated the only man who had bested him as a professional. He desperately wanted a rematch with Max Schmeling—and as early as possible.

Louis was the first black fighter to hold the world heavyweight championship since Jack Johnson's infamous title reign ended 22 years earlier. It was estimated that about one-fifth of the crowd in Comiskey Park was comprised of black fans. There was no trouble about Louis' victory reported anywhere in the United States. This was not anything like Jack Johnson in the aftermath of Sydney or Reno a generation earlier. In fact, Louis was mobbed by well-wishers of all races after being declared the winner. It took him ten minutes to escape the back-slapping to get to the solitude of his dressing room. In a touch of irony, Louis was assigned the entire Chicago White Sox clubhouse

Joe Louis on a bleacher seat, circa 1938.

as his personal dressing room. Major League Baseball was still racially segregated in 1937. Still, the possibility of racial conflict at some point in the uncertain future was in the back of anyone's mind who was at least 30 years old. The day following Louis' victory over Braddock, Ed Baker, the sports editor of the *Ottawa Citizen*, penned some thoughtful and hopeful remarks on having another black world champion:

> Just what effect Louis' victory ... will have on the colored population of the United States will remain to be seen, of course. Maybe none because the tan-colored heavyweight is really a spurious champion. But if you go back to that period between 1910 and 1915, it will be recalled there were race riots in many different parts of the States.
>
> Maybe people today are more tolerant. Maybe members of Joe Louis' race are more enlightened and better behaved than they were when the black man, Jack Johnson, was champion....[30]

In Germany, Schmeling's 1936 win over Louis was a terrific propaganda coup. The Nazis had embraced Schmeling after his victory over Louis, touting him, of course, as verifiable proof of German racial superiority. Schmeling, however, seemed to avoid politics in his daily life. Whether he was apolitical or not is a matter of debate. Schmeling never joined the Nazi Party himself.

He refused to wear a swastika emblem on his trunks. But from the moment Hitler had risen power in Germany in 1933, Schmeling had to toe a difficult line. As a German he had to please the Nazis. Yet he had to maintain positive relations in New York City, the epicenter of professional boxing. That was where Schmeling earned most of his money as an athlete. It was also where a large percentage of the boxing community resided—and a significant portion of it was Jewish. In fact, Schmeling's manager, Joe Jacobs, was an American Jew. Schmeling steadfastly refused to sever ties with him despite ongoing pressure to do so from the Nazi regime back home. Jacobs was once photographed alongside Schmeling while giving the Nazi salute with a lit cigar in his right hand. Berlin was not happy about that image.

To pass the time until a second match versus Schmeling could be arranged, Louis continued to be active. He recorded three victories in title defenses. In his first outing since winning the world heavyweight title, Louis faced Tommy Farr of Wales before a throng of 33,469 souls at Yankee Stadium on August 30, 1937—just ten weeks after demolishing Braddock. To many fans' surprise, Farr, rated somewhere between a 10:1 and 15:1 underdog depending on one's bookmaker, lasted the full 15 rounds. Moreover, the challenger won the crowd's approval with his game performance. Many spectators booed when Louis was awarded the unanimous verdict, although most observers firmly thought Louis had done sufficiently well to win. Referee Arthur Donovan erred in nearly raising Farr's arm in victory. Donovan also scored the fight, as referees often did during the 1930s. However, eyebrows were certainly raised when it was learned that Donovan gave the champion 13 of the 15 rounds (with one round even). The two ringside judges had it 8–5–2 and 9–6, both for Louis. Their scores were much closer to what the chaps in press row believed to be a fair and reasonable assessment of the bout.

Donovan's one-sided scoring of the bout caused the British correspondents to question both his integrity and his eyesight. Wrote one irked scribe from the United Kingdom, "The verdict is that of a man either blindly partisan or afflicted with astigmatism. It ... justifies the beliefs that nothing short of the annihilation of Louis would have given Farr victory. That Louis won may not be disputed, but as I read the fight, there was only a fractional difference in his favor at the finish."[31] Even American boxing writers were unimpressed with Louis' narrow triumph over the unfashionable but feisty Welshman. Henry McLemore of United Press wrote, "Joe Louis still held the world's heavyweight boxing championship today, but that was about all. His glamor was gone. No one spoke of him as the 'Dynamite Killer.' No one compared him to the stubble-bearded Dempsey of Toledo."[32] Louis had injured a knuckle on his right hand in the second round, but few observers were willing to accept that reason for Louis not knocking out a perceived no-hoper.

The aforementioned Dempsey, now age 42, attended the Louis-Farr contest and frankly did not think much of either combatant's abilities. He nostalgically quipped, "Fifteen years ago against that sort of fighters I would have sent [my manager] Jack Kearns out to do the fighting and I would have stayed in the corner."[33] Another ex-titlist, 59-year-old Jack Johnson, concurred. "Give me three pork chops and a breath of fresh air, and I'll challenge 'em both!"[34] Max Schmeling was, of course, a keen observer too. "I will beat Louis every day in the week—and twice on Sundays," he declared after being thoroughly unimpressed by the champion's first troublesome title defense. Benny Leonard, the retired former lightweight champ, who was widely considered the greatest 135-pounder ever, expressed his views on Louis-Farr succinctly: "I was born too soon and too light."[35]

To regain his diminished stature, Louis engaged in two more title fights in short order. They featured results that were more typical of the Brown Bomber. On February 23, 1938, Nathan Mann was starched in three rounds at Madison Square Garden. Mann, a New England farm boy, was competitive for about one round before the difference in class became apparent. ("Louis Proved Guilty of Mann-Slaughter" read the punny headline in the *Pittsburgh Press*.) After "the fall of Mann" (another *Press* play on words), journalist Joe Williams reported that the smiling challenger had confidently entered the ring "draped in a black robe which was later to prove a symbol of fistic mortality." Williams also added, "There had been stories that Louis had lost his zest for fighting, that the big dough had got him, that he wasn't training seriously anymore. This seems to be a slight mistake. Louis never looked better."[36]

Since defeating Mann did not prove overly strenuous for the reigning world champion, Louis was back in action again less than six weeks later, on April 1. Another farmer's son, this time a Minnesotan named Harry Thomas, was convincingly felled in five rounds at Chicago Stadium. Wins they were for the world champion, but they featured neither compelling opponents nor memorable ring battles. Harry Thomas already had 11 losses on his record prior to his shot at Louis' title. Louis was the first fighter to defeat Thomas within the distance, however. "The smoothest piece of fighting machinery in the ring today relentlessly mowed down Harry Thomas," wrote R.G. Lynch of the *Milwaukee Journal*. "The champion was the old invincible Joe Louis who used to send sports writers and fans into deliriums of praise before Max Schmeling's crashing right-hand punches raised doubts in their minds."[37] People were already thinking 12 weeks ahead to what would unfold at Yankee Stadium on June 22.

On Wednesday, June 22, 1938, Max Schmeling would be attempting to achieve something that four previous heavyweight titlists had failed to do since boxing gloves started to be worn in world championship fights—regain the world championship. Bob Fitzsimmons, James J. Corbett, James J. Jeffries and Jack Dempsey had all come up short in their attempts when they had been given the opportunity. All had been soundly trounced, in fact. If boxing history was to serve as an indicator of what to expect, it was clearly not on Schmeling's side.

Schmeling did his training in the small village of Speculator, NY, in the Adirondack Mountains. Schmeling had trained there before, as had former champions Gene Tunney and Max Baer. It was a serene community of fewer than 300 residents who generally let the challenger and his handlers alone when they ventured away from the camp. Nevertheless, 5,000 boxing fans showed up one day to watch Schmeling spar eight rounds with a variety of opponents. Among the visitors was ex-champion James J. Braddock who left Speculator unimpressed. He predicted Louis would defeat the German challenger inside of seven rounds. "[Schmeling] is slower than ever, his punches are not as fast or as hard, and he is a mark for a left-hand punch,"[38] Braddock stated.

On June 18, Ex-champion Tommy Burns—who had been a bit of an elusive figure since retiring from boxing—told a reporter in Seattle that he favored Louis' chances. "Naturally I'd like to see Schmeling win," the Canadian said, "but if I were a betting man, I'd have to back Louis. Joe has proven his gameness and his age advantage will count."[39] Burns, who turned 57 on the day he was interviewed, was said to be managing a pair of fighters from the Seattle area.

Louis set up his camp in Pompton Lakes, NJ. It and he jointly became tourist attractions. It was not unusual for the daily number of visitors to reach 4,000. One who made a special trip there was Franklin Delano Roosevelt. The chief executive was seated in the back seat of an open car and asked Louis to lean toward him so he could feel his arm muscles. The champion obliged. During one interview, Louis confidently stated he would knock out the challenger inside of two rounds if Schmeling decided to not fight too cautiously. Louis' trainer, Jack (Chappie) Blackburn exuded confidence too. He said his fighter's 1936 loss to the German, though devastating at the time, was really a blessing in disguise. "No fighter can ever be a great fighter until he takes one good licking and learns enough not to let it happen again," Blackburn opined. "Joe's had his and he ain't gonna take another one—at least not from Schmeling. He learned too much to let Schmeling keep whaling away with those right hands again."[40]

When Schmeling arrived in New York City for the rematch, his reception was less than friendly; he needed a police escort to get him and his party safely to their downtown hotel. Schmeling had trouble staying anonymous. He was often recognized on Gotham's streets. From hecklers he was repeatedly subjected to cries of "Nazi!" Passersby mocked him with exaggerated fascist salutes—from a safe distance, of course. It was widely suggested in local newspapers that if Schmeling were to lose to Louis, he would be treated quite harshly if he dared to venture back to Germany. It was clear that the heavyweight championship contest on June 22, 1938, was going to be fought in an atmosphere unlike any other that had ever preceded it.

A June 12 Associated Press story (that ran in the *Montreal Gazette* without a byline) said that Schmeling was undertaking one of the great risks in sports history by challenging for the world heavyweight title at this late point in his career:

> Max is making the supreme gamble in the history of pugilism. Schmeling, at 32, comes near having everything except the heavyweight title. He has plenty of money, a beautiful wife, and he is an idolized citizen of Germany. He and Annie [sic] Ondra have, to all appearances, a supremely happy existence. Max spends most of his time hunting on his huge Bavarian estate. They have a beautiful apartment in Berlin, too, and Max whisks about in a garish American car.
>
> But even close friends of the German have raised the question of whether Schmeling's popularity would last should he lose to Louis. Max, however, is so supremely confident he can beat Louis again that he's ready to take the gamble of losing his place in the sun.
>
> Schmeling would not be going into the ring unless he was absolutely convinced of the outcome. He thinks it will be like shooting a sitting duck.

Five days before the fight, Paul Mickelson of the Associated Press wrote that the German correspondents in New York were predictably in unanimous agreement that Schmeling would defeat Louis for a second time—and do it rather easily too. Alan Gould of the Associated Press wrote on the day of the fight that the Louis-Schmeling bout "has whipped the fight faithful to a high emotional pitch, created more international sporting excitement, and provided the biggest box-office magnet of any title bout since Gene Tunney rode the famous 'long count' to victory over Jack Dempsey in Chicago in 1927."[41]

An editorial in the June 22 edition of the *Montreal Gazette* noted the intense interest the Louis-Schmeling fight was generating across the border in Canada: "Anywhere you went for several weeks past, everyone was talking along the same lines, and the volume of discussion on this particular subject has increased proportionately as the date of the cause of it all drew near. There is probably no event in all sportdom ... which stirs as many millions of pulses and creates such widespread interest as does a heavyweight championship fight. It is no exaggeration to say, figuratively, that the eyes of the world will be focused on Joe Louis and Max Schmeling as they duck through the ropes in Yankee Stadium at 10 o'clock this evening."[42] The *Montreal Gazette* was, of course, more than happy to profit by the Louis-Schmeling hype. The daily broadsheet was planning to capitalize on the bout themselves by printing an extra edition that evening devoted solely to the goings-on at Yankee Stadium. Readers were told to look for it at newsstands and from special street vendors a few minutes after the fight's conclusion.

"Joe Louis, Negro holder of the heavyweight championship of the world, and Max Schmeling, a former champion, meet tonight in New York in a fight that at the eleventh hour still had the fans wondering what the outcome might be,"[43] declared Ronald McIntyre of the *Milwaukee Sentinel* on June 22, 1938. Precisely one year before, Louis had beaten James J. Braddock in Chicago to win the world title.

In Germany, top government officials harbored a festering gripe. *Der Angriff* (*The Attack*), the Nazi Party's official newspaper, loudly decried the way Schmeling was frequently being portrayed in American newspaper coverage of the event. It claimed the sporting press in the United States was displaying "an unsportsmanlike attitude." Propaganda Minister Dr. Josef Goebbels said that American journalists were engaging in "baiting of the worst sort and stupid attacks on both Schmeling and Germany." Ridiculing reports that Schmeling would be arrested if he lost, the Nazi Party organ stated that American newspapers were involved in "a great organized campaign of lies" to turn a sporting event into "a racial and political affair." *Der Angriff* asked rhetorically, "Do Americans think so little of their world champion that even in the last few hours before the fight they are trying to destroy Schmeling's fighting morale with such attacks?"[44]

Not that the political aspects of the bout needed any further fuel, but it was provided anyway. On the day of the fight, newspapers across America reported that espionage activities of "Nazi spy rings" had extended far afield to Hawaii and the Panama Canal Zone; Josef Goebbels announced to a tremendous throng in Berlin's Olympic Stadium that new laws to permanently drive Jews out of that city were imminent; Czechoslovakia was preparing its defense against an expected German invasion; and instances of Fifth Column sabotage had been found in the construction of new warships for the nation's expanded navy. War clouds were forming.

An overflow crowd of nearly 80,000 tense fans filed into Yankee Stadium to witness a piece of history that Wednesday night. It had been 733 days since Schmeling had defeated Louis in the same venue. Hitler, confident his countryman would win, had dispatched radio announcers to broadcast the bout back to the Reich. (There were no communication satellites in 1938; the account of the action would come overseas via short-wave radio. The time zone difference meant the 10 p.m. main event in New York City would begin at 3 a.m. on June 23 in Germany.) Hitler made a point of phoning Schmeling to pass along encouraging words just before he left his dressing room and headed toward whatever destiny had in store for him.

After the preliminary matches, various stars from boxing's past and present entered the ring to be acknowledged by the sellout throng. Max Baer—who had been loudly lobbying for another opportunity versus Louis (despite his poor showing versus the Brown Bomber three years earlier)—was roundly jeered. Baer did have some leverage for demanding a title fight, however; he had won 22 out of 24 fights since being thumped by Louis in 1935. Whether Baer stood a chance versus the champion was entirely another matter. A comical incident occurred when ex-world heavyweight champion Gene Tunney was leaving the ring while Tommy Farr was trying to enter it. The two men collided and Farr was nearly flattened by the oblivious 41-year-old Fighting Marine.

When Louis, weighing 198¾ pounds, first appeared on the runway heading toward to the illuminated ring, the baseball park erupted with wild enthusiasm. Louis wore black trunks with narrow white vertical stripes. They bore an interlocking "JL" monogram on the left leg. When Schmeling, weighing 193 pounds, entered the ring, he made a point of going to Louis' corner to exchange pleasantries. He was clad in a colorful robe and purple boxing trunks. He was greeted with a smattering of boos, but mostly with polite, respectful applause. Some ticketholders were more enthusiastic toward the former champion. Many fans in the distant $5.75 cheap seats of Yankee Stadium were openly rooting for Schmeling to return the world heavyweight title to the white race—and were utterly unabashed about it. They cheered loudly for the German. For the vast majority of boxing fans crammed into the famous ballpark, the upcoming fight represented a clear morality play between good and evil.

Just before the main event, Arthur Donovan, age 46, learned he was to be the third man in the ring. (As an anti-corruption measure, it was commonplace at the time for boxing's governing bodies to appoint their referees for important bouts just a short time before the matches began. This way referees could not be bribed or otherwise intimidated by the fight game's unsavory characters.) This was a return engagement for Donovan as he had refereed the first Louis-Schmeling bout two years earlier. (He had, of course, also refereed the Louis-Farr title bout nine months before where his lopsided scoring of the fight came under fire.)

Donovan was part of a distinguished sports family. Arthur was the son of 19th-century American bare-knuckle middleweight champion Professor Mike Donovan—a man who had once given private boxing lessons in the White House to President Theodore Roosevelt. A good choice to handle such a monumental fight, Arthur Donovan's significant experience would be put to the test more than once on June 22, 1938. Donovan was, in reality, the only man considered to referee Louis-Schmeling II. For 50 years Donovan's main line of work was as a physical fitness/boxing instructor at the New York Athletic Club. Promoter Mike Jacobs had him on his weekly payroll so he could call upon Donovan's services whenever necessary to handle an important bout. Jacobs also owned 10 percent of Louis' contract. If anyone thought there was a potential conflict of interests, no one said so—at least publicly.

Well respected as a boxing arbiter, Donovan would gain public renown over the years for being "Joe Louis' referee," not because he was biased towards the champ in any way, but simply because he was selected to work so many of Louis' title bouts. (Donovan would eventually referee a total of 23 Joe Louis fights.) Certainly, it helped that he had connections to Mike Jacobs, but it was more of an indication of Donovan's overall competence as a boxing official. Donovan became such a staple at major fights that fans were occasionally heard to complain, "Donovan again?" whenever he was announced as the third man in the ring. Sports journalist Dan Parker was quick to defend professional boxing's most famous referee: "Every time Donovan trips over a fold in the canvas while refereeing a bout, you'll hear the old familiar cry, 'Donovan again!' I hope the cry continues because as long as it's Donovan again, boxing fans will be assured of honest, competent officiating."[45] In his long, distinguished career as a boxing official, Donovan refereed 14 world heavyweight championship fights. His son, Art Donovan, was a National Football League Hall of Famer who starred as a defensive tackle for the Baltimore Colts when the pro version of the game began to rapidly ascend in popularity. Off the field he was renowned as one of the liveliest characters and best interview subjects in his sport.

Interestingly, during Donovan's final instructions to both fighters, he used the opportunity to give both Louis and Schmeling a brief lecture. "I want to impress upon you men now the terrific responsibility you have in the ring tonight,"[46] Donovan began. He reminded them that the packed baseball stadium and millions of people listening on the radio were expecting a memorable battle. It was an unusual and wholly unnecessary statement. The stakes and the circumstances were obvious to all.

NBC had secured the radio rights to broadcast the fight throughout America on its vast network of stations. Clem McCarthy, a 55-year-old gravelly-throated sports announcer from New York, was behind the microphone to call the action. His was a familiar voice to American sports fans in the 1930s. Over the years McCarthy had attained fame as both a boxing and horse racing broadcaster, but Louis-Schmeling II would be his biggest stage by far. He would never have a larger audience. It was estimated that 70 million Americans were tuned in to NBC affiliates when the opening bell clanged. It is believed to be the most listened-to radio broadcast in American history. Accordingly, McCarthy's call has been rightly preserved in the National Recording Registry (NRR). "There are some events and some broadcasts, some sporting activities, that reach out to millions of people and touch them in a very deep way and express a lot of their deepest cultural, racial, political hopes and aspirations," noted NRR radio historian Lewis Erenberg says. "This is one of those events, and we have it preserved here and I think that's a wonderful thing."[47]

No sporting event in American history created such excitement and anticipation. Future U.S. president Jimmy Carter, who was not quite 14 in June 1938, mentioned the Louis-Schmeling rematch in his 1975 autobiography. He wrote in *Why Not the Best?* about the night of the fight in his boyhood home in Georgia. "All our black neighbors came to see daddy when the second Joe Louis-Max Schmeling fight was to take place. There was intense interest and they asked if they could listen to the fight. We propped the radio up in the open window of our house and we and our visitors sat and stood under a large mulberry tree nearby...."

As it turned out, announcer McCarthy had a very short night's work behind the NBC microphone. So did the telegraphers who were sending round-by-round descriptions to various eager news agencies around the globe. Those fans who settled down near their radios in expectation of a long, strategic bout—or those who tuned in just a trifle late—would be disappointed. The fight was not even remotely competitive. Schmeling only landed two blows of any significance while, conversely, Louis rarely missed at all.

Louis, normally a cautious boxer-puncher during the opening round of a fight, immediately pursued Schmeling relentlessly—but not recklessly—in attacking his nemesis. It was controlled aggression at its brutal finest. Schmeling, stunned by Louis' unexpectedly fierce assault, went into a defensive posture. Louis pounded Schmeling's head and body with a barrage of punches. Schmeling did manage to land one solid counter right—the blow he had connected with so often in 1936—but Louis was unfazed by it this time.

The champion varied his attack when Schmeling ventured close to him and tried to work on Louis' body. Louis' punches to the German's head were interspersed with damaging shots to his midsection. One body blow to the challenger was so punishing that Schmeling let out a discernible howl. Wrote Gayle Talbot of the Associated Press, "A terrible right to the kidneys that caused Schmeling to scream in pain and that partially paralyzed his 32-year-old legs, gave Louis the revenge he had sought since the German knocked him out in 12 rounds two summers ago."[48]

Schmeling retreated to the ropes. A quick combination to the head staggered Schmeling. The challenger attempted to find a safe place by grabbing the top ring rope with his right glove. Referee Donovan watched closely to see if Schmeling was violating the rules. He was not. It is legal for a fighter to hold onto the rope with one hand—but he cannot throw a punch with the other. Since there was no advantage to what Schmeling was doing, Donovan did not intervene. Louis continued to belt the challenger, landing half a dozen clean blows to Schmeling's body and his conspicuously unguarded head. Schmeling began to crumble to the canvas. Only his hand on the rope stopped his complete descent.

Referee Donovan promptly and quite properly ruled it to be a knockdown even though Schmeling never actually hit the deck. Donovan pushed Louis away and began a count. It was brief. When Donovan reached one, Schmeling had regained his feet and tried to prepare himself to resume the fight. He moved toward the center of the ring where Louis promptly clubbed him with a straight right hand. There was no technicality in the knockdown this time: Schmeling toppled to the canvas for all to see. He unwisely only took a count of two before rising.

Groggy, Schmeling was now a very easy target for the Brown Bomber who could smell victory and vindication. A three-punch combination, culminating with a right hand to the ribs, sent Schmeling down again. His knees did not quite touch the canvas but his gloves did. Again, Donovan correctly ruled the sequence to be a knockdown. Because Schmeling regained his feet so quickly, Donovan's count had barely begun. Donovan waved Louis forward—and the battering from the unstoppable world champion continued unabated.

The champion moved in for the kill. Louis stuck out his left jab to straighten out Schmeling. He stuck a stiff right hand to Schmeling's body, a follow-up left to his face—and a sizzling right hand to his jaw. It was a textbook combination, as pretty as it was powerful. Schmeling collapsed in a heap but got to his hands and knees by Donovan's count of five. A towel came fluttering in from Schmeling's corner from trainer Max Machon. Under New York State rules in 1938, this symbol of surrender was not permitted. Donovan knew the rule, of course. He picked up the towel and flung it away. By the time it had landed on the ropes, the fight was over. Schmeling almost certainly would have been counted out, but Schmeling's seconds had rushed into the ring to end the bout themselves. Machon took a moment to berate Donovan for not stopping the fight on his own when it was obvious that Schmeling was a beaten man. Donovan, and Louis' seconds also helped Schmeling back to his stool. Because Schmeling had not officially been counted out by Donovan, the bout went into the books as a technical knockout. Louis had successfully—and decisively—defended his world heavyweight crown for the fourth time.

Midway through round one, with Schmeling floundering badly and on his way to certain ignominious defeat, the broadcast to Germany was disconnected by Nazi officials who had clearly heard enough from New York City—and figured everyone else in the Reich had too. Four knockdowns and two minutes and four seconds after it began, the latest "Fight of the Century" was in the books. Here is Clem McCarthy's verbatim call of the final few seconds of the one-sided battle for NBC's vast radio audience: "Louis ... a right and left to the head ... a left to the jaw ... a right to the head, and [referee Arthur] Donovan is watching carefully. Louis measures him. Right to the body, a left up to the jaw—and Schmeling is down! The count is five! Five, six, seven, eight. The men are in the ring! The fight is over! On a technical knockout. Max Schmeling is beaten in one round!"

Schmeling left both the ring and Yankee Stadium on a stretcher. The result of the fight produced huge headlines throughout most of the world. In German newspapers, the story of Schmeling's loss appeared in print encased in mournful black borders. One German boxing executive, K. Metzner, who was listening to the fight on the radio with other high-ranking members of the European Boxing Federation, said—with apparent seriousness and with some very twisted logic—that because the bout ended so quickly it did not give a clear picture of whether Louis or Schmeling was the better fighter!

Millions of Germans forfeited a good night's sleep to listen to the shortwave radio broadcast at 3 a.m. Restaurants and other businesses stayed open well beyond their usual hours to accommodate fans who expected Schmeling to achieve the unprecedented feat of regaining the world heavyweight title. German bookmakers had made Schmeling a 2:1 favorite, so the one-sided nature of his defeat took most of the country by complete surprise.

The fight received major press coverage all over Europe. In Great Britain, special newspaper editions were printed to meet public demand for immediate and detailed reports. In some publications, the story of Louis' big triumph pushed the death of King George VI's mother-in-law (Cecilia Nina Bowes-Lyon, Countess of Strathmore and Kinghorne) off many front pages. The *Evening Standard* devoted six full pages to the fight's coverage. A United Press story declared that newspapers in all the European capitals had been saturated with fight coverage.

There was some controversy about what had happened in the ring. Schmeling believed the devastating body punch he received was "a foul blow to the kidneys." Most observers dismissed the claim immediately, including referee Arthur Donovan and Bill Brown of the New York State Athletic Commission. Brown explained the difference between a legal and an illegal kidney punch: "A punch to the kidney is not a foul blow if delivered from out in the clear. The only time a kidney punch is illegal is when it is deliberate, as when the men are in a half clinch and one deliberately hits to the kidney. Any punch delivered from out in the clear is legal if it lands anywhere above the belt. When a fighter lets a punch go, his opponent may twist or turn and so receive the punch in the kidney. Certainly, you can't blame the man throwing the punch."[49]

An International News Service report that appeared in the *Rochester (IN) News-Sentinel* the day after the fight said the "seriously hurt" Schmeling was under close observation at New York City's Poly Clinic Hospital as he was "in danger of a kidney hemorrhage." The blurb indicated the German boxer had arrived at that medical facility shortly after midnight—about two hours after the fight had ended.

Schmeling did indeed suffer some unique damage to his midsection. After a thorough examination by Dr. Robert Brennan, it was confirmed that Schmeling had suffered a fracture of the transverse processes on his back just below the right kidney. They are bony wings that extend from each side of each vertebrae and serve as anchors. Attached to them are muscles and ligaments that are used to keep the body upright. The following day, it was revealed that Schmeling's recuperation regimen would likely require him to lie flat on his back for three weeks. He was scheduled to sail home from New York aboard the German passenger liner *Bremen* on Saturday, July 2. A little more than four months later, on November 9, Max Schmeling, the man who was portrayed in America as a cold-hearted Nazi minion, would stealthily hide two terribly frightened Jewish boys in his home on Crystal Night as a blood-thirsty anti–Semitic mob rampaged across Berlin burning synagogues and Jewish-owned shops and homes.

Louis and his wife were also planning a post-fight ocean trip—a triumphant one. The couple was headed to both Paris and London for a 12-day vacation. Upon his return to America, Louis would resume his usual training for a projected September title defense. His next opponent's identity was yet to be determined.

R.G. Lynch of the *Milwaukee Journal* concluded that Louis' easy victory over Schmeling had created an unexpected problem for him: Louis had convincingly eliminated the last fighter who could possibly provide him with any real competition. Max Baer seemed to be the next in line, but after how poorly he had fared versus Louis in 1935 and the amount of boos Baer received at the Louis-Schmeling fight, knowledgeable boxing people legitimately wondered if anyone would pay to see a Louis-Baer rematch. (One scribe humorously figured if Baer deserved a second crack at the champion, so did King Levinsky—a journeyman heavyweight whom Louis had annihilated in one round in a dreadful mismatch in August 1935. Baer had faced Louis immediately after the Levinsky farce.) Lynch, who could have been the champion's press agent, claimed Louis had no rival, past or present: "The Louis who blasted Schmeling into oblivion on Wednesday night could have licked any heavyweight this writer has ever seen—and that goes back to [Jack] Dempsey's time. Perhaps Joe will never again attain that peak. He was spurred to his greatest efforts by factors which seldom enter into a fight."[50]

Lynch was not alone in his opinion. Nobody could now seriously doubt that Louis was the best heavyweight fighter in the world. "Now I feel like the champ,"[51] Louis happily admitted to reporters. The films of the fight confirmed his excellence. "The slow-motion picture of the 124 seconds of the Louis-Schmeling fight," wrote Henry McLemore of United Press, "is probably the most faithful recording ever made of human savagery."[52] A careful examination of the fight film shows that Louis landed 31 of the 41 punches he attempted. Schmeling only managed to throw two insignificant blows.

Jeff Moshier of the *St. Petersburg (FL) Independent* spoke for a great many boxing fans when he wrote on June 25 after viewing the fight film, "Louis simply outclassed Schmeling. I'm still trying to figure out how he knocked out Louis the first time they fought."[53]

In his description of the short bout, the eloquent Bob Considine wrote, "Louis was like a spring—one pregnant package of coiled black venom."[54]

Henry McLemore further joked that Louis had proven to be the world's fastest executioner. "The brown-skinned boy finished of Max Schmeling in 124 seconds," he wrote. "The [electric] chair takes four minutes to finish a man. The noose takes longer. Only the guillotine can match him as a killer." All levity aside, McLemore had great sympathy for the vanquished German, which was not a common sentiment among American boxing writers that night: "Schmeling's defeat was not something one would like to see again. The utter disintegration of an athlete is painful to watch, even when it takes years. Schmeling's disintegration, from a superb physical specimen to a helpless, hopeless, bleeding object took just two minute and four seconds. One moment the spotlights picked him out and accentuated the brightness of his eyes, the rhythm of his muscles, the eager life in him. One moment Schmeling was a sculptor's model, the next he was something that had to be carried away...."[55]

Gayle Talbot was thoroughly impressed by Louis' performance. The journalist wrote of the one-sided affair,

> Joe Louis, 24-year-old Alabama Negro, today is the incomparable destroyer that the world thought he was two years ago.
>
> Last night, before 80,000 witnesses at Yankees Stadium, the champion removed the last doubt of his greatness by blasting Max Schmeling, one of his formidable rivals, into fistic oblivion in two minutes and four seconds....
>
> Today there isn't truly a man left to debate Joe's right to the crown he won last summer from James Braddock.[56]

Dave Dryburgh of the *Regina Leader-Post* wondered if the fans had gotten their money's worth from the brief ring battle. In his June 23 sports column he wrote, "You probably know as much about the abbreviated fight today as those who shelled out $30 for a ringside seat. They couldn't have been any more than seated when the end came, which would make it expensive entertainment for the lads who traveled all the way from Germany to see Bomber Louis batter the confident Maxie Schmeling."

The Canadian Press reported excited but orderly victory festivities breaking out in Harlem once the fight's result was known. At its apex, there may have been 500,000 people rejoicing in the streets. The report declared,

Harlem went crazy last night in a joyous celebration of dusky Joe Louis' victory over German Max Schmeling. There was shagging in the streets, horn tooting, cow-bell ringing, and 7th Avenue between 110th Street and 150th Street was a tidal wave of joy. Cars and trucks filled with young people careened through the street, the occupants singing and laughing.

Richer by thousands and thousands of dollars [from successful wagers], the great Negro settlement in the heart of New York was a bedlam well into the morning. There was no disorder. The hundreds of policemen had nothing to do.

The extent that the district bet on the fight was seen when one young Negro dashed into a store to tell everybody within hearing distance that he had bet his automobile against $200.[57]

About 10,000 revelers took to the streets in the black section of Cleveland, OH, to celebrate Louis' triumph. Things were not nearly as peaceful as they were in Harlem, however, according to this Associated Press report:

Police used tear gas to quell a riotous crowd last night in the negro section here, celebrating Joe Louis' victory over Max Schmeling. Charity Hospital was filled with injured, and the attendants notified police to take others to other hospitals.

One man was shot, probably fatally, doctors said. Two policemen were felled by flying bricks, a streetcar was stoned, passengers were hurt, and sirens screamed at many false alarms.

At one busy intersection, jammed with celebrants and spectators, general fighting broke out. Knives flashed, clubs swung, and missiles flew. All available police squads rushed to the scene. Tear gas scattered the melee.[58]

Indiana Avenue in Toledo's black section had similar spontaneous outbreaks of merriment just moments after Louis finished off his German challenger in the first round. An unnamed city fireman gave this first-person account to a reporter from the *Toledo News-Bee*: "Right after the knockout they went plumb nuts. People poured out of gathering spots and houses, and in a minute the street was blocked with them. If there was one, there were 6,000. It was the wildest night in years. The first thing we heard was a sort of 'wheeeee' and then there were people. They rocked cars. They stopped people. They yelled. They threw bottles. They threw streamers over the light wires. Nobody was ugly. They were just playful."[59]

Celebrations elsewhere in the United States were generally peaceable and good-spirited. The *Milwaukee Journal* amusingly reported that a local Joe Louis supporter had been fined $1 for violating the city's noise ordinance. He had ben joyously and repeatedly honking his horn after listening to the fight on his car radio.

Esoterica about the fight filled the June 23 newspapers across America. Here are a few samples:

- No representative from the camp of Max Schmeling went to the winner's dressing room to offer post-fight congratulations. How-

ever, two years earlier, when Schmeling upset Louis, two members of Louis' staff made a point of congratulating the German in his dressing room as a gesture of sportsmanship and goodwill.
- In Seattle, a 56-year-old black waiter named Elzia B. Jones (whose name was reported as "Ed Jones" in some reports) apparently could not handle the excitement surrounding Louis' overwhelming defeat of Schmeling. After listening to the brief bout on the radio, Jones happily exclaimed, "Boy, Louis won the fight!" He then immediately dropped dead.
- There was another fatality closer to the action: Jim Eustace, the man in charge of the gate attendants at Yankee Stadium, died of a heart attack while on duty.
- Joe Louis' mother missed the radio broadcast. Lillie Brooks, who had been ill recently, went for an automobile ride near her Detroit home with her family physician as fight time drew near. She had planned to listen portions of the NBC broadcast, but by the time she tuned in, the fight had already ended. She got the first inkling of what happened from newsboys were shouting the result as they attempted to sell extra editions.
- According to an Associated Press story with a Tokyo dateline, the fight was followed with huge interest by the Japanese public. The story of Louis' win was front-page news. However, it was probably unwelcome news. Pre-fight polls showed the people of Japan were overwhelmingly hoping for a Schmeling victory. All things American were not particularly popular in Japan in 1938.
- Former world bantamweight champion, 42-year-old Pete Herman, attended the fight, making the long trip to New York City from his home in New Orleans. Herman never saw a thing, though, as he no longer had his eyesight due to a degenerative ocular disorder. His wife dutifully described the action to him as it occurred.

Between January 1939 and February 1942, Louis became the most active champion in heavyweight history. He defended his title in rapid succession and multiple locales. Opponents with more hype than fistic skill were brought forth and summarily slapped down by the Brown Bomber at a dizzying rate. The sporting press unkindly—but not necessarily inaccurately—called the obscure coterie of concussed no-hopers "Joe Louis' Bum of the Month Club." Game but overmatched fighters such as Johnny Paychek, Bob Pastor, Red Burman, and nearly a dozen others served as cannon fodder. Only Billy Conn, a slick Pittsburgh boxer better suited for light heavyweight competition, gave Louis any real trouble. On June 18, 1941, Conn was dispatched in the 13th round after getting the better of the 27-year-old champion for the first 12 stanzas. With America entering the Second World War, the army came calling. Sergeant Joe Louis did his bit for Uncle Sam by boxing exhibitions for the troops. In 1946, in his first two postwar title bouts, Louis continued his winning ways. He was 32 now, but he still defeated Conn in a rematch that did not come close to matching the original fight for competitiveness or suspense. Three months later the world champion thrashed Tami Mauriello in one round, flooring him twice after being staggered himself. There was hardly anyone left for Louis to knock out.

Surprisingly, a father of six from Camden, NJ, by the name of Jersey Joe Walcott tested Louis twice. On December 5, 1947, after a 15-month layoff, Louis faced the unheralded challenger who figured at the end of 15 surprising rounds that he had done enough to win—including knocking down Louis twice. Somehow Louis came out on the winning end of a stunning split decision that rankled most fair-minded fans who witnessed it. It was a decision largely based on expectations and reputation rather than what occurred in the Madison Square Garden ring that memorable evening. As a consolation prize, Walcott was given a rematch in 1948. Louis won on an 11th-round knockout. Louis retired in March 1949 after holding the world heavyweight championship for nearly 12 years.

Fate often takes strange twists, and that was certainly true with both Joe Louis and Max Schmeling. Louis managed his ring earnings badly and naively. He was constantly trying to get out of an enormous income tax debt that was partly his fault and partly the fault of a heartless, immovable Internal Revenue Service bureau-

Joe Louis was out of the ring for about 51 months while serving his country during the Second World War. A man of few words, Louis nevertheless famously noted that the Allies would win the war because "we're on God's side" in this poster from 1942.

cracy. Joe's IRS troubles began when he donated an entire purse from a title fight to a war charity, but somehow it was ruled that he still had to pay income tax on what would have been his earnings. The end result was that Louis was compelled to fight long after he should have been happily retired from boxing. For the rest of his life he could never escape even the interest that was accruing on his massive tax debt.

On September 27, 1950, Louis unretired and challenged the man who had won his vacated crown: Ezzard Charles. Charles won by a unanimous decision at Yankee Stadium fairly handily. (The judges' scores by rounds were 12–3, 13–2 and 10–5.) It was Louis 27th fight with the world heavyweight title on the line—and it was the only one he lost. He retired from the ring again. One news story had him joining a circus to earn a regular paycheck. Boxing paid better. Undeterred—and still very much in debt—Louis kept battling away, hoping for another chance to regain the championship and satisfy the IRS too. He won eight straight bouts against generally decent opposition. Louis' last fight was at Madison Square Garden on October 26, 1951. That night he was blasted into retirement a second and final time in under eight rounds by a young Massachusetts slugger named Rocky Marciano. Referee Ruby Goldstein saved the 37-year-old Louis from a certain knockout defeat by mercifully stopping the fight without a count after Louis had been roughly pounded through the ropes. Goldstein later said he could not bring himself to count ten over the fabled Brown Bomber, whom he called an old friend.

As for Max Schmeling, he was not shot, hanged, or strangled with piano wire when he returned to Nazi Germany. The German government distanced itself from Max—which was absolutely fine with him. He had one more bout before the outbreak of war. Thirteen months after the humbling loss to Joe Louis, Schmeling defeated fellow countryman Adolf Heuser in Stuttgart to gain both the German and European heavyweight titles. The venue where the fight was held was named after Adolf Hitler. During the war Schmeling served the Third Reich as a paratrooper. A rumor circulated in Allied countries that the ex-champ had been killed in action. It was inaccurate—and the Nazi Propaganda Ministry made a point of debunking the story, showing Schmeling to be very much alive and well. Schmeling survived the Second World War despite being injured and hospitalized for several months in 1941.

Immediately after the hostilities in Europe ceased, Schmeling lost virtually everything of value that he possessed. His palatial home in Berlin was seized. (It exists now as the Libyan embassy.) Needing money, in 1947 and 1948 Schmeling, now into his forties, returned to the ring and fought five more times before hanging up the gloves. His last bout, a decision loss to Richard Vogt in West Berlin, was on October 31, 1948. Joe Louis was still world heavyweight champion at the time. In postwar and post-boxing civilian life, Schmeling rebounded in true championship form and embarked on a highly successful career as a businessman. In fact, he became one of his country's wealthiest citizens. He invested his late-career ring earnings well. The ex-champion was profiting from all the Coca-Cola products manufactured in West Germany. He owned a major bottling plant and was one of the soft drink company's chief executive officers in his homeland. He also found there was significant money to be made in Germany and elsewhere by just being former world heavyweight champion Max Schmeling. He cagily trademarked his name and profited by selling it for various projects.

Years later, when Louis was in serious financial trouble, he was hospitalized with one of his frequent illnesses. An overseas admirer volunteered to pay the former champion's hefty medical bills. Louis' generous benefactor was none other than ... Max Schmeling! (Schmeling had made a surprise visit to see Louis at the latter's Chicago home in 1954. Louis was utterly dumbfounded to see Schmeling on his doorstep 16 years after their last bout. The two old ring foes reunited again in 1966 when Muhammad Ali defended his world title against West Germany's Karl Mildenburger in Frankfurt. The ex-combatants got along splendidly, laughing and joking with one another as they reminisced about their historically famous shared experiences.) Schmeling explained his selfless actions towards the downtrodden Brown Bomber by saying that he had always considered Louis to be a friend. Accordingly, Schmeling's conscience could not allow him to neglect the frail ex-champion when he desperately needed monetary help.

Schmeling lived to the ripe old age of 99, dying on February 2, 2005, in Wenzendorf, Germany. To date, no other former world heavyweight champion has lived such a long life. Schmeling's wife of 54 years, Anny Ondra, had predeceased him in 1987. (Because Anny and Max had frequently been portrayed as the ideal Aryan couple by Nazi propaganda, neither felt comfortable visiting Anny's former Czech home after the war, so they never did. Their marriage was childless; Schmeling died with no direct descendants.) "I had a happy marriage and a nice wife. I accomplished everything [one] can," he stated philosophically when he was in his eighties. "What more can you want?"[60] In 1988 Schmeling received more than 50 percent of the votes in a national poll to determine Germany's "Athlete of the 20th century," finishing ahead of tennis champion Boris Becker, among others. That same year in a *New York Times* interview, Schmeling, then age 82, said he was still busily working five days a week.

Always gracious with autograph requests, upon his passing Schmeling was properly eulogized as one of professional boxing's greatest gentlemen and ambassadors. He reputedly remained an avid follower of the sport until the day he died. In many sporting locales, the dignified Schmeling was awkwardly more popular outside of Germany than he was within his own country. It was particularly true among the boxing communities in the United States and elsewhere. This was somewhat understandable. "Unser Max" had been a living reminder of an era that a great many postwar Germans wished to forget. Still, the government of Germany did not choose to conveniently forget their late boxing champion. Their once-beloved "Unser Max" was pictured on a German postage stamp in 2005. Schmeling was also the subject of a stage play, written by Brian C. Petti, titled *The Measure of a Man*. In a 1975 interview, Schmeling reflected on his one-sided loss to Joe Louis in 1938. "Looking back, I'm almost happy I lost that fight," Schmeling said. "Just imagine if I would have come back to Germany with a victory. I had nothing to do with the Nazis, but they would have given me a medal. After the war I might have been considered a war criminal."[61]

Schmeling was born nine years before Louis and out lived him by nearly 24 years. Joe Louis, the great Brown Bomber, died suddenly on Sunday, April 12, 1981, a month shy of his 67th birthday. He had been unwell for years and was badly enfeebled before his time. His last public appearance, appropriately, was the night before his unexpected death. In his wheelchair, he had a ringside vantage point for the Larry Holmes-Trevor Berbick heavyweight championship fight. He seemed to be in good spirits. The bout took place at Caesars Palace in Las Vegas where Louis had been employed for the final years of his life—whenever he was well enough—as a casino greeter. When the sickly-looking Brown Bomber was introduced by ring announcer Chuck Hull, he smiled and politely acknowledged the cheering of the 4,000 fans with a gentle wave of his left hand. Shortly before 10 o'clock the following morning, he collapsed at home in his bathroom. An ambulance was quickly summoned, but all attempts to revive the old champ proved fruitless. He died of cardiac arrest at Desert Springs Hospital at 10:05 a.m. Las Vegas time. Louis had suffered from major heart issues since 1977 and had been basically confined to a wheelchair since that time. Four months before he died, Louis had had a pacemaker installed. Louis' closed casket was placed in the Caesars Palace Sports Pavilion. Thousands of fans and ordinary citizens waited in long lines to pay their respects to a departed American icon.

Just six days before his unexpected death, Louis was feted at a gala testimonial attended by numerous celebrities. (Frank Sinatra was pushing Louis' wheelchair!) There were more than 1,500 people present for the occasion. Muhammad Ali, one of the attendees that night, told a TV news crew that the vast New Orleans Superdome could have been filled five times with all the people who would have liked to have been on hand to honor the ailing champion because of Louis' timeless popularity and the volume of respect he had earned over his remarkable lifetime.

When the news of Louis' death was announced at Tiger Stadium in Joe's longtime hometown, the Toronto-Detroit baseball game was temporarily halted so everyone in the ballpark could observe a moment of silence. A similar scene was played out at Yankee Stadium—the site of so many of Louis' ring battles—where the Texas Rangers were playing the New York Yankees.

At the Sean O'Grady-Hilmer Kenty world lightweight championship bout that afternoon at an Atlantic City casino, the bell at ringside was ceremoniously struck ten times as a sign of mourning and respect for the fallen champion. Jersey Joe Walcott—the man whom Louis had beaten in the final two of his 25 title defenses—was present as an official with the New Jersey State Athletic Commission. He was inconsolable when he heard the sad news from Las Vegas.

Jack Sharkey, another of Louis' old ring adversaries, offered his condolences from his Massachusetts home. "I'm sad to hear it, awfully sorry to hear it," declared the 78-year-old former champion who lamented the loss of another "old friend."[62] Louis' one-sided victory over Sharkey in 1936 had concluded the Boston Gob's 12-year professional boxing career.

Jack Dempsey's wife Hannah, who knew Louis personally, spoke on behalf of her ailing 85-year-old husband. "Joe Louis was a fine gentleman and Jack was very fond of him. I'm sorry he had to pass away at such an early age. He was about 20 years younger than Jack."[63]

Arthur Donovan, the referee who became famous mostly for working so many of Louis' title bouts, predeceased the Brown Bomber by seven months, passing away at age 89 on September 1, 1980. In the last interview he gave, Donovan specifically praised Louis' "superlative weapons of attack."

Commenting on Louis' passing, renowned boxing broadcaster Howard Cosell recalled the memorable night of Wednesday, June 22, 1938, labeling it "the most important prize fight ever to take place. The political and sociological implications [were] unparalleled."[64]

Louis' obituary in the *Baltimore Afro-American* also predictably recalled his famous second clash with Max Schmeling and the extraordinary circumstances behind it. (Virtually all the Louis obits of any length did.) It stated, "For Louis, it was a personal triumph. For America, it was a night which transcended sports and became permanently etched in the minds of millions. As the ominous rumblings of the pre–World War II years grew louder, Schmeling had become the embodiment of Nazi Germany. Louis was America's hero."[65]

In a feature article about Louis' passing in that same publication, Sam Lacy, a black sports writer who had witnessed 18 of Louis' 25 title defenses from press row, wrote what many veteran scribes and fans believed in their hearts, "Set aside all the Muhammad Ali rhetoric, the clichés and the speculation. The real champion is dead. [Louis] was also one of the finest men I've known. He was THE champion."[66]

Of course, Max Schmeling, age 75, was asked to comment on Louis' death too. From his home in Hamburg, West Germany, Schmeling graciously provided these kind words about his most famous ring foe: "Joe was a boxing genius. He was the kind that only comes, at most, one time in a generation. He was the greatest opponent I ever faced."[67]

By executive order of President Ronald Reagan, Joe Louis was interred at Arlington National Cemetery with the full honors typically reserved for American heroes—for that was what he was. His stylish headstone identifies him as world heavyweight champion from 1937 to 1949. Max Schmeling, true to his nature, helped defray most of the costs associated with Louis' funeral. President Reagan personally stated, "Joe Louis was more than a sports legend—his career was an indictment of racial bigotry and a source of pride and inspiration to millions of white and black people around the world."[68]

In delivering Louis' eulogy, Jesse Jackson stated, "Usually the champion rides on the shoulders of the nation and its people, but in this case the nation stood on the shoulders of its hero."[69]

September 23, 1952

Rocky Marciano vs. Jersey Joe Walcott
One Devastating Punch

"[You] may not have seen the good young heavyweight yet, but at least the fight game is looking with hope toward a young man named Rocky Marciano. He has won all of his professional fights—24 of the 27 by knockout—and while there is still much he must learn, he is the kind of fighter people pay to see. He can punch, take a punch, and he likes to fight."—W.C. Heinz in the June 1950 issue of *The Ring*

"Chances are Marciano's ability to take a punch will be tested early, perhaps in the first round, for he is easy to hit. If Walcott lands that Sunday punch—his long right out of the old Jersey Shuffle—the fight may be over. If Marciano shakes it off … we will probably have a new champ."—Jack Hand of the Associated Press in the September 23, 1952, issue of the *Schenectady Gazette*

"It was by far the best heavyweight championship fight I've seen in many years, a throwback to the days of Dempsey, Jeffries, and Jack Johnson, days when gory, heart-throbbing ring battles were the rule rather than the exception. Thrills, sustained action, suspense, expectation, and a dramatic finish. What more could one ask?"—Nat Fleischer, editor of *The Ring*

The man who would become internationally famous as world heavyweight boxing champion Rocky Marciano was born on September 1, 1923, as Rocco Marchegiano. He was the son of first-generation Italian immigrants Pierino Marchegiano and Pasqualina Picciuto. The family resided in Brockton, MA in the area around Brooks Street. Pierino earned his living as a shoemaker. Rocco was the oldest of six children.

As a youth, Rocky could be routinely found at a local park, the James Edgar Playground, playing baseball or football—and getting into an occasional scrap. A seminal day in Marciano's youth was the day he actually lost a fight. He came home crying and defeated.

"This one kid beat me up," Marciano recalled. "My uncle told me not to be a sissy. He said he'd teach me everything he knew about boxing, so he got this bag and put it up in the cellar."[1] After training for about three months, Marciano tracked down the kid who beat him up and handed him a pair of boxing gloves and challenged him to duke it out. Rocky's former tormenter had had enough inside of five minutes.

Rocky had two years of high school education before he dropped out. "I didn't care for school much, anyway," he said in a 1950 interview with *The Ring* magazine, "and I thought I could help the folks out [financially]. The shoe shops were going bad, and a couple had moved out of the city. My uncle was close to me. He advised me to go to work and help out [my parents]."[2] Rocky ended up working a variety of odd jobs for short stints: ditch-digger, candy-mixer, dishwasher and truck driver.

In 1943, in the middle of the Second World War, Marciano was drafted into the army. During hostilities he was stationed in Swansea, Wales. The unit he was assigned to was responsible for ferrying supplies to Normandy after the D-Day landings. When the war ended, Marciano completed his military service at Fort Lewis near Tacoma, WA. He discovered his crude boxing skills and powerful punching benefited him in an unexpected way: His unit frequently held amateur boxing tournaments for the enlistees. The winners would receive three-day passes. Marciano won so often—and used the accrued furloughs to travel back home to Brockton—that his parents actually wondered if their eldest son was still in the service. Rocky was mustered out of the army in 1946.

Despite his natural pugilistic gifts, Marciano did not fancy himself a professional fighter. Baseball was more to his liking. Marciano was a capable enough amateur baseball player to be invited to the spring training facility of the Chicago Cubs' farm team in Lafayette, NC, in 1947. He thought he was good enough to be a professional catcher. He lasted three weeks before being cut from the squad. According to Rocky, his hitting was more than adequate—he was a slugger, of course—but his throwing arm was not what it once was. He blamed it on hitting the homemade heavy bag in the family cellar too often.

Marciano seriously took up boxing at his uncle's suggestion. He did not have a long amateur career. In its June 1950 issue, *The Ring* magazine reported that Marciano had about 30 fights in the amateur ranks; boxing researchers have only been able to track down 13. The inflated figure may include the various tournament bouts he fought while in the army that were not officially recorded anywhere. Rocky figured if he was going to fight, he sensibly reasoned he might as well be paid for his difficult and painful labors. Somewhere along the line Rocco Marchegiano adopted his ring moniker. On the advice of manager Al Weill, he changed a vowel in his first name and dropped a syllable and slightly altered his surname to make it more easily pronounceable. Henceforth he would be known as "Rocky Marciano"—one of the great ring names in boxing history.

Marciano's pro debut came on March 17, 1947, at the Valley Arena in Holyoke, MA. He was 23 years old, somewhat late for an aspiring boxer to begin a professional career. It was against another first-timer, Lee Epperson, who fell inside three rounds. (Epperson must have found better and safer career avenues as there is no record of him ever having another professional bout.) Rocky fought nine of his first 11 bouts in Providence, RI—scoring knockouts in them all and winning a growing fan base there too and elsewhere in New England. It was not until his 17th pro bout that an opponent, a Canadian named Don Mogard, managed to last the scheduled distance with Marciano. The sporting public became fascinated with the stocky, young, hard-hitting heavyweight. Newspapers on a national level began to regularly report the results of the big banger from Brockton.

Marciano was not especially pretty to watch; he seemed awkwardly unbalanced and labored in his ring movements. His footwork was not especially good, either. To critical boxing purists, Marciano lacked the polish one normally associated with great fighters and potential champions. Yet he was one of boxing's most dominant fighters, often overwhelming those who possessed superior ring skills. Marciano's trainer Charley Goldman once stated, "A lot of people say Rocky don't look too good to them, but the guy on the floor don't look too good either."[3] Renowned sports journalist Shirley Povich concurred. He once wrote in the *Washington Post*, "Rocky Marciano can't box a lick, his footwork is what you'd expect from two left feet, he throws his right hand in a clumsy circle and knows nothing of orderly retreat. All he can do is blast the breath from your lungs or knock your head off."[4]

Despite the plentiful criticisms directed his way, Marciano certainly was an exciting fighter who gave the fans a good, entertaining scrap for their money. Marciano would gladly absorb two punches for the chance to land one of his stunning thunderbolts. He carried lethal knockout power in either hand. Marciano could end fights with a single left hook or smashing right— and he often did. Furthermore, he was not above bending the rules by landing close-quarter blows that were more along the lines of elbows and forearm whacks to the head than legitimate punches. (In discussing Marciano's fighting style years later in his book *The Great Heavyweights*, former British Empire champion Henry Cooper theorized that Marciano's management team wisely never permitted their man to fight outside of America because his roughhouse tactics may have gotten him disqualified in Europe if a referee chose to strictly enforce boxing's rules.)

In his 25th professional outing, on December 30, 1949, Marciano nearly killed his opponent, 20-year-old Carmine Vingo, at Madison Square Garden. Vingo, who had turned 20 two days before the bout, was no slouch, having compiled an admirable 16-1 record and a reputation for being reckless in the ring. The winner of the bout could assuredly look forward to bigger things in the near future.

In what was described in the following day's newspapers as a "savage fight," Marciano floored Vingo in both the first and second rounds, but by the fifth round Vingo seemed to be gaining the advantage. Marciano, however, retook control of the fight for good in round six. He knocked out Vingo at 1:44 of that round with a vicious uppercut. According to an Associated Press report, Vingo's chief second wanted to surrender before the thumping final blow was landed by Marciano. "We wanted to stop the fight," said Jackie Levine, "but under the rules we aren't allowed to enter the ring while the fight is on."[5]

Vingo's head slammed hard onto the canvas rendering him unconscious. He regained his senses briefly but fell into a coma. No ambulance was available—and none was required to be present at New York City boxing cards in 1949—so Vingo was carried on a stretcher two blocks to nearby St. Clare's Hospital where the initial prognosis was grim. Vingo was given only a 50 percent chance of surviving, according to Dr. Vincent Nardiello, the longtime house physician for Madison Square Garden, who first attended to the injured boxer. A chaplain was summoned to administer the last rites. United Press reported that approximately 250 fans attempted to visit the stricken Vingo in the hospital immediately after the fight. There had been 18 boxing fatalities in 1949; the well-wishers hoped and prayed that Vingo would not be number 19.

Vingo underwent brain surgery and eventually pulled through. Nevertheless, Marciano was shaken by the ordeal. He became a regular visitor to the hospital, pacing the hallways and pondering his own future. Vingo was discharged from the hospital in February 1950, but he suffered partial paralysis and had to give up his boxing career. (His $1,500 purse for the Marciano fight was seized to offset part of his $4,000 hospital bill. Vingo never learned who paid the balance. He spent the rest of his life employed in private security.) A relieved Marciano only resumed his boxing career once Vingo was out of danger. Marciano and Vingo became good friends. Vingo was a regular attendee at Marciano's training camps. He was also a guest at Marciano's wedding in 1950. In a 1971 interview Vingo described Marciano as "one of the nicest guys you'd ever want to talk to."[6] Largely forgotten by the boxing community in his later years, Vingo lived to be 85 years old, passing away in June 2015.

Less than three months after the Vingo fight, in a terrific marquee matchup between two undefeated heavyweight prospects, Marciano won a disputed split decision over Roland LaStarza on March 24, 1950, at Madison Square Garden. LaStarza, a native of the Bronx, was 37–0 entering the fight. The fight was extremely competitive and closely contested. The judges' scorecards were 5–4–1, 4–5–1, and 5–5. Today, that scoring would mean the fight was a draw. However, under New York State's boxing rules in 1950, a supplemental points system was used to break ties. (For some reason, a draw was considered an unpalatable result.) Marciano was given the nod, by a 9–6 edge, by referee Jack Watson, the man who had scored the fight five rounds apiece. Despite suffering a knockdown in the fourth round from a looping right hand, LaStarza figured he had not gotten a fair shake despite being a New Yorker. He told the *New York Herald Tribune*, "The fact is [Marciano's] manager Al Weill is the matchmaker for the Garden. I would say that had a lot to do with the decision."[7] LaStarza maintained he had been robbed until the day he died in 2009 at age 82. A United Press correspondent agreed with LaStarza. He wrote, "LaStarza had such an edge in the in-fighting that most of the boxing writers scored for the New Yorker."[8] The Associated Press also had LaStarza winning the bout, by a 5–4–1 count. Be that as it may, Marciano was the fighter who exited the ring with his undefeated record still intact. Although he was now 26–0, Marciano had failed to impress the unnamed UP scribe, who critically wrote, "As yet, the 25-year-old [sic] slugger cannot be rated a formidable contender for the heavyweight crown because of his awkwardness."[9]

More wins followed in 1950 and 1951 for "the Brockton Blockbuster," as the press liked to call Marciano. Rex Layne, who was something of a Pacific northwest terror, was knocked out in six rounds at Madison Square Garden on July 12, 1951. Layne had only lost once in 34 fights—and had beaten Jersey Joe Walcott eight months before the latter won the world title—before being mowed down by the unstoppable Marciano. Now most everyone involved in pro boxing was beginning to believe Marciano could become a future world champion. The fact that Marciano was a white man was undeniably good for publicity too. The world heavyweight boxing championship, once the zealously guarded possession of the Caucasian race, had been held by three successive black fighters since the summer of 1937. Marciano, it was thought, would restore some life and vigor to a division that was becoming drab.

Fewer doubters remained after Friday, October 26, 1951—the night Marciano stepped into the ring versus ex-champion Joe Louis in a highly anticipated crossroads fight. One man was ascending, the other man was seemingly in decline. Common sense said that the 37-year-old Louis—who looked years older—should have been comfortably retired. He had been, twice. However, the persistence of the omnipresent tax man was unwavering, so Louis was obliged to keep on boxing to pay off his debt to the Internal Revenue Service. He was no longer the man who had thoroughly outclassed Max Baer and Max Schmeling in the 1930s. That was ancient history. Marciano blew Louis away in the eighth round. It was a tough night for both men. Louis' career was clearly at an end. Marciano, who had to knock out his hero, wept in his dressing room afterwards. Louis' resounding defeat was front-page news in many American newspapers, including the *Pittsburgh Press*. It ran a dramatic photo of the groggy former champion about to fall helplessly through the ring ropes. The accompanying story began this way:

> It was a bitter end for a great champion.
>
> Joe Louis lay under the ropes, his head lolling over the apron of the ring, and the most remarkable career in ring history was finished by the black oblivion of a right hand to the jaw.
>
> He had hoped, in his financial extremity, that he still had the old magic and once again he would be king.
>
> But the king was dead at 2:36 of the eighth round at Madison Square Garden last night.
>
> His hopes and his dreams were slain by the flailing fists of a rugged young Italian named Rocky Marciano, proving once again that "they never come back."
>
> "I felt sorry for him," the winner said.
>
> So did everybody.

By the time the summer of 1952 had ended, Marciano had notched more impressive victories over a trio of seasoned veterans. The triumphs came against Bernie Reynolds (stopped in three rounds) who had 51 wins on his record; Lee Savold (did not come out for round seven) who had 105 victories; and west-coast phenom Harry Matthews (flattened in two rounds) who had won 81 fights. The Matthews bout at Yankee Stadium on July 28, 1952, was an especially impressive triumph for Marciano. Matthews had won the first round by outboxing Rocky, but Marciano blasted him out in the second round with a nifty left jab-left hook-left hook trio of punches. Marciano's record was now a flawless 42-0. After Marciano's victory over Matthews—which guaranteed him a championship fight—Jack Kearns, who had guided another fearsome banger to the world heavyweight title 33 years earlier, told Nat Fleischer of *The Ring* magazine, "This guy Marciano is a throwback to Jack Dempsey. He hits hard with either hand, comes in tougher and harder when hurt, and is the best puncher since Jack."[10]

Indeed, Marciano's next logical opponent—the only logical opponent, really—was reigning world heavyweight champion Jersey Joe Walcott. There was no one else left for Marciano to beat on his way up the heavyweight ladder—and there was no one else whom the public wanted to see challenge the present champ.

Jersey Joe Walcott was born Arnold Raymond Cream in Pennsauken,

NJ on January 31, 1914. (At least that is the date accepted by most boxing historians. Walcott's true age was frequently a matter of debate among boxing buffs.) His father had emigrated from St. Thomas, a tropical island in the West Indies that was under Danish administration at the time. Arnold had an American mother, hailing from Jordantown, NJ. Theirs was a large family; Arnold was the oldest of 12 children. Arnold was only 15 years old when his father suddenly died. With his family in dire financial need, Arnold dropped out of school and worked in a local soup factory to earn what he could to help his mother financially support his siblings. At about this time he also began training as a boxer. Arnold's father had regaled him with the exploits of Joe Walcott, a former world welterweight champion from Barbados who had been active from 1892 to 1911. Thus, when Arnold eventually took up the sport, he also adopted his hero's name—with the addition of "Jersey" to honor his home state. When the American version of Joe Walcott became a famous boxer in his own right, ring historians began referring to the old welterweight champ (who had died in 1935) as "Original Joe Walcott" or "Barbados Joe Walcott."

Walcott began his pro boxing career as a 16-year-old in 1930. His march toward fistic fame was not exactly a smooth one. He compiled a solid but not spectacular record, so he stayed mostly off the radar for most casual fans of the sweet science.

By August 1936 Walcott had attained a decent 16–2–2 record, mostly competing as a middleweight against virtual unknowns in the fight game. From that point until the end of the Second World War, Walcott became a highly streaky pugilist, winning and losing in spurts. His style often worked against him. Walcott had an elusive boxer-puncher mentality. He was a mobile heavyweight; he preferred not to stay flat-footed and slug it out with his opponents—which was unusual among the top-flight fighters in boxing's upper divisions. Walcott's fights could be tough for judges to score. He probably lost more than a few decisions that should have gone his way. By 1945, Walcott seemed far away from becoming world heavyweight champion. Meanwhile, Joe Louis, discharged from the army, was resuming his career as world heavyweight champion after a four-year hiatus from the ring. In 1947 the Brown Bomber was now 33—the same age as Walcott, give or take three or four months. The champion's best days were behind him—and Walcott would be the man to prove it.

On Friday, December 5, 1947, at Madison Square Garden, Joe Louis defended his world heavyweight championship for the 24th time since winning it from James J. Braddock 10½ years earlier. His last 15 fights had ended in knockout victories for the beloved champ. His opponent that night would be Jersey Joe Walcott, who had once been employed as a sparring partner for Louis. How did Walcott merit a title fight? Mainly because Louis, who had won 56 out of his 57 professional bouts, needed a payday and he had pretty much vanquished everyone else in the heavyweight division. The *Pittsburgh Press* disparagingly referred to the challenger as "the best of a mediocre crop of contenders" and further noted that he had been "resurrected from the pugilistic scrap heap." It was hardly a ringing endorsement for the unfashionable challenger, but the arena was sold out nevertheless. Despite the scuttlebutt that said the fight would surely prove to be a horrid mismatch, the *Pittsburgh Press* did offer this tiny glimmer of hope for the challenger's few backers: "Jersey Joe is much faster afoot than Louis and also more shifty in his boxing. Walcott's handlers hope that his elusive style might enable him to evade the champion."[11]

Walcott, who sported a 44–11–2 record, was no better than an 8:1 underdog. Some bookmakers were offering 10:1 odds for anyone foolhardy enough to place a bet on the unfashionable challenger from Camden, NJ. Most people thought that was a charitable assessment of the fight since Walcott's most noteworthy ring triumphs were two hairline decisions over Joey Maxim—a light heavyweight. (Walcott had also lost to Maxim once.) According to one report, a sponsor uniquely offered to buy advertising space on the soles of Walcott's boxing boots since the overmatched challenger was likely to end up flat on his back when the fight ended. Most people were debating how long the fight would last rather than who would be the winner. Another successful Louis title defense was considered a foregone conclusion. Indeed, "How Many Rounds Will It Take?" was the headline atop the *Pittsburgh Press* sports section on the night of the bout. Ticketholders were in for a major surprise.

Walcott took a page from Max Schmeling's playbook and studied films of Louis' previous fights. Walcott thought mobility and elusiveness were the keys to upsetting the hard-hitting but aging champion. Louis fought best when his target was virtually immobile. Walcott intended to present to Louis a more difficult, moving target all night long.

When the bell rang to begin the fight, Walcott moved in and out, side to side, and every which way. He stutter-stepped and scored with jabs. He bobbed and moved and side-stepped. Some ringside reporters dubbed the challenger's odd movements "the Walcott Waltz"; other preferred the term "the cakewalk." This was clearly something out of the ordinary. Unused to such a slippery opponent, Louis was having trouble gauging where Walcott was going to be next. Midway through the opening frame, Louis trapped Walcott in a corner and appeared to hurt the challenger with a flurry of blows when the unthinkable happened: Walcott tagged Louis with a short counter right and sent him toppling to the canvas, scoring a flash knockdown. A gasp and a roar came from the sellout Garden crowd. This was going to be a competitive fight for the champion after all! It turned out to be far more than that.

Louis was up quickly, but he now fully realized that Walcott was not one of his typical hopeless challengers. Twice more in the first round Louis was noticeably staggered. In the fourth round Walcott again decked Louis. This time a long, booming right hand caught the Brown Bomber on his jaw. The champion was clearly hurt and smartly took a seven count from referee Ruby Goldstein before regaining his feet. The crowd at Madison Square Garden was in an uproar over the unexpected trouble Louis was facing.

By the end of round 12, most observers figured Walcott had an insurmountable lead on the judges' scorecards. So did his cornermen. They advised Walcott to fight the last three rounds cautiously. They did not want a repeat of the mistake Billy Conn had made six years earlier when he carelessly opted to slug it out with Louis when he could have coasted to a safe decision victory and the title. That is precisely what Walcott did. Walcott was given a huge cheer when the bell ended the 15th round.

The end of the fight had a surreal quality about it. One thoroughly excited spectator, a young man of about 20, eluded both police and Garden security personnel and leapt into the ring to congratulate Walcott on his apparent historic victory. Louis was so certain he had lost, he attempted to leave the ring before the decision was announced. There is no rule that says a fighter must linger around to hear the decision, but it was almost unheard of for a fighter to do such a thing. Louis' handlers and various officials at ringside, for the sake of good sportsmanship, corralled him and persuaded him to remain in the ring. They quietly told him it would be a polite and thoughtful gesture for the old champion to congratulate the new titleholder when the inevitable and historic decision was announced.

Then came the stunning verdict from public address announcer John F. X. Condon whose body language indicated he probably did not believe it himself: Louis had won by a split decision! He was still the heavyweight champion of the world. In 1947 New York State used the simple scoring system of rounds won, lost and drawn (as did most boxing jurisdictions). Judge Frank Forbes scored the bout 8–6–1 for Louis. Judge Marty Monroe also gave the nod to Louis, by a 9–6 margin. Ruby Goldstein, arguably boxing's best referee at the time, had a vote in the scoring too. He provided the dissenting ballot, scoring the fight 7–6–2 in favor of Walcott.

When the decision was announced, Madison Square Garden erupted with boos from unbelieving fans who were certain they had witnessed the rare spectacle of the world heavyweight championship changing hands for the first time in more than a decade. The man who had been declared winner and still champion did not raise his arms in triumph. He too was embarrassed by the debacle. Instead he made his way to Walcott's corner, shook his hand, and said, "I'm sorry, Joe." Later, when asked about referee Goldstein scoring for Walcott, Louis could have claimed it was a very close contest, or that Walcott fought too cautiously in the later rounds. Instead, he uttered just about the classiest comment possible under the circumstances: "I know Ruby," the immortal Brown Bomber stated. "He calls 'em like he sees 'em."[12]

An outraged woman sitting at a ringside seat attempted to belt Goldstein with her heavy purse as he headed toward his dressing room. She was only prevented from doing so by her husband's quick intervention. When the man informed his angry spouse that *Goldstein was the sole judge who had scored the fight for Walcott*, the woman had a complete change of heart: She embraced Goldstein and kissed him. "God bless you!" she told him. In the subsequent weeks Goldstein received dozens of letters from boxing fans everywhere who congratulated him for having the integrity to have scored the fight in the challenger's favor. Sometime afterward Goldstein was the subject of a feature story in *The Ring* magazine. It was titled "I'd Rather Be Right Than Popular." In this case, Goldstein was perceived to be *both* right and popular.

Years later Louis was decidedly less gracious about what had happened. In the mid–1970s he and Walcott appeared together on *The Way It Was*, a PBS-produced sports nostalgia program hosted by Curt Gowdy. Louis said that although he had indeed fought "a bad fight," he was nevertheless certain he had done enough to win the decision. He just wanted to quickly retreat to the privacy of his dressing room because he was disgusted with his performance. The fact that he said he was sorry to Walcott was not necessarily an admission that the judges' verdict had been a bad one. Walcott, sitting beside Louis, seemed incredulous at Louis' odd, self-serving explanation.

That night, for the first time in his professional career, Joe Louis left the ring to a loud chorus of boos. Walcott and his entourage stuck around, however. Once Louis had departed, Walcott raised his hand to salute the crowd. They gave him a heartfelt standing ovation. To most observers the official decision that night was nothing short of highway robbery. According to an article that ran in the next day's *Pittsburgh Press*, 40 boxing writers at ringside were asked who they would have voted for. The majority said Walcott, but it was surprisingly only by a 24:16 ratio.

Walcott was nearly in tears in his dressing room. When a photographer oddly asked him to smile for a picture, Walcott angrily replied, "Smile? What the hell do I have to smile about?"[13] His handlers—and Jersey Joe himself— figured Louis had only won five of the 15 rounds at best. The decision should have been a formality, they said. In recalling the fight on its 70th anniversary in 2017, boxing historian Michael Carbert listed the 1947 Louis-Walcott tilt among the worst decisions in boxing history, given its overall importance as a bout for the undisputed world heavyweight title. Few scholarly fans would argue that assertion. Carbert opined such incidents were a plague on the sweet science and drove potential fans away from the sport: "Bad decisions. Robberies. Ridiculous scorecards. Maybe nothing sickens a fight fan more than the judges rendering a final verdict which makes a mockery of a hard-fought contest. Sadly, such incidents are legion in the history of our beloved sport and, in recent years, have only become more common."[14]

With boxing fans in an uproar over the fight's outcome, a swift rematch was an absolute necessity. On Friday, June 25, 1948, at Yankee Stadium—the same venue where both Louis-Schmeling bouts had occurred—Walcott was knocked out in the 11th round by a crisp volley of Louis' blows. Louis looked far more focused than he had in the fight six months earlier, and he certainly did not underestimate his opponent this time. For one last glorious night, Louis looked to be the champion of old. It was Louis' last fight as the heavyweight champion of the world. Eight months later, the Brown Bomber officially relinquished the title on March 1, 1949, ending a remarkable reign of nearly 12 years at the top of the heavyweight heap.

Like Gene Tunney's retirement in 1929, Louis' departure from boxing left a gaping hole in the heavyweight division. It was determined that Walcott and Ezzard Charles would meet for the vacant world heavyweight championship. Charles was a capable fighter who had done especially well in the light heavyweight division. He had notched wins over Archie Moore and Jimmy Bivins. (However, Charles was likely best known for a victory over a young contender named Sam Baroudi who died after being knocked out. Baroudi's death greatly affected Charles who pondered retirement after the tragedy.) Charles beat Walcott on a unanimous decision on June 22, 1949, at Comiskey Park in Chicago to claim the vacant world heavyweight title. After three successful defenses, Charles was pitted against Joe Louis who was making an ill-advised comeback because of financial issues. Charles comfortably beat Louis by another unanimous decision on September 27, 1950, to eliminate any doubt that he was the legitimate world heavyweight champion.

The pool of heavyweight contenders in the early 1950s was not especially strong, so Jersey Joe Walcott, who was becoming a sentimental favorite with boxing fans, again worked his way back into title contention. On March 7, 1951, in Detroit, he faced Charles for a second time. Again he lost on a decision. Walcott was now winless in four world heavyweight title fights—a dubious record for championship futility matched by no other fighter in boxing history. Still, their bout was competitive enough to merit yet another rematch.

On July 18, 1951, at Forbes Field in Pittsburgh, Walcott finally broke his personal title-fight jinx. He won the world heavyweight championship with a spectacular seventh-round knockout of Charles. The finishing punch was a surprise because it came from a precisely delivered compact left hook. Walcott was supposed to only have knockout power in his right fist. The terrific blow sent Charles face-first to the canvas. The champion tried to rise but fell backwards in a stupor—and the fight was over. *The Ring* magazine named Walcott-Charles III as its 1951 Fight of the Year. At the advanced age of 37—

perhaps older—Jersey Joe Walcott became the oldest man to win boxing's most cherished title. The next day in the *Pittsburgh Press*, Edwin Beachler wrote, "Jersey Joe Walcott, the old pappy guy, was more surprised to find himself on the heavyweight throne today than ex-King Ezzard Charles. People he never met grab him, shake his hand, and slap him on the back harder than Charles did. He's an inspiration to old-timers, especially, who have been plugging away at a goal they never reached. They haven't stopped mobbing him since he threw that lightning seventh-round kayo punch."[15] It was definitely a feel-good story for sports fans who did not have a specific rooting interest—and for those who remembered the injustice of Walcott's 1947 disputed loss to Joe Louis at Madison Square Garden. "It was a long road to reach the title," Walcott happily stated after his victory. "Each [of the previous championship fights] I thought I was going to win. I've been fighting for 21 years. It's a 21-year dream that finally came true."[16]

Of course, Charles' surprise defeat created interest for yet another rematch, so Walcott-Charles IV had to become a reality. Eleven months later, on Thursday, June 5, 1952, the final installment of heavyweight boxing's most common title matchup occurred at Municipal Stadium in Philadelphia. Like the combatants' first two fights, it went to a decision. In a lackluster contest, Walcott got the votes of all three judges by counts of 8–7, 9–6, and 7–6–2, but it did not mean the decision was without controversy. Many fans and boxing scribes thought Charles was deprived of a victory that would have made him the first boxer in history to regain the world heavyweight championship. For once, it was Walcott who got the benefit of the doubt from the official judges.

The *Pittsburgh Press* reported on its front page, "Jersey Joe Walcott, combining showmanship and a fighting heart, retained his world heavyweight boxing crowd here [in Philadelphia] last night because 'you can't take a man's title away on such a close fight as that.'"[17] The comment came from one of the judges, Buck McTiernan of Pittsburgh, who expressed the general feeling of boxing insiders, who, rightly or wrongly, believe in the tradition that a champion should always be given the edge when a decision is close. Despite a United Press poll of ringside scribes who thought that Charles should have gotten the nod by a 21:17 ratio, Chester L. Smith, the sports editor of the *Pittsburgh Press*, was one individual who thought otherwise. He wrote in the following day's paper under the headline "Walcott Deserved Victory,"

> ... Our heavyweight champion, Joe Walcott, and his challenger, Ezzard Charles, put in 15 full rounds of honest and earnest endeavor last night. They earned their pay.
> When it was all over, the officials came to sufficient agreement to allow old Joe to keep his title.
> There were dissenting cries, even sharp in some quarters, over this verdict, but weighed in the aftermath, it probably was fair enough. A crown, and especially a

heavyweight crown, should not be brushed off a man's shoulders as though it were a fly; it should be forcibly taken away from him. And this Charles did not do to Walcott, even though his more rabid partisans may say he did.[18]

Judging a prize fight is certainly an inexact science, but the opinions of sportswriters regarding Walcott-Charles IV showed some truly wild disagreements. Joe Nichols of the *New York Times* had Walcott winning 13 of the 15 rounds. Conversely, Whitey Lewis of the *Cleveland Press* scored the fight in Charles' favor by an 11–3–1 tally!

The closeness of the fight did not make it a thriller, however. Smith duly noted,

> This was a hard-tugging fight, as you could see by watching the faces of Walcott and Charles, yet through it all there were only a precious few moments when you sat erect in your seat and said to yourself, this might be it. There were rounds when you thought you might be looking at a yacht race on a day when the wind refused to blow. Or a scoreless tie in football when the ball never gets inside the 20-yeard line.
>
> For those who prefer the gory kind of fist-fighting, the night was almost a complete disappointment.[19]

People watching the fight on television got a nasty surprise after the 15th round: The pictures from Philadelphia cut out just before the judges' decision was announced. It was later explained that a small boy at the stadium had accidentally stepped on a switch and, in doing so, temporarily shut down NBC's national broadcast. Of course, the network and its affiliates were bombarded with angry telephone calls from viewers who missed hearing that Walcott had been declared the winner and still champion of the world.

Another embarrassment was the ghastly work of ring announcer Pete Miller who seemed to have trouble pronouncing common words and the name of a revered former heavyweight champion. According to Chester L. Smith, Miller "stunned the more scholarly of those present by introducing Mr. Gene Tunney as Mr. Gene Tooney." Miller also referred to the venue as "Munny-sippel Stad-yum."[20]

Boxing history was made when Zach Clayton was appointed as the third man in the ring. He became the first black man to referee a world heavyweight championship bout. Most writers thought he did a passable job, with the notable exception of Charles' corner. They thought Clayton was especially harsh in his rulings regarding how Charles was allowed to do battle. "He picked on Charles all night," complained chief second Ray Arcel. "He was constantly warning him. And I never saw a referee part heavyweights so fast."[21] Clayton had also scored the fight 9–6 for Walcott—the widest margin of any of the three judges.

The Walcott-Charles series had run its course after four championship fights. Each participant had won twice. A fifth bout did not seem particularly appealing. Despite the rivalry being very competitive, boxing fans had grown tired of the series and wanted to see a new face vie for the crown. "[I] can't make any money with Charles,"[22] Walcott acknowledged. Next up for the winner and still champion: a lucrative title defense versus 42–0 Rocky Marciano on September 23, 1952. Philadelphia's Municipal Stadium would again be the venue.

During a visit to Cincinnati on September 16, former champion Joe Louis picked Walcott to defeat Marciano. According to a United Press story, the famed Brown Bomber said, "I pick Walcott for a knockout in six rounds. Louis explained that Marciano can be hit often with left hooks—the type Walcott had defeated Charles with in their third fight. "I hit Marciano plenty of times with my left," Louis recalled, "but my left went out on me and I didn't knock him out."[23]

Less than a week before the fight, there were already discussions about a rematch—provided that Marciano won the title on September 23. In was commonplace at the time for a "return-bout clause" to be included in any boxing contract in which the champion was putting his world title on the line. Basically, it insured the man who lost the title would be offered the first opportunity to knock off the new champion. Such a clause was becoming a sticky issue for Marciano's camp, however. Rocky's manager Al Weill issued an ultimatum from Marciano's training camp in Grossinger, NY. He declared that Walcott's manager, Felix Bocchicchio, must sign "our original return-bout agreement" or risk not having that provision in any revised deal. When asked what would happen if Bocchicchio refused to sign it and pulled Walcott out of the September 23 fight, Weill replied, "Then I'll claim the title for Marciano."[24] Although Weill doubted Bocchicchio would pull out of the bout because of the huge gate that it was certain to generate, the Pennsylvania Boxing Commission was threatening to cancel the affair unless the two camps could reach some sort of return-bout agreement. To no one's surprise, an agreement was reached. There was no chance the September 23 fight was going to be imperiled. There was too much money at stake for everyone involved.

On September 20, an amusing story came out of Walcott's training camp in Pleasantville, NJ: One of Jersey Joe's sparring partners fled the ring after angering the ex-champion and facing his wrath. Oakland-based light heavyweight Billy Smith lived up to his nickname of "Disappearing Billy" after absorbing a volley of hard combinations from Walcott. The incident began when Smith walloped Walcott with a hard punch to his exposed chin during a sparring session. Walcott took umbrage and proceeded to clout Smith around the ring with what a United Press correspondent said were six consecutive one-two punches that "nearly knocked Smith groggy." Smith had had enough and wanted to leave the ring, but Walcott's trainer Dan Florio signaled Smith to continue the one-sided sparring session. "What do you want? My brains knocked out?"[25] asked Smith as he crawled through the ropes to safety—and, presumably, unemployment. Smith had been tabbed with the unflattering moniker "Disappearing Billy" when he unexpectedly fled from the ring in the eighth round during a main event versus Archie Moore in Portland, OR on January 2, 1951.

Two days before the Marciano-Walcott championship fight, the challenger was perceived by oddsmakers to have the edge; Marciano was listed as a 3:2 betting favorite. By the time of the bout, significantly more Marciano money than Walcott money was being wagered, driving the bookmakers' odds of a Marciano win up to 9:5 and finally to 2:1. Stories of overly confident Massachusetts fans betting the titles to their homes and automobiles on Rocky were circulating. Such developments did not worry or impress the Walcott camp, however. They continued to believe that Rocky was an overrated, unskilled fighter whose weaknesses would be exposed. They argued that Joe Louis was a hollow shell of his former greatness when Marciano blasted him into permanent retirement the previous year. Similarly, Marciano's dominant victory over Harry Matthews ought to be discounted because, according to Walcott's fans, Matthews was little more than a blown-up light heavyweight. They, of course, also thought Roland LaStarza should have gotten the decision over Marciano in their 1950 encounter.

The day before the championship bout, United Press polled 35 of its sportswriters. Four-fifths of them favored Marciano to win—the vast majority by knockout. Only one scribe picked Marciano to win by decision. On the flip side, only one writer foresaw Walcott winning by a knockout. Regardless of the outcome, Walcott told reporters he absolutely planned on continuing his boxing career. "I have six children to support,"[26] he explained. During training Walcott had sparred just 50 rounds. Marciano had almost double that amount under his belt; he had boxed 99 rounds in preparation for the big night.

Picking Walcott to win by knockout was a bold statement. Entering the fight, Marciano had never even been decked in his entire professional career. Carmine Vingo had come the closest, staggering the Brockton Blockbuster in their brutal 1949 slugfest at Madison Square Garden, but he, of course, could not achieve the feat. Walcott said publicly that he believed that Marciano was basically a glorified amateur based on his crude style of brawling. Thus, he figured the challenger would be easy to pick apart with skillful boxing.

On a night when the Brooklyn Dodgers rallied to clinch the National League pennant with a 5–4 home win over the Philadelphia Phillies in the first game of a doubleheader and maligned vice-presidential nominee Richard Nixon deftly salvaged his political career with his famous "Checkers speech," a large portion of America's collective attention was firmly centered on a boxing ring in the middle of Philadelphia's Municipal Stadium. There was no free TV or live radio descriptions of the Marciano-Walcott bout, which was to begin at 10 p.m. in the Eastern time zone. To follow the action instantly, one either had to go to the actual fight venue or attend one of the 50 closed-circuit television screenings showing the championship tilt in 31 cities across America's eastern regions. Based on advance ticket sales, early estimates of the closed-circuit revenues were about $125,000—a sum that pleased co-promoters Jim Norris and Herman Taylor. If the fight happened to be competitive, even more revenue could be generated by showing the films afterward. Closed-circuit telecasts were a new source of revenue for boxing impresarios. Within a very short time, closed-circuit receipts would become *the* major source of revenue for important boxing matches. With satellite technology soon to be a reality, it also meant that a major fight could now be held just about anywhere as long as people could pay to watch it in a theater somewhere near their homes.

One of the two closed-circuit venues in Pittsburgh was offering a nifty movie/boxing double feature: For the price of a $3.50 ticket, one could go to the J.P. Harris Theater on Sixth Avenue and see *Les Miserables* (starring Michael Rennie and Debra Paget) followed by the live screening of the Marciano-Walcott bout.

For those wanting to see the much-anticipated title fight via this wondrous new medium, a bargain could be had if one attended a certain drive-in theater situated in Rutherford, NJ. The Associated Press reported that the usual movie showplace was charging $10 per car to watch the bout—regardless of how many occupants were inside each vehicle! The generous offer drew an unruly caravan of discount-seeking fight fans whose enormous size was estimated to be somewhere between 20,000 and 30,000. The figure almost rivaled the paid admissions at Philadelphia's Municipal Stadium—40,379. Chaos ensued, of course. "They double- and triple-parked on two main highways, tied up traffic for hours miles around; brawled among themselves; built bonfires to keep warm; swigged beer, played poker and practically wrecked the place,"[27] said the AP article. Seymour Weiss, the theater's manager, said 3,500 people would usually be considered an excellent turnout at his place of business on a typical night. But this was not a typical night. Things got out of control early at the drive-in. Hours before the fight was to be screened there were thousands of vehicles lined up to take advantage of the special bulk admission prices. The result was "a rampaging mob." People were badly overcrowding small vehicles, testing their maximum load capacity to the extreme. Several fans were stuffed in the trunks of some cars. One "midget automobile" (as it was described) somehow accommodated 15 occupants.

At a closed-circuit venue in New York City, fans who had paid between

$3.60 and $4.80 per ticket to the see championship fight got less than they expected. The picture failed just before the fight began, leaving only a weak audio description of the goings-on in Philadelphia. The disgruntled fans were told they could obtain refunds—provided they had kept their ticket stubs.

Walcott weighed in at 196½ pounds. Marciano tipped the scales a dozen pounds lighter than the champ at 184½. The fight would take place in the same ring where Gene Tunney took the crown from Jack Dempsey in 1926, which seemed to be a good omen for the challenger. Three weeks earlier Marciano had celebrated his 29th birthday. Walcott, the oldest heavyweight champion to date, was supposedly approaching his 39th birthday. Youth was on the side of the challenger, while experience was clearly an asset of the champion. When Walcott had faced Joe Louis for the title in December 1947, Marciano had just a single pro fight under his belt.

In round one Walcott, wearing white trunks with a dark stripe up the sides, took the fight to Marciano. The challenger, wearing dark trunks with a white vertical stripe, seemed both nervous and tentative despite most of Municipal Stadium supporting him. (A large contingent of New Englanders had made the trip to Philadelphia to root for their man.) Walcott started well and was rewarded for it. He rocked Marciano with several shots from close in and dropped him for a count of three with a nicely thrown left hook. Hitting the canvas was a new experience for Rocky, but he got up and gamely continued to battle away. Rocky suffered a slight cut inside his mouth too. Marciano's fans, who had bet sizable amounts of cash on him to take the title from Walcott, had to be worried by their man's shaky start.

Round two saw Walcott inflict more damage with hard lefts and rights. Marciano's best punch was a solid body blow. Still, Walcott appeared to have won the first two rounds fairly comfortably. An examination of the scorecards after the fight showed that referee Charley Daggert remarkably scored the second round for Marciano.

Marciano had a better showing in round three when he connected with several good body shots and had Walcott regularly backing up. A grazing blow at the end of the round seemed to stagger Walcott just slightly. Anything positive that Marciano did was greeted with tremendous noise by the partisan crowd. In round four most of the fighting was done at close quarters. Again, Rocky landed some solid body shots, but Walcott countered well. It was a tough round to score. Referee Daggert was needed to break up clinches several times. Two of the three judges scored round four for the challenger.

Round five saw Marciano rewarded for his persistence. His general aggressiveness won him the round on all three officials' cards. Round six provided several flurries from both fighters. Walcott preferred to dangerously linger on the ropes and counterpunch. Marciano was happy to assume the role of the aggressor. Marciano suffered a slight cut on his forehead, perhaps from an accidental clash of heads. Walcott suffered one above his left eye. Walcott appeared to get the better of the exchanges, but he also seemed more tired than the challenger at the end of the sixth round.

Both men had their moments in round seven. Marciano landed a good right as did the champion. For a moment, it appeared that Marciano was about to go down again, but he managed to maintain his balance. Walcott's pristine white trunks were showing the effects of the rugged battle—they had splotches of blood on them. It probably came from both men. The cut on Marciano's forehead, while not especially serious, did generate a small stream of blood that trickled onto the challenger's face. Round eight saw no clear domination by either man. Marciano was constantly moving forward, but he was largely ineffective in doing so. Walcott seemed to be bothered by the cut above his eye. Marciano was the fresher of the two men. However, Marciano was noticeably blinking rapidly late in the round.

Between the eighth and ninth rounds, Marciano's manager and chief second, Al Weill, complained to referee Daggert in a heated exchange. To some observers the argument seemed to be about the excessive salve that had been applied to the cut above Walcott's left eye. After the fight, Weill revealed that his complaint was actually about liniment that Walcott's corner was applying to their man's shoulders. It was getting into Marciano's eyes and causing a stinging sensation. Indeed, Marciano was blinking badly in his corner. Daggert did not take kindly to Weill telling him how to do his job, and brusquely sent him back to his own corner. In the ninth round, Marciano was the pursuer and focused his attack mostly to Walcott's midsection. Walcott was mostly able to thwart the challenger's offensive, but Marciano did connect with a solid right to the jaw late in the round. It was, perhaps, the best punch Marciano had landed thus far in the contest.

In the tenth round, Marciano three times landed substantial right hands to the champion's face. Each time Walcott grinned back at the challenger as if to say the punch had not bothered him. It was certainly a psychological ploy to unnerve and confuse Marciano, but tiredness was setting in and Walcott was slowing down. He was fighting more flat-footed than he had been. As long as Walcott was shifty and mobile, Marciano would have trouble landing big, damaging punches. Two-thirds of the scheduled 15 rounds had been completed. Walcott was clearly ahead on points based on his superior counterpunching ability. Marciano was headed into uncharted territory. Never before had any of his fights lasted more than ten rounds.

As the 11th round began, Walcott's face was noticeably puffier than in the previous round; the few solid blows Marciano was landing to the champion's head were having a noticeable effect. The pace of the round was slow until Walcott got the best of an exchange in the center of the ring. Two left hooks were especially damaging to the challenger. A cut opened below Mar-

September 23, 1952—Rocky Marciano vs. Jersey Joe Walcott   153

ciano's right eye and Marciano seemed to stagger slightly. Marciano seemed unnerved by the fresh cut and pawed at it several times. Walcott pressed his newfound advantage and took to the offensive. He had Marciano in trouble for a while and had the challenger's back to the ropes. By the end of the round, however, Marciano had weathered the storm, but Walcott seemed to be in control of the fight. The 11th round was Walcott's most dominant since the opening frame.

The 12th round was another good one for the titleholder. Walcott landed several solid left jabs and left hooks on Marciano's face and body. Marciano was now ineffectively lunging at Walcott, trying to score with roundhouse punches. Few came close to hitting the target. Walcott seemed to be catching his second wind. He became more mobile and was able to keep away from the charging challenger with little difficulty. Marciano, sensing time was not on his side, appeared to be getting desperate. With three rounds remaining, Walcott seemingly had an insurmountable lead on the scorecards. If the fight went the distance, Walcott would certainly get the decision. Between the 12th and 13th round, Walcott's handlers exuded confidence. His manager, Felix Bocchicchio, seemed so unconcerned about the fight's outcome that he began to calmly chitchat with his reporter friends seated at press row. Meanwhile Marciano's cornermen were making it clear to the challenger that he definitely needed to register a knockout to win. They were not quite correct. All three judges' scorecards at that point properly had Walcott in the lead. Referee Daggert had the champion ahead in rounds, 7–4–1. Judge Pete Tomasco had Walcott leading 7–5. Only judge Zach Clayton had Walcott with an insurmountable edge over the challenger, 8–4. If the fight went the full 15 rounds with Marciano winning the final three, the bout would have ended in a draw.

The bell rang for round 13. Nothing significant happened for the first 30 seconds. Marciano pursued the champion, bobbing in and out of a crouch. Walcott retreated but his hands were held low. As Walcott's back touched the ropes near Marciano's corner, the challenger feinted with a left hook to the body. It appeared that Walcott was going to try for a counter right hand blow to the oncoming challenger. He never got the chance. Walcott dropped his left hand even farther, exposing his jaw. Marciano wound up and delivered a quick, short, powerful right hand that landed flush on the champion's chin. The crowd gasped at its obvious great force. Marciano knew the punch was lethal; Walcott was senseless. For good measure Marciano landed a grazing left hook that barely connected with the champion's forehead just before referee Daggert intervened to begin a count. The left was superfluous. Marciano properly moved toward a neutral corner as was required by the rules. Walcott sagged towards the canvas. In a somewhat grotesque scene, his left arm became entangled in the ring ropes, preventing him from completely falling face-first to the canvas. Daggert picked up the count at five. It was merely a formality. Daggert could have counted to 1,000 or 10,000. Walcott was not budging. He was out cold.

"There was never a twitch from Walcott as he lay crumpled on the canvas," wrote Nat Fleischer in *The Ring*. "The spectators looked on in awe. Many feared that old Jersey Joe had been fatally injured, so tense was his body."[28] Amid the clamor of an approving crowd, Rocky Marciano was acclaimed the new heavyweight champion of the world—the 17th of the modern era. The official time of the knockout was 43 seconds—an appropriate stat as the victory coincidentally gave Marciano his 43rd win without a defeat in 43 outings.

The end came so suddenly that some reporters missed what had actually felled Walcott. Jack Cuddy of United Press incorrectly wrote, "An explosive left that followed a setting-up right smashed dusky Joe to the canvas and made Rocky the first white heavyweight champion in 15 years."[29] The vanquished Walcott, of course, was not quite sure how the fight ended, either. In his dressing room after the battle he told reporters, "I don't know what he hit me with, but he did hurt me whenever he hit me and wherever he hit me."[30]

Oscar Fraley, another United Press scribe, said that Walcott, like many champions before him, could not defeat the inescapable ravages of time. He wrote:

> Jersey Joe Walcott joined boxing's legion of the past today.
>
> Gallantly courageous to the end, the old man of mysterious years finally bowed to the shackles of time Tuesday night, when he joined the list of humbled ancients who stretch from Bob Fitzsimmons to Joe Louis.
>
> It will read, in the record books, that he fell before the shocking blows of Rocky Marciano. The story was the decade—and maybe more—that he spotted The Brockton Blockbuster.[31]

The Ring magazine's coverage of the bout (which ran in its December 1952 issue) had on its cover artist C.R. Scharre's clever rendition of both Marciano and former champion Jack Dempsey in similar attacking poses. The caption atop boxing's most prestigious periodical read "New Mauler Champion" and asked "Marciano Another Dempsey?" For its historic significance as a title-changing contest, the bout would be named *The Ring*'s Fight of the Year for 1952, along with the 13th round being selected as the publication's Round of the Year.

Nat Fleischer, the editor of *The Ring*, praised Walcott's terrific effort in defeat. "A remarkable fighter went to the post the underdog in a world heavyweight championship bout and almost succeeded in making suckers out of those who belittled him, but Father Time caught up with him just as it seemed he would be acclaimed as 'the winner and still champion.'" Fleischer qualified his statement, however, by noting, "It wasn't so much old age that beat Jersey Joe. It wasn't a decrepit old man who faced the Brockton Blockbuster. Walcott put up one of the best fights of his long career."[32]

In describing the knockout blow, Fleischer evoked the name of a revered past champion from Marciano's neck of the woods. "The manner in which [Marciano] ended a tough, brawling, furious battle in 43 seconds of the thirteenth round was a reminder of the days when another New Englander, John L. Sullivan, ruled the roost by virtue of his mighty fists."[33] As for the thunderous Marciano knockout punch, Fleischer wrote, "The clout struck its mark with such suddenness and such swiftness that many in the vast assembly didn't see it land. But what they saw as they stood up thunderstruck, with eyes focused on the ring as old Jersey Joe was sprawled in a grotesque position, against the ropes, an inert mass, was convincing proof to them that an explosive fist must have landed with TNT force to make a human hulk so helpless."[34]

Fans and writers alike praised both fighters' gutsy performances and the great sports entertainment they had each provided. "It was truly a great and grueling fight," declared Fleischer. "Almost until the final blow was struck, the ageless cutie from Camden, NJ was as dangerous an opponent as was the challenger. Walcott had repeatedly thrilled the spectators, his own partisan rooters, and the Massachusetts adherents by trading punches with his younger and powerful rival."[35]

Fleischer also foresaw a long title reign for the new champion. "By his victory," boxing's foremost scribe wrote, "Marciano proved he can take it as well as dish it out; that he possesses a fighting heart and the greatest asset of a crowd-pleaser—the sock. Though he has much to learn, Rocky, with youth and strength to aid him, should be able to retain his crown against the assault of any of the present crop of heavies and will probably hold onto his title for a long time."[36]

Walcott, bitterly saddened by the loss of his title, seemed keenly interested in an immediate rematch with the new champion—which his contract with Marciano entitled him. However, Walcott's manager Felix Bocchicchio was not nearly as enthusiastic about such a contest. He suspected Marciano's brutal and devastating knockout punch had done irreparable damage to Walcott's chances of ever regaining the title. In fact, Bocchcchio said if Walcott wanted to continue as a fighter, he would do it without his guidance. Yet, within 24 hours, Walcott managed to change Bocchicchio's mind. "I have always been guided by my manager's judgment," Walcott noted, "and there is no doubt that his advice has brought the championship to Camden. While I have the same admiration for him, I know in my heart that I can make boxing history by recapturing the championship."[37] Accordingly, Felix Bocchicchio would again be in Walcott's corner for the return bout versus Rocky Marciano. Like the two famous Dempsey-Tunney fights in the 1920s, Marciano and Walcott would move their rivalry from Philadelphia for the first bout to Chicago for the second.

Two days after Marciano had won the title, John Douesnard of the *Granby (QC) Leader-Mail* expressed serious concern about Walcott fighting Marciano again. He feared for the former champ's safety. Douesnard wrote, "Rocky Marciano's spectacular knockout of old man Jersey Joe Walcott gives promise that he will be a colorful champion. The fans have always gone all out for a slugger and Marciano is all of that. Walcott, after announcing his retirement in his dressing room immediately after the fight, changed his mind and announced he would attempt to regain the crown. It is too bad the boxing commission wouldn't step in and save the old man from a terrific beating he is without a doubt due to receive if the return bout comes off as planned."[38]

By the time that rematch was held in Chicago Stadium on Friday, May 15, 1953, Walcott was 39 years old (at least). Within the space of eight months Walcott had gone from being the oldest world heavyweight champion ever to the oldest fighter to ever challenge for the world heavyweight crown. Marciano entered the ring with more confidence than he did the previous September. His body language was palpably positive. Marciano was again a solid betting favorite with a 16:5 line being offered by bookmakers in favor of the defending world champion retaining his laurels. A pre-fight poll of 36 sports writers had an overwhelming 34 of them predicting a second Marciano triumph over Walcott. Even the black press offered little support for Walcott. The *Baltimore Afro-American* barely acknowledged the fight was happening. It printed merely the tale of the tape on the night of the fight; there was no accompanying story. Even with a one-sided fight expected, strong television viewership was anticipated. The fight would air live on NBC-TV in the United States and on some CBC affiliates in Canada.

Marciano was clad in white trunks for the rematch. (It was becoming something of a tradition for the champion to wear the lighter shade of ring attire.) For the first two minutes of the opening round, Marciano recklessly charged and Walcott boxed. It was basically looking like a rerun of the first fight, but with Rocky doing far better in the first round this time than he had done in Philadelphia. Little of note happened in the first 130 seconds of action.

However, just past the two-minute mark, Marciano landed a quick two-punch combination, the key blow being a strong right hand. Walcott plopped to the canvas on the seat of his dark trunks; his backward momentum caused his legs to lift above his prostrate body as if he were about to perform a reverse somersault. Referee Frank Sikora picked up the count and began tolling over Walcott who seemed to be fully alert. However, Walcott reacted slowly and oddly to Sikora. As the count reached eight, Walcott was still in a sitting position with one glove on the bottom rope and one on the canvas. That was still the case at Sikora's count of nine. When Sikora tolled ten, Walcott was in the process of rising, but his left glove was still touching the canvas. Sikora quite properly signaled the fight was over. Rocky Marciano had retained his title by a knockout at 2:25 of the opening round (despite the ring announcer erroneously declaring that the fight had ended at *1:25* of the first round).

Writing in the *Pittsburgh Press* the following day, reporter Roy McHugh accurately stated, "Walcott at first looked bewildered. Then he smiled and walked straight to his corner shaking his head. He appeared to be fresh and unhurt, perfectly able to fight." In another part of his report, McHugh commented that a great many fans both at Chicago Stadium and watching the bout on television believed that "Walcott, the marvelous Methuselah, had no real desire to get up."[39]

Marciano told the press that he was not surprised that the fight ended so quickly. "At first I thought he would get up—and then I looked at his eyes and they were glassy.... I knew then he was finished."[40]

The 13,266 fans in attendance—mostly a pro–Marciano bunch—were mystified by the weird ending and the shortness of the bout, but they were generally pleased that their man was the winner and still heavyweight champion of the world. McHugh further noted, "[The spectators] seemed to be halfway expecting an announcement that this had only been a warmup and that now the real fight would begin." The headline above McHugh's coverage of the pitiful contest read, "Walcott's career ends with flop."[41]

The boxing website BoxRec describes the bout's odd conclusion this way: "With less than a minute remaining in the first round, Walcott threw a jab and Marciano countered with a left hook and a right uppercut that sent the off-balance Walcott sprawling on his back, his feet flying high above him. The challenger pulled himself up to a sitting position, one hand on the ropes, and appeared unhurt. He then sat there and let the referee count him out. Once the fatal ten was reached, Walcott hoisted himself to his feet and complained that he had received a fast count."[42]

Walcott's angry cornermen claimed their man had been victimized by a quick count and filed an official protest the following day with the Illinois Boxing Commission. It was swiftly rejected. Marciano's manager Al Weill could not fathom what all the fuss was about. He said, "The referee counted him [Walcott] out as plain as day."[43] Interestingly, the abbreviated fiasco made more money for Walcott than it did for the champion. Walcott received a $250,000 flat payment for his 145 seconds of work, while Marciano was given 30 percent of the Chicago Stadium gate. When the receipts were counted, Walcott had negotiated the better deal. He made about $84,000 more than Marciano did. Ringside seats for the unsatisfactory bout had a face value of $50. An Associated Press correspondent (who received no byline the *Calgary Herald*) did the arithmetic and proclaimed Walcott was paid "approximately $1,724 a second for his 145 seconds of surprisingly inept performing."[44]

That same journalist displayed an excellent grasp of boxing history when he alluded to the Dempsey-Tunney rematch in that city nearly 26 years before. "The home of boxing's famed 'long count,'" he wrote, "today had a short-count controversy raging after heavyweight champion Rocky Marciano's first-round knockout of Jersey Joe Walcott at Chicago Stadium."[45]

Walcott—who became the eighth ex-heavyweight champion to fail in an attempt to regain the title—wisely never fought again. He likely realized his box office appeal would have been next to nothing after the strange and highly unsatisfactory ending to Marciano-Walcott II. He retired with a laudable but not extraordinary professional record of 51–18–2. Walcott is the only man in boxing history to lose six world heavyweight title matches—two each to Joe Louis, Ezzard Charles, and, of course, Rocky Marciano. No one else has lost five. (Charles and Floyd Patterson are tied for next highest on the list with a mere four). The next time there was a controversial first-round knockout in a world heavyweight title rematch, it would be 1965 and it would involve Muhammad Ali and Sonny Liston. In a strange and ironic twist of fate, Jersey Joe Walcott would be the referee.

In 1971 Walcott was elected sheriff in Camden County, NJ—the first black man to ever hold that office. He had worked with the Camden County Corrections Office since quitting the ring. Beginning in 1968 he served as the director of community relations for Camden. Walcott continued to stay active in boxing as an official and later as the chairman of the New Jersey State Athletic Commission—the governing body that oversees pro boxing in that state. He died on February 25, 1994, about a month after his 80th birthday—or thereabouts. Despite Walcott being a former world heavyweight champion and playing a significant role in the careers of both Joe Louis and Rocky Marciano, his death surprisingly received very little attention from the mainstream media.

Marciano went on to defend his world heavyweight crown five more times. Twice he beat Ezzard Charles. Their first bout, on June 17, 1954, was a terrific contest. Charles, although he lost a unanimous decision, managed to go the 15-round limit with the champion—the only man ever to do so. Marciano knocked him out in eight rounds three months later in a rematch. Both fights were held at Yankee Stadium. Marciano also knocked out Roland LaStarza who had been clamoring for a rematch since their split-decision bout in 1950. British Empire champion Don Cockell and light heavyweight kingpin Archie Moore also fell before the powerful punches of Rocky Marciano. (Moore did manage to score a flash knockdown against Rocky in the second round, duplicating the feat of Jersey Joe Walcott.) The ninth-round knockout victory over Moore on September 21, 1955, was Rocky's 49th professional win against no losses. Despite the brief knockdown he suffered, Marciano looked as capable and as dominant as ever. He floored Moore four times. Immediately afterward, however, Marciano hinted about hanging up the gloves. When Marciano was interviewed in the ring toward the end of the close-circuit telecast, a reference was made about his trying for 50 wins. Marciano avoided the subject by making no comment.

"There's a lot of pressure from my family for me to retire," Marciano told Murray Rose of the Associated Press shortly after the fight. "My mother wants me to quit. So does my dad and my wife. It's been a pretty bad ordeal for them. I don't know what I should do. Personally, at this point, I don't feel I should retire."[46] His manager Al Weill certainly didn't want his meal ticket to walk away from boxing. There was more money to be made—plenty more. He insisted to reporters that Marciano would stay active. "No, he's not quitting," Weill told a handful of scribes. "There are other contenders who should get a shot. There are Bob Baker, Nino Valdes and Hurricane Jackson. He could fight one of them in June [1956]."[47]

Nevertheless, Marciano eventually bowed to familial pressure. On April 27, 1956, he retired from the ring with a perfect 49–0 record (with 43 knockouts) at age 32. A photo in the next day's *Pittsburgh Post-Gazette* showed Rocky's wife and three-year-old daughter looking wistfully at a picture of Rocky. The caption said, "They're going to get acquainted with Pop."[48] It was only a slight exaggeration. During his stint as champion, Marciano was wholly dedicated to his profession. He estimated (and regretted) that he had only spent about five months with his family over the 43 months he had reigned as the world heavyweight titlist. Marciano confirmed his main reason for retiring from the ring was to spend more quality time at home.

Unlike many of his predecessors, Rocky stayed retired. To date he is the only undisputed world heavyweight champion to have gone through his entire career without a loss. He allegedly was offered $1 million to make a comeback versus Floyd Patterson, a 1952 Olympic gold medalist who had won the vacated title, but Rocky declined. When Sweden's Ingemar Johansson took the title from Patterson in an upset in the summer of 1959, Marciano prepared for a possible comeback for about three weeks but ultimately decided against it.

Marciano spent the rest of his life making public appearances and involving himself in new business ventures. He enjoyed doing both. On August 25, 1969, Marciano was warmly received in Milwaukee. The ex-champ arrived to promote a golf event and an Italian spaghetti house he had recently invested in. "He had seemed so full of life," a columnist from the *Milwaukee Journal* lamented. Marciano also told local newsmen that boxing desperately needed the return of Muhammad Ali to inject some needed renewed interest in the declining sport.

On Sunday, August 31, 1969, one day before his 46th birthday, Marciano perished when the small private airplane he was flying in crashed near Newton, a town in Jasper County in central Iowa. The accident site was a mile and a half short of the runway of a small airfield in that rural community and about 30 miles short of the aircraft's actual destination.

Marciano and a friend, 23-year-old Frank Farrell, were flying from Chicago to Des Moines—a trip of about 2½ hours. They were the only two passengers on the plane. A medical examiner determined that both men and the pilot, Glenn Belz, were killed instantly. Farrell and Belz were both Des Moines residents. Belz was an amateur pilot who operated a local construction business. Investigators later blamed pilot inexperience and error for the tragic mishap. The beloved former champion was making a special stop en route to his home in Fort Lauderdale, FL where a birthday party in his honor had been planned. Rocky's stopover in Des Moines was to help publicize Farrell's new insurance business. Farrell had been an outstanding high-school athlete in his hometown.

The single-engine Cessna was running short of fuel in cloudy and drizzly conditions. The pilot, 37-year-old Belz, radioed that foul weather was preventing him from seeing Des Moines, some 30 miles away, but he could see the lights of Newton and would attempt to land at a small airstrip there. Belz frantically tried to safely land the aircraft in a field belonging to farmer Henry Eilander. Witness Colleen Swarts, age 30, said she saw the small plane stall in the sky near her home. "I was scared to death it would fall on us," Swarts told the media. "I could see the lights on the plane. Then it sort of drifted away and I heard an awful thud. I knew what had happened." Swarts added, "I hope I never hear anything like it again. I never dreamed anyone like Rocky Marciano was in it."[49] Swarts was the first person to report the crash to the police.

A little over a month later the National Transportation Safety Board (NTSB) released its report on the accident. It assigned blame on the pilot, concluding that Belz was neither experienced nor qualified enough to cope with the weather that night. In short, he should never have attempted the flight given the conditions and his inexperience. The NTSB revealed that Belz had logged a little over 230 hours of flight time since obtaining his private pilot's license, 107 of which were in Cessna 172 aircraft, but only 35 hours were at night. He was not qualified to fly by instrument alone. The NTSB's report concluded, "The pilot followed the first cardinal rule of safe flight by obtaining a weather briefing, but he did not follow the second—carefully weighing the forecast conditions against his piloting skill, and the capability of his aircraft, and then making a conservative decision. That decision, in this and many other similar cases, should have been not to make the flight."[50]

The airplane struck an oak tree on its descent. A wing and its motor were torn loose upon impact. The disintegrating plane bounced for about 80 yards across farmland before it came to rest in a creek bed. The result was an especially grisly crash: Rocky, seated alongside Belz at the front of the aircraft, suffered a gruesome and fatal head injury. It fell to Rocky's younger brother, Peter, to relay the awful news to his parents in Brockton that their eldest son had died a horrible but sudden death in Iowa.

Marciano left behind his wife of 19 years, Barbara; a 16-year-old daughter, Mary Anne; and a 17-month-old adopted son, Rocco Kevin (sometimes referred to as Rocky Jr.). He would grow up having no memories of his father. Kevin had just learned how to walk the previous week while Rocky was away on business. The former champion never got the chance to see his son take any baby steps.

Barbara Marciano (née Cousins) would die young too, passing away on September 9, 1974, at age 46 from lung cancer. After his mother's death, six-year-old Rocco Kevin would be raised by his maternal grandmother and his sister. Barbara was interred beside Rocky at Forest Lawn Memorial Gardens Central in Fort Lauderdale. Mary Anne Marchegiano (she preferred to use her father's true family name) died suddenly in 2011, age 58, from a respiratory illness.

The obituary that appeared in Associated Press stories on September 1, 1969, said of the popular ex-champion, "Marciano, whose savage punching and courage gained him fame and fortune inside the ring, and whose clean living won him respect outside it, was killed Sunday night."[51]

"This is the saddest news I've ever heard," said a shaken 55-year-old Joe Louis when he was informed about Marciano's tragic passing. "When he beat me in 1951, I think it hurt him more than it hurt me. He was always talking about it. After the fight he sent a message to my dressing room saying how sorry he was the fight turned out the way it did. Everything I remember about Rocky Marciano is good."[52] When Louis, a man of few words, attended Marciano's funeral in Fort Lauderdale, he chose the right ones to say. After kissing Rocky's closed casket, Louis told everyone within earshot, "God is getting Himself a beautiful man."[53]

Jersey Joe Walcott said the entire sport of boxing suffered when Rocky's airplane fell out of the sky. "I am very sorry," said the man who lost his heavyweight crown to the Brockton Blockbuster 17 years earlier. "I consider him a close friend. He was good for boxing. The sport cannot afford the loss of a man like Marciano. Inside the ring he was a lion; outside it he was a lamb."[54]

Carmine Vingo—the Brooklyn heavyweight contender whom Marciano had nearly killed in the Madison Square Garden ring almost 20 years before—unhesitatingly traveled at his own expense from New York to Florida to attend Rocky's funeral.

Five months after dying, Marciano did make a return to the ring—in a way. In early 1969, he and 27-year-old Muhammad Ali (who was in exile from pro boxing because of the legal entanglements associated with his refusal to be inducted into the army during the Vietnam War) agreed to participate in a hypothetical "computerized" fight versus each other. Data from both undefeated fighters—some 129 variables altogether—were fed into a state-of-the-art NCR 315 computer. The machine analyzed the data to generate a fictitious 15-round championship bout between Ali and Marciano. The fighters' ages were irrelevant. The computer assumed that each man was at his respective physical peak. The whole concept was quite a novel idea for its time.

The two fighters worked out the details. Each said he was eager to reacquaint himself with the other. They got together at a television studio in North Miami in front of four movie cameras to act out various possible scenarios. They would be spliced together to match whatever the computer determined would unfold in each round—had there actually been a real match between the boxing legends at their respective peaks. The filming began before the computer had generated the fight's result, so no one involved in the production knew what the eventual outcome would be. In deference to his age and receding hairline, Marciano wore a toupee (as he did in his later years). Thus, Marciano had more "hair" in the 1969 movie than when he fought Archie Moore at Yankee Stadium in 1955. He also lost 50 pounds to make his physique look more athletic and youthful. The last of the 75 one-minute scenes was shot less than a month before Marciano's untimely death.

Five former world heavyweight champions—Joe Louis, James J. Braddock, Jersey Joe Walcott, Jack Sharkey and Max Schmeling—were recruited to provide expert commentary. Sound effects to augment the boxers' faux punches and canned cheering from an invisible crowd added a level of believability to the whole affair. Chris Dundee was hired to be the referee. The computer would act as sole judge and would announce its scoring—and the explanation of its scoring—at the end of each round. Of course, Marciano had died before the film's release, so he never knew how it turned out. According to his brother Peter, though, Rocky fully expected to emerge as the winner.

The completed film, titled *The Super Fight: Marciano vs. Ali*, was shown in the United States, Canada and in many parts of Europe in about 1,500 venues on closed-circuit television on one evening only: Tuesday, January 20, 1970. It did very good business, much better than was expected. It grossed in excess of $5 million. Marciano's recent death, in a perverse way, probably increased the public's interest in the unusual "boxing match" between two of the sport's legendary figures.

Who won the hypothetical fight? It was a split decision of sorts: At the North American theaters, Marciano duplicated his title victory over Walcott in 1952 with the same result over Ali: The NCR 315 said The Brockton Blockbuster won the hypothetical clash of undefeated world heavyweight champions with a 13th-round knockout. (Ali—who was often referred to as Cassius Clay in the film—scoffed at the unfavorable result. "That computer was made in Alabama!"⁵⁵ he humorously quipped.) Oddly, however, at the European closed-circuit venues, Ali won by a technical knockout, also in 13 rounds! (The fight was stopped on cuts.) The case of two endings appears to be the producers pandering to what they perceived the audiences wanted the outcome to be based on where they resided. Of course, it leads to an obvious question: Whom did the computer actually select as the winner between Rocky Marciano and Muhammad Ali? The truth may never be known. Based on how the film was distributed, the producers, in a sense, called the bout a draw.

The fight, fictitious though it was, was still big news in 1970. It was covered in the sports sections of many daily newspapers as if it were real. Describing what he saw at a local screening, Roy McHugh, the sports editor of the *Pittsburgh Press* comically wrote, "In what Clay said was his last fight, a dead man won the heavyweight championship of computerland. It was surrealistic hokum, somewhat less persuasive than violence on television. But when Rocky Marciano, with a left hook that sounded like two boards coming together, knocked out Cassius Clay in the 13th round last night, the crowd at the Stanley Theater whistled and whooped...." McHugh continued, "Marciano would be 46 now. To turn back the clock he wore a snug, black toupee and layers of tan makeup. Except when his waistline was in focus, Rocky looked good."

McHugh described the Pittsburgh patrons as "predominantly male, white, and young. [They] had come on a snowy, subzero night, filling possibly two-thirds of the downstairs seats at $5 a head. It was a good-natured crowd, cheering facetiously at the first unconvincing exchanges, exploding in a semblance of real excitement when the action heated up toward the end."

Ali's dramatic skills were lauded by McHugh. "Clay is a consummate actor," he wrote. "Trying to beat the count, he scrambled halfway up and then collapsed to his knees. At the fadeout, with the referee lifting Marciano's hand, Clay hung like wet wash on the top strand of rope, his head bowed in forlorn dejection."⁵⁶

People who attended a screening at a Philadelphia venue were pleasantly surprised to see Muhammad Ali himself among the 700 ticketholders. (He had recently purchased a home there.) Like everyone else in that theater, Ali did not know what the outcome would be, of course.

Ali's presence certainly added a bonus level of entertainment to the proceedings with his antics. He gleefully carried on a good-natured running banter with the other customers. A United Press International reporter said Ali was "verbally sparring" with fans. Early in the fight when he absorbed several of Marciano's best punches, Ali proclaimed, "Rocky never hit a man that many times who did not go down!" When Ali had an especially good tenth round he delightfully hollered at the screen, "You're cooking, champ!"

When he was later floored by Marciano, he screamed, "Can't no 45-year-old man put me down!" When Marciano won the fight in round 13, Ali grabbed his coat and comically covered his head in mock shame. "I'm leaving!" he shouted before the replay of the knockout could be shown. As he departed he said, "Don't you believe that!" Later he told a local reporter, "Sure [the result] upsets me, but it's just a fiction, a make-believe fight." He also added with a smile, "It takes a good champ to lose like that." As a postscript he said, "People have seen me in the ring for the last time tonight. I'll never fight again."[57]

For legal reasons, all prints of *The Super Fight: Marciano vs. Ali* were supposed to have been destroyed shortly after the one-time-only January 20, 1970, broadcast date. This was clearly not the case. Some theaters continued to advertise screenings well after January 20. *ABC's Wide World of Sports* aired the film later in 1970. *CBS Late Night* did the same in 1977. *The Super Fight: Marciano vs. Ali* definitely appeared on Canadian television as late as 1979. One surviving print was located and used to produce a commercial DVD in 2005. The DVD includes a documentary feature about the making of the unusual film.

In eulogizing the fallen champion two days after his death, Roy McHugh eloquently wrote of Marciano on September 2, 1969,

> He was cheerful and unassuming and eager to please, and his exterior belied what he could do in the ring. At weigh-ins he looked out of place. One was tempted to feel apprehension for him.
>
> Most of his opponents were taller and heavier than he was. Even they could not believe—until Rocky demonstrated it to them—that a man of his size could be so strong.
>
> Easy to hit, Marciano was hard to hurt. A thick neck anchored his formidable jaw.
>
> Rocky Marciano lacked the animal magnetism of Joe Louis or Jack Dempsey, which kept him from duplicating their hold on the public's imagination. But he was the only heavyweight champion who never lost a fight as a professional—and who is to say for sure that any fighter at any time could have beaten him?[58]

Rocky Marciano has now been dead longer than he was alive. He is not close to being forgotten, though—especially in his place of birth. Forty years after Rocky's tragic passing, it was announced in 2009 that a bronze statue of Marciano would be created for public display in Marciano's hometown of Brockton, MA. Renowned Mexican artist, Mario Rendon, was selected to be its sculptor. The groundbreaking ceremony was held on April 1, 2012, on the grounds of Brockton High School. The statue was officially unveiled on September 23, 2012. Fittingly, the date chosen was the 60th anniversary of Marciano defeating Jersey Joe Walcott for the world heavyweight championship with one mighty wallop.

March 8, 1971

Muhammad Ali vs. Joe Frazier
The Fight of the Century

"Ali, of course, has set himself up as a symbol of the times, a defiant man in the face of heavy criticism for his refusal to step forward when he was called by the armed services. He also wants to prove desperately that he, not Frazier, is the heavyweight champion of the world."—Ray Grody, *Milwaukee Sentinel*, March 8, 1971

"The thrust of this fight on the public consciousness is incalculable. It has been a ceaseless whir that seems to have grown in decibel with each new soliloquy by Ali, with each dead calm promise by Frazier. It has magnetized the imagination of ring theorists and flushed out polemicists of every persuasion. It has cut deep into the thicket of our national attitudes, and it is a conversational imperative everywhere…"—Mark Cram, *Sports Illustrated*, March 8, 1971

"It was called The Fight of the Century—and 20 years later the billing still holds true. No fight before or since has carried the same significance. Its impact transcended boxing, crossing social, economic and racial barriers. It was a sporting event that turned into an obsession. And the lines were clearly divided."—Robert Cassidy in the July 1991 issue of *The Ring* on the 20th anniversary of the first Ali-Frazier fight

On March 8, 1971, the war in Vietnam was grinding on with no end in sight; leftist revolutionaries in Turkey had released four American airmen they had kidnapped and held under the threat of death for six days; the military leader of Syria, General Hafez Assad, was calling for a "war of liberation" against Israel; and Harold Lloyd, the wonderful silent movie comedian from the 1920s, passed away from prostate cancer at his Beverly Hills home at the age of 77.

However, that Monday most of the free world's attention was focused on something much more captivating: a boxing ring in Madison Square Garden in New York City. In it the most eagerly awaited professional prize fight in history was about to take place. It featured two undefeated fighters, Joe Frazier and Muhammad Ali. Each man claimed to be the true world heavyweight champion—and each had a compelling case. Anyone who routinely read a newspaper or who owned a radio or television had at least some inkling of the enormity of this sports event. So colossal was its magnitude that it was promoted simply as "the Fight." No further description was necessary. As *KO Magazine* noted in 1991 on the 20th anniversary of the occasion, "You had to be on Mars not to know this fight was happening."

Cassius Marcellus Clay, Jr.—who, as Muhammad Ali, would eventually become the most famous man on the planet—was born on January 17, 1942, in Louisville, KY. One of five children, Clay came from a lower-middle-class black family. In 2016, the British newspaper *The Guardian* claimed that "penury was taken for granted" in the Clay household. It was untrue: His father was a capable sign and billboard painter. His mother, Odessa, was a domestic helper. Together they made ends meet plus a little bit more.

Odessa was the anchor in the Clay home. She raised Cassius and his younger brother (Rudy) as Baptists. Both became regular churchgoers and rarely got into any trouble. Cassius was just an average scholar. School held no particular allure for him. Nevertheless, he did graduate from Louisville's Central High School in 1960 but he was nowhere near being an honor student. Academically he ranked a dismal 376th in his class of 391 pupils.

In 1954, Cassius Sr. gave his namesake son an expensive gift for his 12th birthday—a shiny new red bicycle with chrome trim. It was young

A pensive and annoyed-looking Muhammad Ali is shown in a photograph circa 1969. This was during the period when Ali had been stripped of the world heavyweight title because of his refusal to be inducted into the U.S. Army. Still, he was largely considered to be the legitimate titleholder. *The Ring* magazine continued to list Ali as the rightful world champion until early 1970.

Cassius's most beloved possession. He did not possess it for long, however. One day he attended a community bazaar in his hometown and parked the bike outside the venue—only to find that it had been stolen when he went to retrieve it. Furious, Cassius reported its theft to a local policeman, Joe Martin. He also told the officer that he intended to whip whomever had taken his bicycle. Martin happened to be an amateur boxing instructor who ran a racially integrated gymnasium in Louisville's Columbia Auditorium. He advised the young crime victim to learn how to box before picking a fight with anyone. Martin invited the youngster to attend his gym to learn boxing basics. Clay did not immediately agree, but eventually concluded that Martin's idea was sound. Cassius' missing property was never recovered. However, in a roundabout way, because of a bicycle thief the world discovered Cassius Clay/Muhammad Ali.

Cassius learned the basics well enough to be featured on a local amateur boxing television program, *Tomorrow's Champions*, that Joe Martin had a hand in producing. His first opponent was 14-year-old Ronnie O'Keefe, another Louisville boy making his ring debut. Clay, weighing 90 pounds, won the three-round bout on a split decision. Twenty-four years later, at the end of 1978, O'Keefe and the world's most famous person would be reunited on the British version of *This is Your Life*. Clay (by that time he was Muhammad Ali, of course) was thoroughly delighted to shake hands again with his very first ring adversary. "We done got old," he told O'Keefe with a chuckle.

Young Cassius tried a variety of sports as a youth, but invariable drifted towards boxing and only boxing. Ironically, he found American-style football to be excessively brutal compared to pugilism. Clay lasted one down as a ball carrier. He did not like helplessly absorbing blows from all directions and from multiple opponents. "You've got to get hit in [football]," he once said, "It's too rough! You don't have to get hit in boxing. People don't understand that."[1] Indeed, as Cassius Clay became more and more accomplished as an amateur fighter, he became a more elusive target for his opponents to strike. He could move in the ring like few others. Mobility and speed became the trademarks of Cassius Clay.

Clay progressed quickly and had a stellar amateur career. He won 100 of 105 bouts. He would eventually capture six Kentucky Golden Gloves titles, two national Golden Gloves championships, and an Amateur Athletic Union national title. His amateur career came to a climax at the 1960 Olympics in Rome—the first Summer Games to be televised to a wide audience. As a brash 18-year-old, Clay won the gold medal in the light heavyweight division. Poland's 25-year-old Zbigniew Pietrzykowski, who had been a bronze medalist at the 1956 Melbourne Olympics, was thoroughly outclassed in the final. (Pietrzykowski, a multiple European amateur champion, would win another bronze medal at the 1964 Tokyo Olympics.) Writing in the *Times of London*,

Neil Allen presciently described Clay and his domination of Rome's light heavyweight field: "The American has given the impression of being so much a showman that we have waited throughout the tournament for someone to wake him up with a solid punch. Nobody has, and in the final last night, Clay, like some loosely strung marionette, put his punches together in combination clusters and pummeled the Pole about the ring. Only great courage kept the triple European champion on his feet. We still have not seen whether the new gold medalist can take a punch, but I expect him to be among the professionals next year so we shall know his worth soon enough."

Despite being the apparent star of the boxing tournament, Clay did not receive the Val Barker Trophy for the best boxer at the 1960 Olympics. Instead it went to Nino Benvenuti, an Italian, who, as a professional, would become a popular world middleweight champion. Like Ronnie O'Keefe, the thoroughly beaten Pietrzykowski was also reunited with Ali 18 years later during that same British television program in 1978—much to the latter's surprise. A professional boxing career obviously beckoned for the talented Olympic gold medalist from Kentucky.

With the backing of a Louisville investment group, Cassius Clay had his first professional bout seven weeks after his Olympic triumph on October 29, 1960, at Louisville's Freedom Hall. He weighed 182 pounds and wore the same white trunks he had worn at the Rome Olympics. His opponent was 30-year-old Tunney Hunsaker, who had lost his last six fights. Clay extended Hunsaker's losing streak to seven, easily winning a six-round decision. Years later, in an interview with *Sports Illustrated*, Hunsaker recalled that Clay was a quiet and polite young man—he had not yet become the loquacious and outrageous "Louisville Lip" whose verbal antics would turn boxing on its ear.

Clay was quick to realize that pro boxing was sadly lacking in colorful characters that captured the imagination of the public—and lack of interest meant poor gate receipts and disappointing paydays. By watching professional wrestling—especially the matches featuring the outlandish gimmickry of Gorgeous George—Clay realized that people would be drawn to the arena to boo a man as frequently as they would to cheer him. Soon after turning pro, Clay began flamboyantly boasting about his abilities, denigrating his opponents' abilities, and, most outrageous of all, predicting the round in which his adversary would fall! Often Clay would combine all of the above into grammar-school-level poetry. Newspapermen loved Clay; he made for good copy. Boxing traditionalists were not so sure about him. They thought his cockiness was over the top and labeled him "Gaseous Cassius." Be that as it may, Clay's plan worked: Within a short time, Cassius Clay was the best known heavyweight boxer outside of world champion Floyd Patterson. He was also drawing crowds and reviving interest in a stagnating sport.

By the end of 1962 Clay was 16–0 and had beaten a handful of name fighters—most notably Archie Moore, who was 46 years old at the time. Clay suggested that Ancient Archie was in need of a pension plan and would fall in the fourth round of their Los Angeles bout—and he did. Forward-thinking boxing fans saw Clay as a possible challenger to the new fearsome titleholder Charles (Sonny) Liston who, earlier in 1962, had roughly separated Floyd Patterson from the world heavyweight championship with a crushing first-round knockout at Chicago's Comiskey Park—the same venue where Joe Louis had won the title in 1937.

Clay had a breakthrough year in 1963. Liston had again thrashed Patterson in one round in their rematch, and there were not too many capable heavyweights on the horizon to challenge the fearsome, heavy-hitting new world champion. Opportunity seemed to be presenting itself to the cocky young contender. Not many fight buffs truly fancied his chances versus Liston, but no one other than Clay seemed to be a plausible title challenger. So onward Clay plodded. A week after his 21st birthday, on January 24, 1963, Clay knocked out Charlie Powell in three rounds at Pittsburgh's Civic Arena. As was becoming Clay's custom, he stopped his victim in the round he had predicted. (A large cartoon about the fight in the *Pittsburgh Press* referred to the beaten Powell as a "Clay pigeon.") A record indoor fight crowd for Pittsburgh was on hand. They booed the ending lustily, believing Powell did not try hard enough to beat referee Ernie Sesto's fatal ten count. Clay had a ready response: "The way I was hitting him, it would have been too bad for him if he'd gotten up."[2]

Clay had two more fights planned in 1963 before he hoped to dethrone Sonny Liston. Clay wanted to do it before his 22nd birthday to eclipse Floyd Patterson's record as the youngest world heavyweight champion ever. First would be Doug Jones in Madison Square Garden—then British (and British Commonwealth) champion Henry Cooper in London, England.

The Doug Jones fight on March 24, 1963, was a disappointment on two levels for Clay. First, a newspaper strike in New York City meant the press coverage it received before and afterwards was far below the level of what Clay was now accustomed to receiving. Worse, Jones did not fall at all. Refusing to chase the much more mobile Clay around the ring, Jones just stood flat-footed and dared Clay to brawl with him. The end result was an unpopular unanimous decision win for Clay that featured a severe disparity in the scoring. Referee Joe LoScalzo had Clay comfortably in the lead at 8–1–1, while both ringside judges had Clay only marginally ahead at 5–4–1. The unimpressed crowd at Madison Square Garden threw peanuts into the ring. Clay picked up a few, unshelled them, and shoved them in his mouth all the while looking contemptuously at the paying customers.

The Clay-Cooper bout—which would be the first of two matches between these fighters—was held in London's Wembley Stadium on June 18,

1963, and drew nearly 50,000 spectators. Scheduled for ten rounds, Clay predicted a fifth-round victory, which the British sporting public considered to be just a tad arrogant. The bout fell on the 148th anniversary of the Battle of Waterloo—and Clay almost met his. The fight has gone down in ring lore for a famous and often misunderstood sequence of odd events that happened at the end of the fourth round.

During the first round, Cooper did well, even bloodying Clay's nose slightly, greatly pleasing his home-country rooters. Cooper landed a couple of good punches in the second round too, but the tide was shifting toward Clay's overall edge in boxing ability. Cooper, always susceptible to cuts, suffered a slight gash under his left eye. In the third round, Cooper suffered a serious cut over that same eye. "Cooper's left eye is a very sorry sight indeed," declared BBC television commentator Harry Carpenter at the end of the round.

In the fateful fourth frame, Clay was boxing well. He was content to keep Cooper at a safe distance, doing his best to avoid being tagged with Cooper's terrific weapon—'Enry's 'Ammer, one of the best left hooks in all of boxing. At the very end of that memorable round, Cooper connected with a beauty of a left hook. Clay never saw it coming and was clearly hurt. He slid down the ring ropes and landed on the seat of his trunks near a neutral corner. He got up at the count of three just as the bell rang. This is where things got interesting and controversial in Clay's corner.

Clay had certainly been jolted by Cooper's left hook. When he got back to his corner on unsteady legs, he sat down but tried to rise immediately. "He still doesn't know where he is! He's still half out! They're working furiously on him in the corner!" shouted Harry Carpenter over the clamor engulfing Wembley Stadium.

One of Clay's seconds popped an ammonia capsule and smelling salts under Clay's nose in an effort to rush him back to his senses. Both were considered illegal stimulants under British boxing rules but the transgressions were not noticed by any officials. Clay's chief second and trainer Angelo Dundee noticed a slight tear in one of Clay's boxing gloves and brought it to the attention of referee Tommy Little. (Dundee always denied that he caused the rip—news photos taken in round three confirm the glove was already torn—but he never denied making it slightly larger.) Little went to British Boxing Board of Control officials at ringside to ask if there were another pair of gloves nearby. The answer was no. The fight continued.

Over the years wild stories circulated that the bout was delayed five, six, or even ten minutes while officials scurried about for a replacement glove. The actual truth was that the interval between rounds four and five was about 65 seconds—just five seconds longer than usual. The time was verified by a journalist from *The Ring* magazine in 1975 who, in writing a retrospective story about the fight, interviewed the timekeeper and checked the unedited BBC broadcast tapes. Nevertheless, what occurred between the fourth and fifth rounds in Clay's corner has always been fodder for boxing history buffs.

Clay emerged from his corner at the start of the fifth round with a dramatic sense of urgency—as did Cooper, each for different reasons. Clay took the offensive with the clear intent of trying to end the fight in the fifth round—as that was when he had predicted the bout would end. The gash above Cooper's eye was "in a shocking state," Carpenter told his audience. "It's pouring blood. I think referee Tommy Little will have to stop this because Cooper's eye is really in an absolutely appalling state." Moments later that was precisely what happened.

Clay was bombarded with programs from ringside ticketholders when he quickly reminded them that he had again correctly called the round when his opponent would be dispatched. He always got along splendidly with Henry Cooper, though. Fifteen years later, when Muhammad Ali was being honored on the British version of *This is Your Life*, Ali confided to Cooper, "You hit me so hard you rocked my kinfolks back in Africa." The aftermath of the Clay-Cooper fight was a revised policy mandating spare sets of gloves are always kept near the ring at all professional boxing cards in Great Britain.

Now no one was separating Cassius Clay from a world heavyweight championship bout with Sonny Liston. Despite not looking exactly invincible in his final two bouts of 1963, Clay was the only logical contender out there.

Charles (Sonny) Liston was an unpopular champion. He had a perpetual scowl, a surly personality, and a prison record for armed robbery. In fact, Liston had learned to box while incarcerated. Liston's career was also managed by characters whose reputations were less than stellar. His true age was always a bit of a mystery. No one has ever been able to find Liston's official birth record. He was born to sharecropping parents in rural St. Francis County, AK. Liston was allegedly one of 25 children. At the time he drew his first breath Arkansas did not require births to be documented. In some boxing record books, 1932 is listed as the year Liston was born. Others list no date whatsoever. Liston was listed in the 1940 U.S. Census as a ten-year-old, but skeptics suggest that figure may have been a rough estimate. Shortly before Clay and Liston met for the world championship in 1964, a news story emerged indicating that Liston had a 19-year-old daughter, heightening the doubts about the true year of his birth. In his attempt to generate public interest in the contest, Clay poetically taunted the champion about his mysterious age: "You're 40 if you're a day—and you don't belong in the ring with Cassius Clay!"

Meanwhile, Clay's notoriety for being the best interview in sports (along with his penchant for boasting and poetizing) got him some television time far beyond the usual boxing telecasts. He appeared on both Jack Paar's and Jerry Lewis' respective new talk shows to promote both himself (of course) and his upcoming heavyweight title challenge versus Liston, whom Clay dubbed the "Ugly Bear." Paar (who had handed off *The Tonight Show* to Johnny Carson the previous autumn) was absolutely delighted to have the confident young challenger as a guest. He had Clay recite one of his self-aggrandizing poems with piano accompaniment from Liberace! The amusing doggerel ended with, "If Cassius says a mosquito can pull a plow, don't ask how! Hitch him up!" Lewis thought considerably less of Clay, however. The comedian was rudely abrupt with the boxer and called him "a big bag of wind." Clay had the last laugh, however. By the time Clay and Liston fought for the world championship, Lewis' program was history. ABC canceled *The Jerry Lewis Show* in December 1963 after just 13 disappointing weeks.

When Clay-Liston fight finally occurred on Tuesday, February 25, 1964, at the Miami Beach Convention Center, few people had much affection for Liston—but even fewer thought Clay had a chance against Liston's scary punching power. The venue was nowhere near sold out and Clay was a 7:1 betting underdog, 8:1 in some places. Howard Cosell, who was just beginning to make a name for himself as a sports journalist, found Clay to be an engaging personality, but he confidently predicted Liston would win by a first-round knockout—just what he had done to Floyd Patterson twice. Cosell was among the vast majority. Of 60 journalists polled before the fight, just three picked Clay to win. Two of them—Leonard Koppett of the *New York Times* and Bob Waters of *Newsday*—would appear as contestants on the game show *I've Got a Secret* six nights later.

The opening round was a revelation. Clay easily eluded Liston's crude attempts to corner him. By the end of the round Clay had landed a serious flurry of punches on the befuddled champion and had ably demonstrated that Liston could be outboxed by someone who was not afraid of him. By the end of the second round Clay had the fans in the half-filled arena solidly behind him as an upset was in the offing.

Clay's apparent cakewalk to the heavyweight title was nearly scuttled after the fourth round, however. Clay returned to his corner and said a terrible burning sensation was affecting his eyes. He screamed at Angelo Dundee to stop the fight. Dundee refused and tried to cleanse his fighter's face. Whether some coagulant that was being applied to Liston's cuts had accidentally gotten into Clay's eyes or whether something more nefarious had occurred is a matter of debate. What was perfectly clear was that Clay was in big trouble as he still was blinking frantically when the bell for the fifth round sounded. He headed out to face the fearsome power of Sonny Liston with his vision severely impaired. Clay retreated for most of the round, barely doing anything offensive. He pawed at Liston and tried to keep away. Liston managed to work Clay's body, but he was unable to take advantage of the odd situation. Clay's eyesight cleared up in the final minute. He had survived.

In the sixth round Clay resumed his dominant boxing. The flat-footed and tired Liston looked to be the 40-year-old that Clay said he was. Clay jabbed, scoring repeatedly. He followed with occasional combinations. Liston did virtually nothing. When both fighters headed back to their respective corners, no observers knew that Sonny Liston's championship reign was done.

But it was. When the warning beep sounded for the seventh round, Clay rose and prepared to continue wearing down Liston's resistance. However, Clay was among the first to realize that Liston was not going to continue. Clay started a gleeful celebratory dance. When the bell sounded, Liston's seconds were still surrounding his stool. Referee Barney Felix went to investigate what was happening. He got his answer: Liston could not answer the bell for round seven, becoming the first world heavyweight champion since Jess Willard in 1919 to surrender the crown between rounds. Liston had dislocated his left shoulder—at least that was the story coming from his corner. Cassius Clay was the new heavyweight champion of the world—and he enthusiastically proceeded to let announcer Steve Ellis and the people at the closed-circuit venues know it: "I'm so great. I don't have a mark on my face. I just upset Sonny Liston and I just turned 22-years-old. I must be the greatest! I shook up the world! I am the king of the world! I'm pretty! I shook up the world! I can't be beat. I am the greatest!"

Writing about the astonishing result in the next day's *Pittsburgh Post-Gazette,* journalist Al Abrams was both praiseful of the new champion and dismissive of the deposed one. "[Clay] burst the Liston bubble and proved him no more than a hard-punching tyro who made it big because [Floyd] Patterson, a smaller man, had a china chin and was knocked out in less than a round in two meetings."

The next day, with the sports word still reeling from the unforeseen upset in Miami Beach, Clay shook up the world again. He announced he had adopted the Islamic faith, he was renouncing his "slave name," and would, for the time being, be known as "Cassius X." Shortly thereafter he accepted the name Muhammad Ali from his spiritual leader, Elijah Muhammad. Years later, Ali's personal physician, Dr. Ferdie Pacheco, said that Cassius Clay was such an impressionable youngster that he (Pacheco) could have converted him to Judaism if he had been so inclined.

That news of Clay's new name and new religion was not particularly well received in the heartland of America where people harbored suspicions about the black Muslim movement and its various leading figures. A headline on the cover of the July 1964 of *The Ring* magazine proclaimed "Clay Story Turns Sour." By the time Ali and Liston were ready to meet in their rematch 15 months later, the bout had basically been chased out of Boston because civic leaders there disapproved of both fighters' outside-the-ring associates.

Instead of Boston Garden, a small high-school hockey arena in Lewiston, ME hosted the bizarre May 25, 1965, rematch. Ali won by a dubious first-round knockout that still evokes passionate discussion today about how legitimate the finishing blow was. (When asked for his opinion of Ali-Liston II, former champ Jack Dempsey replied, "Let's not dignify it."[3]) Sonny Liston's days as a contender were over, and professional boxing had Cassius Clay as its world heavyweight champion—with precious few contenders anywhere close to his caliber to give him serious competition. Floyd Patterson was resurrected again and lost his fourth world title bout. Henry Cooper was given a deserved second chance at Ali and lost on cuts again. Ali looked tremendous in dispatching aging Cleveland Williams and the overmatched Brian London—both in three rounds. Canada's George Chuvalo, known for his incredible durability, managed to last the distance in Toronto and gained everlasting fame in his home country because of it. Overmatched West German champion Karl Mildenburger was blasted out in Frankfurt. Ernie Terrell was beaten on a decision at the Houston Astrodome. Zora Folley was flattened in Madison Square Garden. Howard Cosell suggested in a television interview with Ali, after nine successful title defenses in three years, there was really no one left for the champion to beat.

Then international affairs intervened in the boxing world. The United States still had a military draft in the 1960s. In accordance with federal law, Ali had registered for national conscription on his 18th birthday in 1960. He been originally classified as 1-A, but it was dropped to 1-Y in 1964. (Interestingly, the world's most famous amateur poet had scored poorly in the language section of the test.) The 1-Y designation meant that Ali would only be called to duty in the event of a national emergency. But with the increased American need for soldiers to serve in the Vietnam War, the standards were reduced. Ali's score was revised upward as a passing grade, qualifying him for military service. Accordingly, he was ordered to report for induction in Houston, the city where he now resided, on April 28, 1967. Citing religious objections to the war, three times he refused to step forward when his name was called. He also added, "I ain't got no quarrel with them Viet Cong. None of them ever called me nigger."[4] Ali immediately became the most polarizing public figure in America. He was arrested later that day. He was charged and convicted of evading the draft and faced a possible $10,000 fine and potentially five years in prison. However, he launched an appeal, claiming to be a conscientious objector and a minister of his faith.

With Ali facing a possible jail term, professional boxing's various governing bodies stripped him of his heavyweight title. *The Ring* magazine did not, however. To its credit, *The Ring*—advertised as "the bible of boxing" and generally respected as the authoritative publication on the pro game—continued to list Ali as its world heavyweight champion in its monthly rankings based on its policy that a champion can only lose his title in the ring or voluntarily relinquish it; it cannot simply be taken from him. Editor Nat Fleischer, age 79, was personally no supporter of Ali's stance against the Vietnam War, nor was he an advocate of Islam, but Fleischer steadfastly stuck to Ali's claim as world heavyweight champion in accordance with his publication's principles. Fleischer received a great deal of hate mail on the issue—with some fans irrationally claiming the elderly Jewish boxing scribe was in cahoots with the black Muslims—but he never wavered in applying *The Ring*'s laudable standards in Ali's unusual case.

Exiled from the wealth he could accrue in professional boxing, in the late 1960s Ali earned his living more modestly than he had since becoming a pro athlete. He stayed in the spotlight by making paid public appearances. He was especially in demand at college campuses where he drew terrific crowds as a "guest lecturer." Ali was regarded as a heroic figure by most of the students who paid to see his lively addresses. Ali's shtick was basically an open forum where he would appear on a stage and answer the audience's questions on just about any subject. In a 1968 interview with Howard Cosell, Ali derisively referred to all other world heavyweight title claimants, such as Joe Frazier, Jimmy Ellis and Jerry Quarry, as "homemade champions" and their crowns as "Mickey Mouse titles."

But the world heavyweight crown—vacated as far as the power brokers in boxing saw it—had to be filled. One promising up-and-comer was the aforementioned Joe Frazier of Philadelphia.

Joe Frazier was born on January 12, 1944. He came from a black, sharecropping, Baptist family of 13 children in Beaufort, SC. He was the 12th child born to Dolly Alston-Frazier. The Fraziers lived in a rural area of Beaufort called Laurel Bay. Their ten acres of land was not especially bountiful, but it did produce watermelons, cotton and valuable corn. The latter crop was converted into bootleg liquor. Its sale provided the necessities of life for the large Frazier clan. Joe was especially close to his father, Rubin. Rubin nicknamed Joe "Billy Boy." Making life even tougher for Rubin was a tractor accident that occurred when Joe was less than a year old. Part of Rubin's left forearm had to be amputated.

One luxury item the Fraziers eventually acquired was a television set. Professional boxing was an omnipresent attraction on the tube during the early and mid–1950s; in 1954 it aired six nights of the week. The Fraziers permitted their friends neighbors to watch the professional bouts on their set— and Dolly would sell drinks for a quarter apiece to earn some extra money. One night while the fights were on TV, Joe's Uncle Israel made an offhand remark that changed the boy's life: He took a look at his eight-year-old nephew and said his stocky physique could make him another Joe Louis. Joe already had the reputation at his elementary school for being a tough customer. He would often accept money or food from classmates in exchange for protecting them from bullies. The day after his uncle's comment, Joe made a homemade heavy bag out of rags, Spanish moss, and corn cobs. "For the next six or seven years," Joe recalled in his 1996 autobiography, "damn near every day I'd hit that heavy bag for an hour at a time."[5] Crude though it was, the daily heavy-bag workout provided the first real training Joe Frazier ever had as a boxer.

One day a mishap of his own doing permanently injured Joe's left arm. He poked his family's 300-pound hog with a stick and it began to chase him. Joe stumbled while running and ripped open the arm on an exposed brick. Unable to afford a doctor, Joe's family relied on stopgap first aid. The arm did not properly heal and Joe could never quite straighten it out for the rest of his life. Yet it would become his greatest weapon inside a boxing ring.

By the time Joe was 15 he had experienced enough of Beaufort's gripping poverty to know he needed to leave if he were to have any meaningful future. He boarded a northbound bus, settled in Philadelphia, and found work in a slaughterhouse. He quickly took up amateur boxing as a pastime.

At nearly 6' tall, with a bobbing and aggressive style reminiscent of Henry Armstrong, Jack Dempsey and Rocky Marciano, Frazier enjoyed a terrific amateur career, capturing the Golden Gloves heavyweight title three times in succession (1962 to 1964). Prior to the Olympic Trials for the 1964 Games in Tokyo, Frazier's only amateur loss was to portly Buster Mathis. At the Trials, which were held as part of the World's Fair in New York City, Mathis and Frazier met again in the heavyweight final. It was a peculiar setup: The two boxers wore headgear and ten-ounce boxing gloves despite the fact that Olympic competition used no headgear and eight-ounce gloves. According to Frazier's recollection of the bout, Mathis wore his trunks abnormally high, and the referee kept warning Frazier about low blows that should have been absolutely legal. Eventually Frazier was penalized for low blows—which proved decisive. Mathis won on points. Frazier's Olympic dreams seemed to be over.

However, Frazier was persuaded to accompany the American boxing team to Tokyo as an alternate. He happily served as a sparring partner for any boxer—from any country—who approached him. Frazier's patience was rewarded when Mathis had to withdraw from the tournament with an injured hand. Frazier stepped in and won the heavyweight gold medal with four victories. In his last bout, Frazier himself was competing with an injured hand which limited his power. (He had damaged his thumb versus his semifinal opponent, Vadim Yemelyanov of the Soviet Union, whom he defeated by a second-round technical knockout.) Using mostly his right hand, Frazier won a close decision against Hans Huber of Germany. Frazier was the only American boxer to win a gold medal in Tokyo. Like Cassius Clay four years before, professional boxing was Frazier's obvious next step after winning an Olympic championship.

Similar to Clay, Frazier's foray into pro boxing was also sponsored by a local group of businessmen and investors. (One of them was Larry Merchant who would later gain prominence as a television boxing analyst.) The group, known as Cloverlay, was organized by Frazier's amateur trainer, Yancey (Yank) Durham. The financial backing allowed Frazier to train fulltime. In a 1970 interview with the *New York Times Magazine*, Durham said of Frazier, "I've had plenty of other boxers with more raw talent, but none with more dedication and strength." Durham also accidentally gave Frazier the nickname "Smokin' Joe" before a sparring session, telling him he wanted to see smoke come out of his gloves.

Joe Frazier's first professional bout was in Philadelphia on August 16, 1965. Opponent Woody Goss did not last a round. Not one of any of Frazier's other three ring foes in 1965 managed to last three rounds with the 1964 Olympic kingpin.

By 1966 Frazier was a heavyweight worth watching—and one that boxing insiders were watching closely. Eddie Futch, a well-respected trainer from Los Angeles, joined the Frazier team as an assistant to Durham. Eddie Machen, a fringe contender, was the most noteworthy notch added to Frazier's collection of victims that year. Machen fell 22 seconds into the tenth round of a scheduled ten-rounder on November 21. In 1967, Frazier toppled six more opponents including Doug Jones (who had given Cassius Clay fits in 1963) and George Chuvalo (who went the full 15 rounds with Ali in a valiant though lopsided championship fight loss). At the end of the year, Frazier's professional record was an impressive 19–0 with 17 of his opponents failing to last the distance.

On March 4, 1968, Frazier defeated his old amateur nemesis, Buster Mathis, in Madison Square Garden with an 11th-round technical knockout to gain partial recognition as "world heavyweight champion." (He was recognized as the titlist in New York and five other states. It was definitely a small world.) Over the next 15 months Frazier defended his slice of the crown four times with Oscar Bonavena and Jerry Quarry giving him the toughest tussles. At Madison Square Garden on February 16, 1970, Frazier defeated Jimmy Ellis, who held the WBA version of the world heavyweight title, in four easy rounds in what was billed a unification fight.

There was always the specter of Muhammad Ali hanging over Frazier's crown, however. Interestingly, Joe supported Ali's position about refusing to be drafted. In fact, Frazier lent Ali money when he needed it and publicly came to his defense regarding his religious objections to the Vietnam War. In early 1970, Ali became frustrated at the delay over his legal appeals. He figured his boxing days were over and announced his retirement. Eighty-two-year-old Nat Fleischer took Ali at his word and stopped listing him as world heavyweight champion in *The Ring* magazine. *The Ring* quickly recognized Frazier as new champion for having beaten all the legitimate active claimants. In early 1970, while his appeal was being examined, Ali was granted a boxing license in Atlanta thanks to the efforts of a sympathetic senator. After more than three years away from the ring, Ali could resume his boxing career. Not long afterward, Ali won his case in the United States Supreme Court, 8–0, with one abstention. The court's ruling was based on a legal technicality rather than a full vindication of Ali's claim to be a conscientious objector. Few people, including Ali, cared about why he was not being sent to prison. His freedom did allow for the important question to be settled in the ring regarding who the true world heavyweight champion was: Ali or Frazier.

Ali's first opponent was no slouch. It was Jerry Quarry, the best white heavyweight in the United States. Quarry had lost a title bout to Joe Frazier in 1969. Ali and Quarry fought in Atlanta on October 26, 1970—a locale where Ali was not especially popular. In fact, Georgia's governor Lester Maddox had declared a "day of mourning" to mark the fight and urged a general boycott of the bout. According to a UPI news story, about ten threatening phone calls were received at Ali's Philadelphia home on the day of the bout. However, on the night of the fight, there were no picketers outside the Municipal Auditorium, a dingy old opera house built in 1909 that had clearly seen better days. About 5,000 enthusiastic fans showed up to see Ali's return to professional boxing. The mostly black crowd was openly hostile to Quarry and loudly cheered Ali. Ali won the abbreviated fight rather handily. The bout ended when Quarry suffered a nasty cut over his eye in the third round and was unable to come out in the fourth round. At least Quarry's chief second Teddy Bentham thought surrender was the wisest option. Quarry was furious when Bentham tossed in the towel to referee Tony Perez. *Pittsburgh Press* sports editor Roy McHugh reported, "For a moment it seemed that Quarry wanted to punch Bentham. Wrenching away from the old man's restraining arm, he stamped around the ring, bellowing, 'No!'" Quarry needed 11 stitches to close the gaping, bloody wound on his forehead.

Ali showed no visible signs of ring rust in his first bout since defeating Zora Folley at the Houston Astrodome in 1967. Ali's professional record was now 30–0. McHugh was impressed by what he saw from the ex-champion. He wrote, "Ali had been as masterful as ever. Dancing in and out, staying on his toes, he had popped left jabs into Quarry's face, peppered him with hooks, and nailed him with straight rights. In the first round Quarry hardly touched the bounding Ali."

Quarry was still irked when he met with reporters the following morning. "I went out there thinking [Ali] was going to be the greatest," Quarry admitted. "Heck, he's a good fighter, but he ain't great. He couldn't whip my four-year-old kid. If I don't get this cut, there ain't no way Cassius Clay could beat me—and he knows it. I wasn't beaten by a better fighter; I was beaten by a miracle. He has slowed up an awful lot from what I expected—and his punches don't have any sting."[6]

As for Ali's chances versus Joe Frazier? Quarry scoffed at the idea of Frazier losing to Ali. "Frazier will kill him," Quarry bluntly opined. "I've fought an awful lot of guys and Joe Frazier is the toughest and gamest man I've ever fought."[7] The loss to Ali dropped Quarry's record to 37–5–4 and was a major setback in his quest for another title shot.

Ali was not especially pleased with how the fight ended, but for an entirely different reason. He felt its stunning shortness had not given him an adequate test. Nevertheless, Ali's mind was already drifting towards his planned encounter with Joe Frazier sometime in 1971. "Frazier can't box. He's got no jab. He's just got the one style,"[8] Ali declared. Ali's fans seemed completely satisfied with the victory—regardless of the circumstances. McHugh reported that at the enormous Regency Hyatt House hotel, "In a scene of extraordinary emotion, midnight crowds of exotically dressed black people rendered a champion's homage to Muhammad Ali."

Six weeks later, on December 7, 1970, Ali was back in the ring. He recorded a 15th-round knockout over an awkward, long-haired Argentinian heavyweight named Oscar (Ringo) Bonavena who had a large following in his homeland. The fight drew more than 19,000 fans to Madison Square Garden. (To the delight of many New York City public transportation users, Ali and his entourage traveled by subway to the fight and happily chatted with other passengers.) The bout had a title attached to it—albeit one that few fans cared about: the vacant North American Boxing Federation heavyweight crown. (How an Argentinian qualified to fight for a North American title is anyone's guess.) Still, it was a noteworthy contest because of Ali. It was even available in closed-circuit theaters in some boxing-mad locales. While it was a win over a name fighter, Ali did not especially look impressive. Ali had predicted a ninth-round knockout, but he himself was rocked by a solid Bonavena left hook in that very round when he became unnecessarily careless. It was easily the best punch of the night landed by Ringo.

This time Roy McHugh of the *Pittsburgh Press* was not impressed with either Ali, whom he derisively labeled "the heavyweight champion of the social protest movement," nor the crude, caveman-like style of Bonavena, whom McHugh described as a man "who punches like he is swinging oars." Wrote McHugh, "Bonavena's clumsiness, his total absence of style, his repeated low blows … appeared to confuse Ali."[9] Eighty-year-old Dan Daniel, a journalist who had been covering the sports scene in New York City since 1909, readily agreed that Ali showed "deterioration" compared to how he had looked in 1967. He did, however, give Ali kudos in a left-handed sort of way. "One may not like Cassius Clay as a citizen, as an American, as a man who will not step up and sing out 'God Bless America' as a draft-evading felony defender. But one had to admire this former world champion as a competitor. He was alert, mobile, determined and physically and mentally adequate to the task confronting him."[10]

The late stoppage—coming with just 57 seconds left in the fight—was just window dressing. After 14 rounds, Ali held a commanding lead on the judges' scorecards: 12–2, 10–3–1, and 8–5–1. Nevertheless, confusion clouded the bout's conclusion. "The end of the Clay-Bonavena fight was a mélange of bewilderment," declared Dan Daniel of *The Ring*. "Ringo was knocked down three times within 20 seconds and never got the benefit of the compulsory eight-count. The referee was Mark Conn."[11] The loss dropped Bonavena out of the heavyweight elites for good, despite Ringo winning 12 of 14 bouts he contested over the next 62 months. He met an untimely end in May 1976, at age 33, when he was shot to death outside an upscale, 100-room brothel in Sparks, NV. According to news reports, Bonavena had fallen in love with the 59-year-old wife of the proprietor. His sordid demise did not hurt his popularity in Argentina one iota. Approximately 150,000 people filed past Bonavena's open casket at the Luna Park Sports Arena in Buenos Aires.

Ali's next opponent would be the man now recognized as the world heavyweight champion—Smokin' Joe Frazier. It was a unique and unprecedented situation: a fight between two undefeated world heavyweight titlists. Its appeal would captivate the sports world and beyond. The date and location had not been finalized, but Roy McHugh, the prescient Pittsburgh scribe, believed it would "provide the biggest payday in sports history."[12]

Frazier had seen the Ali-Bonavena bout at a closed-circuit venue. The champion was even less impressed by Ali's outing than McHugh was. Amazingly, Frazier had Bonavena pitching a shutout when the fight ended 57 seconds into round 15—proving that great boxers do not necessarily make competent fight judges. "The way I saw it, Bonavena won every round," Frazier somehow concluded. "Furthermore, I thought Clay fought a dirty fight. I thought Bonavena would fight dirty, but Clay's actions were unsportsmanlike, especially coming from a former champion."[13] Back on September 21, 1966, Bonavena had given Frazier all sorts of trouble in a fight at Madison Square Garden. Frazier only won the contest on a split decision. In 1968 Frazier beat him again in a title defense on a unanimous decision.

When he was not busy pounding his opponents in the ring, Frazier embarked on a side career as a singer, making occasional nightclub appearances with a group of female backup vocalists called the Knockouts (or the Knockabouts depending the billing on any given night). Was he any good?

The Ring magazine cheekily commented, "As a singer, Frazier is a great fighter."[14] While not pursuing musical aspirations, Frazier himself kept active in the ring by crushing world light heavyweight champion Bob Foster in Detroit in just two rounds on November 18, 1970. Shortly thereafter, the inevitable match was made: On Monday, March 8, 1971, Joe Frazier would defend his world heavyweight championship versus "the other champion" Muhammad Ali. It was the only heavyweight matchup anyone anywhere wanted to see. By the time the two men stepped into the ring, no fight in boxing's history—before or since—had ever captured so much of the world's attention.

The venue that advertised itself as "the world's most famous arena"— Madison Square Garden in New York City—would have the honor of hosting the most anticipated contest in boxing history. In the March 1971 edition of *The Ring*, correspondent Dan Daniel wrote that it made more sense for the fight to be held at the Houston Astrodome because of its far greater seating capacity and friendlier tax statutes. "Texas has no law taxing profits from ancillary rights, such as closed-circuit TV and movies," the veteran journalist noted. However, Ali's camp favored the Garden because it had hosted the Bonavena fight and the New York State Boxing Commission was perhaps the most supportive of any governing body of Ali's right to possess a boxing license.

Each of the two participants absolutely needed the other for the fight to be the major attraction that it came to be. Thus, they both were paid equally. The remuneration for both men on March 8, 1971, would be staggering—a guaranteed flat fee of $2.5 million apiece regardless of how many tickets were sold at Madison Garden or at closed-circuit venues around the world. This was at a time when the male Wimbledon singles champion received a paltry £3,750 (and the female champion only half that sum) and Major League Baseball players were averaging $31,543 per year.

Because both men were being paid a flat rate, there was really no financial need for either of them to hype the fight—but Ali did it anyway in a way that was especially cruel. He seemed to revel in demeaning Frazier's appearance, intelligence, and ability to match him in verbal sparring exchanges. Frazier seethed about being mocked—and especially hated that he was disparagingly perceived in some segments of the black community as being a white man's black man. Undoubtedly, Ali was embraced by America's counterculture movement while Frazier was generally praised by "the establishment" as its champion. This was an interesting development because Frazier had grown up with far less material wealth than Ali had. Norman Mailer, in his coverage of the bout for *Life* magazine wrote, "Frazier had become the white man's fighter. Mr. Charley was rooting for Frazier, and that meant blacks were boycotting him in their heart. Mailer also added that Frazier "was twice as black as Clay and half has handsome [with] the rugged, decent life-worked face of a man who had labored in the pits all his life."

Both fighters concluded their respective training regimens on Saturday, March 6, with Ali finishing his workouts at Miami Beach, and with Frazier ending his in Philadelphia. Both combatants arrived in New York City on Sunday, March 7. Each went into seclusion to get optimum rest before their highly awaited showdown. The fight was scheduled to begin at 10:40 p.m. eastern time the following night.

For old-times' sake, Ali playfully offered to predict the round in which he would knock out Frazier. He said the end would come sometime in round six. Frazier laughed at the notion. Ali predicted he'd have a generally easy night with Smokin' Joe. "You don't understand," he told one British boxing reporter, "Frazier will be easier than Quarry or Bonavena. I'll just hold his head and I'll tell him, 'Come on, Champ.' I'll just play with him. He'll be trying all those short hooks and not reaching me and I'll be moving and saying, 'Come on, champ. You can do better than that!'"[15]

In his own interviews leading up to the fight, Frazier constantly referred to Ali as "Clay." When a reporter asked him why he did that, Frazier responded with a shrug, "That's what his mama named him!"[16] Clearly, Frazier was irked by Ali's jibes that were both personal and hurtful. He said, "Clay's a big guy but I've fought big guys before. Movers, too. He says I won't reach him but that's a broad statement. He will find the ring will get smaller and I will get bigger. I don't see the job taking more than 10 rounds. I'll be talking to Clay in there. I always talk in my fights and I've got something special to say to him after all this crap about me being an Uncle Tom."[17]

The fight was an event in every sense of the word. It had more than a bit of over-the-top showbiz glitz attached to it. The nearly 20,000 fans arriving at Madison Square Garden passed through a gigantic spotlight as if it were a lavish Hollywood premiere. The array of gaudy fashions was head-turning, according to a report that ran in the March 9 edition of the *Calgary Herald*.

> The spectators had come to see and be seen.
> The soul brothers and sisters, flamboyant in their minks and feathers, rubbed elbows with government chiefs, tycoons, sports heroes, and astronauts.
> City pants, leather suits, mink midi-coats, fancy boots, hats of all colors, shapes and sizes; fringed vests; cartridge belts; dresses; knickers and capes. It looked like an Easter Parade, only it was in the Garden rather than on Fifth Avenue.
> In fact, at times it was difficult to determine just what the gawkers inside the Garden were more interested in: the fighters or the fashions.
> One person they could not help noticing was Lupe Ladino of New York, a 22-year-old singer, who wore a bright orange fur chubby, orange pants and white leather boots with orange fur dangling from the tops.
> "The magnitude of the event merits dressing to the fullest in homage to Ali," said Leroy Nieman, the New York artist who specializes in athletes.

Frank Sinatra was there, tanned and toupeed, sitting beside Burt Lancaster, who looked just like he does at the movies.

Sinatra sat in a press chair next to ringside, snapping pictures of the fight, although no one seemed to know which news organization he represented.

Fans goggled as [New York City] mayor John V. Lindsay arrived with the Apollo XIV astronauts—Alan Shepard, Edgar Mitchell and Stuart Roosa.

Playboy publisher Hugh Hefner arrived with two bunnies—and his ever-present briar pipe.

Will Grimsley, a writer who had covered the fight game for years, was also struck by the colorful attire of the attendees. "It was a far cry from the old-time fight crowds—underworld characters and their flashily dressed molls occupying all the best seats," he noted, "and scarred old fight personalities with cauliflowered ears puffing away on black cigars. The Garden looked like a nesting haven for peacocks—male and female."[18]

There certainly was no shortage of celebrities from all walks of life. Even Colonel Harland Sanders, the face of the Kentucky Fried Chicken restaurant chain, was in attendance. He was wearing his famous white suit and string tie, of course. A Spanish bull-fighting champion, 34-year-old Manuel Benitez, was there too. He told reporters, "I'd prefer to fight Clay and Frazier together rather than a bull—if they wore handcuffs."[19] It was also noted that several delegates from the United Nations were present in their native attire. Another ticketholder in Madison Square Garden that night, attracting no attention whatsoever, was a future president of the United States: 24-year-old Donald Trump. He would become a major figure in Atlantic City's boxing promotions in the 1980s, but this night was the first time Trump ever attended a professional boxing match.

The fans at Madison Square Garden seemed to be more supportive of Frazier than Ali, but Ali's fans certainly seemed to be flashier and more passionate. One, Ann Hines of Pennsylvania, who was dressed in a velvet leopard ensemble, declared, "Muhammad Ali has to win." When asked to elaborate, she said, "Frazier is the black white hope, if you know what I mean."[20]

Passions were running high. There were several threats on Frazier's life that were forwarded to the New York City Police Department—who were already busy investigating general bomb scares at Madison Square Garden. Frazier's children were harassed and bullied at school. His family was receiving special police protection at his home because of threats that had been telephoned there. About 1,000 police personnel were on duty in or near the arena on the night of the fight. The Associated Press reported, "The building was combed from its catacombs to its rooftop prior to the big battle."[21]

In what must have been a bad omen for Ali, his little brother, Rahaman Ali (formerly known as Rudolph Valentino Clay), lost in one of the undercard bouts to Ireland's Dan McAlinden on a six-round majority decision. There were no knockdowns in the preliminary fight, but Ali's sibling was staggered several times by the Irishman. Rahaman Ali was only an occasional fighter, but he had won all seven of his previous professional bouts, dating back to 1964, before the March 8 loss. He had fought on the undercard in Miami Beach the night his brother defeated Sonny Liston for the world title—and also on the undercard of the infamous rematch in Lewiston, ME. Rahaman Ali had voluntarily suspended his own ring career during his brother's exile from boxing. He quit the ring following two successive losses in 1972. His pro record was 14–3–1. In 2015, Rahaman, who was born 18 months after his famous sibling, published his autobiography. It was titled *That's Muhammad Ali's Brother! My Life on the Undercard.*

In a piece for *The Ring* magazine, Jersey Jones noted that half a century earlier, the 1921 Dempsey-Carpentier fight was the first to exceed $1 million in revenues. Fifty years later, "in the Age of Aquarius," the Frazier-Ali tilt was expected to top $10 million with the closed-circuit television monies included. In fact, closed-circuit television revenues surpassed $18 million in the United States alone, with a ticket typically costing somewhere between $12 and $15 at most locales. Fans in New York City who could not get one of the 20,000 tickets for the live event at Madison Square Garden could attend screenings at the nearby Felt Forum or at Radio City Music Hall. Bing Crosby was quite content to watch the fight in this manner. "It's more comfortable this way,"[22] he stated to one reporter who was surprised to find him with the proletariat and not among the celebrity ticketholders at the Garden.

Personal comfort was certainly going to be an issue at some open-air closed-circuit venues. Bitter March evening temperatures fell upon Three Rivers Stadium in Pittsburgh and an outdoor amphitheater in Thunder Bay, Ontario. Nevertheless, both venues reported strong advance ticket sales. (In fact, about 5,500 hearty fans withstood 18-degree weather along with 30-mile-per-hour winds—and the threat of snow flurries—in Pittsburgh's new multi-purpose outdoor stadium. As it was the only closed-circuit venue in that city, boxing enthusiasts had to choose between freezing or missing out on sports history. Photos of Pittsburgh's dedicated but frigid fight fans appeared in many newspapers the next day.) Although the main event would start just before 4 a.m. in Great Britain, huge crowds were expected at the 33 closed-circuit venues there too. Ali had a huge following in that country—despite having a perfect 3–0 record against British heavyweights.

There were glitches at a couple of American closed-circuit theaters that angered unlucky patrons. Some 7,000 ticketholders at the Coliseum Arena South in Chicago saw and heard absolutely nothing from Madison Square Garden due to a major technical malfunction. The manager profusely apologized and politely told the audience to disperse. But when he announced that the patrons should check the local newspapers to find out how to get refunds, the crowd quickly became an angry mob. "We want it now! We want it now!" they roared. Police were summoned to squelch a riot. The gendarmes did not get there on time. By the time law enforcement arrived, chairs and windows were broken, the front door of the venue was ripped off, and the box office was smashed. Disappointment was met with greater civility elsewhere. Four minutes before the main event was to begin at a venue in Duluth, MN, the projector failed. The crowd assembled there could hear the description of the fight but there was no picture to watch. Everyone was offered a full refund. Absolutely no disturbances were reported in Duluth.

There was more trouble at a second Chicago closed-circuit venue that had nothing to do with any sort of broadcast difficulties. About 1,000 hopeful last-minute ticket-seekers were turned away because the 13,000-seat locale was completely sold out. The latecomers vented their frustrations by throwing bottles and rocks at the building's windows. Somehow there were no arrests made at either trouble spot in Chicago.

At one closed-circuit theater in Tampa, FL, one of the 7,100 excited fans had decidedly mixed emotions about the fight. "I'm betting heavily on Clay," he noted, "but I hope he loses. I have a kid in Vietnam right now. They [the American soldiers stationed there] don't think much of a guy who won't put on a uniform. I hope Frazier nails him, but if he doesn't, I'll get $3,000 out of it."[23] The man's assessment was only partially accurate. Reports from Vietnam said the troops, who were anxiously listening to accounts of the bout free of charge on Armed Forces Radio, were generally split in their allegiances based on American geographic and ethnic lines. Many black draftees from urban America were pulling for an Ali triumph.

At that same Tampa venue, one of the few female attendees holding a cherished ticket condensed what she was watching into very simplistic terms. "It's the good versus the evil," she noted with authority. "Frazier's the good; Clay's the evil. Somebody has got to win. I don't really care who. I just want to see some action."[24] Another man, who identified himself as a local electrician, started to wonder if the $15 price of admission was too much—even for the most anticipated prize fight of all time. "I don't know why I paid this kind of money. I'm probably nuts. The darn thing will probably be over by the third round. But, hey, if it's a good [fight] I want to be here."[25] Another fan told reporter Larry Hug of the *St. Petersburg Evening Independent* his ticket was purely an impulse buy. "Heck, I wasn't even going to go," he admitted, "but when I walked by tonight and saw the line, I just followed it in."[26]

Perhaps the most thoughtful patron whom Hug interviewed was an unnamed male University of Tampa student who believed that more than just the undisputed world heavyweight championship was on the line. He surmised that the future of professional boxing could very well hang in the balance too. "If it's a good fight, people will come back to boxing," he said. "But if it isn't, the sport may die. I came here to see how it would turn out."[27]

Many fans on the night of the fight discovered that not only was there no live radio or free television coverage of the fight, but there was also no nearby closed-circuit venue for them to attend either. The sports editor of the *Schenectady Gazette* reported an unceasing and increasingly frantic stream of telephone inquiries from local fight enthusiasts about where they could watch the bout. He had to tell them there were no closed-circuit screenings in either Schenectady or Utica. The closest location was in distant Albany.

Despite some technical glitches and underserviced areas, on March 8, 1971, closed-circuit boxing telecasts had proven their mettle to draw vast sums of money from a public quite willing to pay it. After the fight, Bob Chick, the sports editor of the *St. Petersburg Evening Independent,* saw it as a potentially worrisome trend. "It's purely academic whether [the Ali-Frazier bout] was worth $15 to see," he wrote. "Maybe it was and the door might now be opened to other sporting events. What's to stop promoters, for example, of baseball's World Series or football's Super Bowl to try the same medium?"[28]

Texans who lived in the Rio Grande Valley got a pleasant surprise when they surfed through their television channels that Monday evening. Their cable TV provider was showing the fight free of charge—albeit with Spanish-speaking announcers calling the action. It was the result of a quirky bilingual programming setup. The bout was carried by satellite to Mexico City. The Valley Cable Television Network relayed it to Monterrey, Mexico—which beamed various Mexican television programs into the Rio Grande Valley. One happened to be the Spanish-language feed of the bout from Madison Square Garden. Word of the unexpected boon spread quickly throughout the region. "I don't care a hang about the commentary," said one delighted viewer, "I just want to see the fight."[29]

Veteran boxing announcer, 62-year-old Don Dunphy, who had been calling fights on both radio and television since 1941, was the main voice working the closed-circuit telecast. He was seated alongside boxing great Archie Moore and Hollywood actor Burt Lancaster. (At the time, show business folks routinely served as color commentators at closed-circuit boxing events. More often than not, they added little to the broadcasts.) Dunphy knew that movie stars did not necessarily make good sports announcers. Lancaster was supposed to provide color commentary during the action, but Dunphy, who was mild-mannered by nature, vetoed that idea. "I'm working these rounds solo,"[30] he politely told the closed-circuit producers. "Burt Lancaster can talk between rounds." It was a philosophy he firmly believed in until the end of his days. In a 1996 interview, when he was 88 years old, Dunphy stated, "When two or three people do blow-by-blow, they over-talk and emphasize too much."[31] Dunphy would eventually be enshrined in ten different sports halls of fame, but on this night of nights, Dunphy had his impartiality questioned during the bout—a fight that he would always fondly refer to as "the greatest sports event of all time."[32]

Ali entered the ring wearing dark red boxing trunks with white vertical stripes up the sides—one of the few times in his professional career that he wore anything other than predominantly white ones. Frazier's trunks were an odd shade of fluorescent green with yellow stripes and waistband. Both fighters' shorts displayed the classic Everlast logo. Frazier's cornermen (Yancey Durham and Eddie Futch) were similarly decked out in green shirts that proclaimed in large letters on the back "Joe Frazier World Champion." Referee Arthur Mercante called Ali and Frazier to the center of the ring and gave the two men their final instructions. He reminded them of the neutral-corner rule and that three knockdowns in a single round would automatically end the fight, according to New York State's boxing rules. Without further ado, the "Fight of the Century" began. An estimated 300 million people around the world had anxiously tuned in for the high drama.

Round one had Ali relying on his probing left jab while Frazier plodded forward in his usual aggressive style. Ali scored well with his left, but he missed the bobbing champion's head with power punches. Frazier landed three good left hooks in the opening round. Each one struck Ali with a thud, but they each elicited a scornful and dismissive shake of the head from the recipient who was trying to convince both Frazier and the sellout crowd that the Philadelphia fighter had not hurt him. Ali fought more flat-footed that fans were expecting. Don Dunphy opined that Ali was playing a dangerous game if he planned on standing still and trading punches with Smokin' Joe.

"The Muhammad Ali that we remember from three years ago was a dancer, but he's not dancing tonight. He may be trying to slug with Joe." That was the first comment Dunphy made a few seconds into the second round. Just as Dunphy made that remark, Ali caught Frazier with a solid left jab and a strong right cross. Seconds later Frazier rattled Ali with a straight right and a left hook that appeared to land just under Ali's chin. "We have a real Pier Six bout here," Dunphy said. Ali did most of the scoring, but the best punch of the round was a solid left hook by Frazier in the dying seconds. Again, Ali shook his head. Thus far it had been two fast-paced rounds of intense, crowd-pleasing action. It was a small sample size on which to judge an entire 15-round fight, but Dunphy confidently said, "This fight, so far, ranks with the great ones."

At one point in the second round, referee Mercante cautioned both fighters against talking to one another. Under New York State's rules, a boxer is not supposed to chat with an opponent during a fight—but it is a prohibition that is seldom, if ever, seriously enforced. Over the course of the fight Mercante periodically warned both Ali and Frazier a few times to cut out the rhetoric, but to no avail. "There was a lot of ghetto talk out there," Frazier told newsmen after the fight. "He was saying he was going to kill me. I just said, 'I'll do the same to you.'"[33] According to Frazier, the most interesting verbal exchange in the bout came during a clinch. Ali said to him, "Don't you know I'm God?"[34] Frazier shrugged and retorted, "Well, God, you're gonna get whupped tonight!" After the fight, Frazier claimed that Ali had angrily said to him, "I'm going to kill you, nigger!"[35] Frazier said he definitely wanted an apology from Ali for that particular remark.

Just before the third round was to begin, Frazier spat into a bucket in his corner. Blood was evident; he had suffered a cut inside his mouth. Undaunted, Frazier continued on the offensive in the third frame. Although Ali continued to land frequently with counterpunches, Frazier did have success with punishing body shots and left hooks to Ali's face. Frazier landed a strong left hook with about ten seconds remaining in the round and followed it with a good flurry to Ali's midsection. "Frazier is relentless," declared Burt Lancaster during the break between rounds three and four. "He's a little man, but he's a Sherman tank. He keeps moving in." Nevertheless, when Ali went to his corner, before he sat on his stool, he dramatically raised his arms skyward to indicate he thought he was doing well.

"Neither fighter has ever faced the quality of opposition he is facing tonight. There is no question of that," Dunphy told his vast audience as round four began. The crowd was already in a frenzy. The excitement was too much for one unnamed patron at Madison Square Garden. Afterwards arena officials confirmed a report that one spectator had died from a heart attack during the compelling main event.

In round four, the pace was a tad slower than it had been in the first three rounds. Dunphy thought that the frenetic opening of the bout was already sapping the two combatants' strength. Ali again fared well keeping Frazier away with his jab, but Frazier landed the best punch of the fight. Again the outstanding blow was a hard left hook, as he took control of the final 30 seconds of the stanza. The pattern of the early rounds was clear: Ali was landing blows more frequently, but Frazier was scoring with the more powerful shots by far—but they were fewer in number. It was becoming an interesting fight to score.

The fifth round was something of a turning point in the fight. Ali, at the advice of his cornerman Angelo Dundee, came out of his corner with more movement, dancing and jabbing as if it were 1966. After Ali landed a quick one-two combination, Frazier laughed at him and dropped his hands. When Ali attempted to hit him again, Frazier deftly bobbed his head out of the way. To anyone familiar with Ali's career, it was clear that Frazier had turned the tables and was using Ali's style of showmanship against him. Frazier again rocked Ali with a solid left hook. Dunphy was impressed with Frazier's uncharacteristic show of bravado but thought he was playing with fire by exposing his chin to Ali. "I think [Frazier] is trying to psyche him out," Archie Moore stated between rounds. Burt Lancaster added, "I think Frazier has kept a lot of anger against Muhammad Ali in his heart; now he's going to make him pay for it."

Round six was the round that Ali predicted Frazier would succumb to a knockout punch. He never came close to administering it. Instead Frazier mounted a terrific offensive. Early in the frame he belted Ali with two vicious left hooks seconds apart. Ali was clearly on the defensive. He tried to keep Frazier at a safe distance by holding his left arm straight out. Ali was now instigating clinches and languishing on the ropes. It was Frazier's best round of the fight and it was, perhaps, the first one the champion had clearly captured. "Ali was trying to hold [Frazier] off with cute little tricks," Lancaster noted. "It wasn't working." The crowd was especially vocal when the bell clanged to end the frame. Dunphy agreed that Frazier's overall aggressiveness throughout the first six rounds would certainly benefit him in the judges' eyes.

"This has to be perhaps the most torrid heavyweight championship fight ever," said Dunphy—who had called a great many of them in his 30 years at the microphone. Dunphy made this remark a few seconds into round seven when Frazier was pursuing Ali, driving him to the ropes, and working him over at close quarters. Frazier seemed the fresher of the two. Archie Moore debunked a suggestion by Dunphy that Frazier was perhaps exhausting himself (in boxing parlance, "punching himself out.") For the third time in the fight referee Mercante warned Ali about one of his crafty tricks: In clinches Ali would put his right glove behind Frazier's head and yank it forward. The ploy was designed to tire Frazier as the champion would impulsively expend energy trying to resist the maneuver. Mercante was doing a very good job as third man in the ring. Ali fared better in the seventh round than he did in the fifth or sixth. His punches, while moving backwards, consistently landed more often than Frazier's awkward offensive thrusts. Toward the end of the frame, Ali deliberately positioned himself in a neutral corner and dropped his hands, daring Frazier to try to land a haymaker—and enticing the champion to burn even more energy. Frazier instead chose to focus on Ali's midsection. At the end of the round, Ali waved his right hand contemptuously at Frazier. Between rounds he acknowledged a chant of "Ali! Ali!" that came from his vocal supporters.

"Both men are in splendid condition; great athletes," said Dunphy as the bell rang for round eight. Both men were eager to do battle and came to the center of the ring before the bell. Mercante had to step between them.

Frazier motioned for Ali to engage him rather than run. Frazier continued his attacking ways as Ali fought in retreat. "I don't know anyone who gets the sheer joy of combat the way Joe Frazier does," Dunphy stated. It was a strange round. At one point the fans booed during a weird exchange. Ali laid on the ropes with his hands down and invited Frazier to attack him. Frazier moved in but again opted to go for Ali's body, mostly with light taps. Ali respond with equally harmless jabs to Frazier's head. "Those pity-pat punches aren't going to do much for anybody," said a puzzled Dunphy. Frazier finally tired of the silly sequence. He grabbed Ali by his waist with both hands and flung him into the center of the ring where he preferred to do battle. Between rounds, a chant of "Joe! Joe!" echoed around Madison Square Garden.

Round nine saw a definite improvement in action over the previous three minutes. Ali scored with numerous jabs, but Frazier, as he had done so often in the first eight rounds, made good use of his left hook. After one particularly solid blow from Frazier, Dunphy said that he thought Ali was in serious trouble. Seconds later, however, Ali responded with a jolting combination of his own and looked to have gained a second wind. Archie Moore, who sensed that Ali was tiring far more rapidly than Frazier, called the ninth "a desperation round for Ali." For what it was worth, Burt Lancaster concurred. "I think Muhammad Ali summoned great reserve just as it seemed he might be going out," Dunphy added. "It's been a great fight."

Between rounds nine and ten, Frazier's corner instructed their man to change tactics: He was to avoid fighting in the center of the ring and instead rough up Ali on the ropes. When Ali had space to operate he was doing his best work. If that space were neutralized, Frazier's brawling style would take its toll on Ali. Frazer now had a lump above his left eye. Ali looked to be the more tired of the two men, but still scored with stinging jabs whenever Frazier gave him punching room. For most of the round, Ali had his back against the ropes. Frazier was scoring with the more spectacular blows, but Ali was still accumulating points with jabs and shorter power punches. Dunphy noted that Ali was instigating the clinches which would likely work against him in the scoring. With two-thirds of the fight over, it was still either man's to win— but Frazier seemed the fitter fighter at the end of round ten.

Shortly after round 11 began, Ali fell to the canvas, but referee Mercante quite properly ruled it to be a slip. Frazier pinned Ali to the ropes, and, in a scene reminiscent of round eight, the two men exchanged soft punches with one another. Suddenly, though, Frazier's vaunted left hook found the mark on Ali's jaw. Ali was clearly staggered and nearly slid down the ropes. Ali now backpedaled to buy himself time to recover. Frazier pursued Ali but his attack was both clumsy and wild. He did score with one further hard left hook, but he may have missed his golden chance to score a knockout as Ali survived the onslaught. He was shaky but had lasted the round. After 11 grueling rounds, Frazier now seemed to be in complete control of the fight. Between rounds Angelo Dundee strongly chastised Ali for being careless and getting caught with the powerful Frazier left hook.

Sensing a possible kill, Frazier sprung from his corner at the start of the 12th round and went into attack mode. He knew no other way to fight. Frazier landed several heavy shots, but Ali managed to admirably respond with some solid counter blows of his own. "This may be a tough fight to score," Dunphy cautioned his audience. By the end of round 12, however, the right side of Ali's jaw was noticeably swollen—the cumulative effect of absorbing so many of Frazier's potent left hooks. At one point, Frazier morphed into Ali and eluded his adversary's blows by simply standing still and ducking under them. Frazier also laughed at the badly tiring Ali who could not manage to connect with any meaningful punches. Still, Burt Lancaster commended Ali for making a good show in round 12 after badly losing round 11. "Ali is certainly disproving any doubt that he's not a game fighter," the actor said.

Round 13 saw Ali fare better with jabs and combinations in the center of the ring as Frazier attacked him ineffectively. "He's boxing beautifully for a tired man," Dunphy said. As Ali seemed to be winning the round Dunphy also noted that "Frazier let him get away after that big eleventh round." As they exchanged vicious flurries while Ali was on the ropes, Dunphy said with admiration, "They're fighting like lightweights now." Frazier landed a series of body shots that made the crowd gasp. "The tide turns the other way now!" marveled Dunphy. "If Frazier stays on top of Ali, Ali has no punching room." When the bell sounded Burt Lancaster was quick to praise the champion's obvious mettle. "I think [Frazier] has got more power and stamina than anyone I've ever seen."

Dan Daniel, who had seen every major heavyweight title bout since the days of the Jack Dempsey-Gene Tunney tilts, saw the fight as a slow but steady progression in Frazier's favor: "Round after round the conviction fastened itself on the experts that Clay was being beaten. They weren't fooled by his play-acting, by his head-shaking denials of injury and pain whenever he was hit hard, by spending so much time backed against the ropes, mainly for periods of rest, by his repeated futile sticking out of his left and whirling it under Joe's nose. Clay used his advantage in reach of 6½ inches to some purpose, but not importantly."[36]

At the start of round 14, Frazier continued to set the pace by advancing forward and putting pressure on Ali. It turned out to be a good round for Ali, however, as he connected with several solid blows and continued to pepper Frazier's face with rapid-fire jabs as he moved sideways and backwards. Don Dunphy noted the swelling around both of Frazier's eyes from the accumulation of blows. "For a man who was virtually out on his feet in round eleven, Ali has come back amazingly," declared Lancaster.

When the bell sounded for round 15, referee Mercante had both fighters touch gloves. It was a gesture not required by the rules, but it was an apt sign of respect and sportsmanship wholly fitting a memorable and well-fought battle. Ali fired a few jabs. Joe relentlessly plodded forward. The two men fell into a clinch on the ropes near Frazier's corner. Mercante ordered a break. The fighters obliged and stepped apart. Ali moved to his left and had his back to the ropes again. Frazier pursued him.

About 25 seconds into the final round, Frazier bobbed and rose from his crouch, firing a picture-perfect left hook. It crashed onto Ali's swollen jaw and sent him to the canvas for just the third time in his career. A roar ripped through Madison Square Garden. Ali was up by the count of four, but under New York State's boxing rules he was required to take a mandatory eight count before continuing. "The crowd, needless to say, is in a bedlam," Dunphy proclaimed.

Frazier tried for a knockout. Twice he landed solid blows to Ali's head and he continued to work the ex-champion's midsection. Ali responded well enough to survive, but he was now clearly hanging on, hoping to endure to the final bell. "Muhammad Ali has never taken such a battering," said Dunphy. Ali gamely tried to mount a last-minute offensive—and did score with a flurry or two—but he was a spent fighter. So was Frazier. Both men went into a prolonged clinch with about 30 seconds to go. When the final bell sounded, Frazier chirped at Ali and raised his hands in victory as his seconds rushed out to congratulate him. In contrast, Ali trudged disconsolately to his corner. His body language plainly indicated that he expected to be on the losing end of the decision. It was impossible for fans at the arena or those watching in theaters to see, but some news reports claimed Ali was so disappointed that he was sobbing in his corner.

Don Dunphy urged fans to remember that the scoring in New York was on the rounds system and that the outcome was in doubt, despite Frazier winning the 11th and 15th rounds decisively. In the postmortem of the fight Dunphy was the target of some criticism by Frazier fans and television critics for appearing to root for Ali, and for making the case that he should get the decision.

The usual post-fight chaos occurred in the ring. Numerous reporters and photographers charged in before police and security could stop them. Other interlopers joined them milling about. Somewhere and somehow in the crowd of humanity, Madison Square Garden's longtime ring announcer, Johnny Addie, managed to collect the judges' scorecards. (This night was Addie's last hurrah. By year's end he would be dead at age 69. A stockbroker by trade, Addie, a widower, had been the public-address man for more than 100 world championship bouts.) Addie announced the verdict: Frazier had won the bout by a fairly comfortable unanimous decision: The judges' scores were (Arthur Mercante) 8-6-1, (Artie Aidala) 9-6, and (Bill Recht) 11-4. Recht's scoring seemed a little one-sided to most neutral observers, even to many Frazier fans. For what it was worth, the Associated Press scored the fight 9-5-1 for Frazier. The verdict settled the biggest debate in all of sports. As the AP noted, "The decision finally put to rest the controversy over ownership of the world title which was taken from Ali 43 months ago when he refused military induction."[37]

Dan Daniel, who was no fan of Ali because of the fighter's religion and military issues, nevertheless praised the vanquished pugilist. Daniel wrote in the May 1971 edition of *The Ring*, "If there had been any question about Clay's gameness and ability to take punishment, it was dissipated completely. Some of the outstanding titleholders and contenders of the past would have wilted under Frazier's attack."[38] Daniel scored the bout (unofficially, of course) in Frazier's favor by nine rounds to six.

Jim Coleman, a notable Canadian sport journalist, believed Frazier had won the bout convincingly—and he was thoroughly delighted by the fight's outcome. He cackled in his syndicated story the following day.

> Joe Frazier knocked the Muhammad Ali out of Cassius Marcellus Clay last night. Frazier hammered Yon Cassius all the way from hell to breakfast—and Clay was lucky to escape with nothing worse than a trip to the hospital where surgeons and structural engineers conducted exhaustive tests to ascertain whether his head was still attached to his torso.
>
> Frazier, who has consistently refused to refer to Clay by his adopted Black Muslim name, did something which no other man has been able to accomplish: he silenced Clay by stuffing a left down Cassius' throat. If the surgeons wish to take an encore after operating on Clay's jaw today, they can borrow a plumber's plunger and then can attempt to recover Frazier's left glove from Cassius' esophagus.[39]

Ali disagreed with the decision, of course, but he was not sticking around to discuss it. Bundini Brown fielder reporters' questions in Ali's stead. When asked about Ali's determination to fight hard until the final bell, Brown said, "No soldier quits in the foxhole."[40] Dan Daniel was appalled by the military reference and denounced Bundini's thoughtless comment "as a real rock."[41]

In the wild hype leading up to the fight, Ali had vowed, if he were to lose, that he would crawl across the ring to Frazier's corner and proclaim him to be the greatest. That did not happen. Ali was taken to a hospital immediately after the bout to have the severely swollen right side of his jaw examined. X-rays showed it was not broken, despite some news agencies saying it was. It was merely a very prominent hematoma. Five days after the fight, Ali appeared live on *ABC's Wide World of Sports* to discuss the bout with Howard Cosell. His jaw was still very much swollen.

"[Ali] underestimated me," Frazier cockily crowed. "He thought I was flat-footed and slow, but I showed him. It feels great to be the undisputed champion of the world. I beat everyone they threw in front of me and I can't do anything more."[42]

After the fight Frazier looked more worse for wear than Ali did, however. Still, the undisputed champion was in a jovial mood and joked with reporters, "Let me go clean up my face; I'm not this ugly." Frazier himself spent time in and out of hospitals during the ensuing month. Apart from needing recuperation time from the grueling fight, Frazier, it was reported, was also suffering from hypertension and a kidney infection. (Frazier was forced to miss the *ABC's Wide World of Sports* recap of the fight on March 13 because he was reportedly stricken with the flu.)

Many members of the print and broadcast media still referred to Ali as Clay despite his protestations about the issue. A UPI story that ran on the front page of the *Bangor Daily News* under the banner headline "Frazier Retains Title, Decisions Cassius Clay" thoroughly reveled in Frazier's big victory. It declared,

> Joe Frazier buried a myth to remove the only stain on his world heavyweight crown, laying the ghost of Cassius Clay to rest with a vicious barrage of left hooks that smashed the challenger's jaw and dumped him to the canvas in the fifteenth round for a unanimous 15-round decision.
>
> While 300 million [people] watched around the world, the 27-year-old Frazier finally caught up with the man who had taunted and teased him from outside the ring for four years.
>
> In the eleventh round, the 29-year-old Clay fell apart, and in the last round the myth came to an end as Clay was bashed to the canvas and his face was swollen almost beyond recognition from the barrage.
>
> Staggering from the power of the punches chopping in at him, Clay was lucky to last until the final bell. No dancing steps came to him anymore and he was left sobbing with remorse on the ropes he became a mere punching bag for the man he had hoped to playfully torture.

The *St. Petersburg Evening Independent,* whose sports editor also was clearly no fan of the vanquished fighter, concocted a truly awful pun as a headline for its March 9 sports section: "Clay Crumbled: Defeat Not Up His Ali." The article on the fight gleefully referred to Ali as "the loudmouthed idol of millions" who had his "runaway tongue silenced by a battered jaw."

Frazier's victory was not enough to satisfy one particular Muhammad Ali hater, 66-year-old newspaper magnate William Loeb. The ultraconservative Loeb was so disgusted by Ali's refusal to be drafted that he refused to accept any advertising pertaining to the closed-circuit screenings for the Ali-Frazier contest. He also imposed a "no Clay news" blackout in his papers. Any and all news stories that even mentioned Ali—or Cassius Clay, as Loeb preferred to call him—were not allowed to run in his publications. Thus, no news of the big fight whatsoever appeared in any of the Loeb-owned newspapers on March 9. This extreme action prompted the resignation of David James, the managing editor of the *St. Albans Messenger*. He accused Loeb of "suppression of the news" and "press censorship."

At several closed-circuit venues, an unexpected phenomenon was reported: Some fans who had begun the fight rooting for Ali had, by the end of the match, switched their allegiances to Frazier. Why? It was difficult to determine. Perhaps it was a case of Frazier winning them over by his gritty performance or they simply wanted to be associated with a winner.

Ali skipped the post-fight media conference. He went to the hospital instead. "We'll be back, and this time there won't be three years between fights," loyal Ali soldier Drew (Bundini) Brown said in the defeated man's stead. "You can't put a car in the garage for three years and expect it not to have a few kinks." When Bundini was asked if Ali planned to retire, he defiantly shook his head. "We're already setting the traps [for the next time],"[43] he insisted.

Ali tried industriously to work his way back into title contention. He fought often and in varied locales, becoming a world traveler with fights in Jakarta, Dublin, Vancouver, and other centers not necessarily associated with pro boxing. Whether he meant to do it or not, Ali was becoming a citizen of the world—and the world loved him for it.

Next time for Ali-Frazier would have to be sometime in the future. Frazier took the rest of 1971 off, but he had two easy title defenses in 1972. Terry Daniels was knocked out in four rounds in New Orleans in January. Four months later Ron Stander was knocked out, also in four rounds, in Omaha. Frazier's next defense of his world heavyweight championship was on January 22, 1973, in Kingston, Jamaica versus 1968 Olympic heavyweight champion George Foreman.

Foreman, a huge, powerful and downright scary puncher, entered the fight with a 37–0 record. He blew Frazier away in two rounds, utterly manhandling Smokin' Joe. Frazier was brutally decked six times in a fight reminiscent of the 1919 Dempsey-Willard clash in Toledo. Boxing is largely a question of styles—and Frazier's head-first attacking style was tailor made for Foreman's frightening raw power. Arthur Mercante, who had capably refereed the epic Ali-Frazier fight two years earlier, looked terribly confused and indecisive in Kingston. He allowed Frazier to take a horrible beating well after the bout should have been stopped. Ali, who was on the comeback trail with ten straight victories, watched the Frazier-Foreman bout in horror. He figured a potential $5 million rematch with Frazier had just gone down the drain. Two months later, Ali suffered a more direct setback by losing a split decision to Ken Norton. Ali barely eked out a victory over Norton in a return engagement six months later. Thus, by January 28, 1974, when Ali and Frazier clashed for a second time, it was not for the world championship. It was basically to decide which one would remain as a viable heavyweight contender.

Ali emerged with a hard-fought victory, boxing better than he did in 1971. He seemed more purposeful—and Frazier seemed weaker than he had in their first bout. Jeff Samuels of the *Pittsburgh Press* noted,

> Fighting about as well as any man 32 years old should be expected to fight, Ali won a unanimous decision over Joe Frazier, the man who beat him three years ago in a classic battle which was to send each man on a sudden downhill skid.
>
> But Ali made it stunningly obvious last night that he is not nearly as far downhill as the world had believed.
>
> "Do I look anything like I'm 32?" Ali shouted to a horde of reporters after his dramatic victory.

The judges' scores were 8–4, 7–4–1, and 6–5–1. The third score was submitted by referee Tony Perez who did not have a great night. In the second round, Ali had staggered Frazier but was prevented from pursuing him by Perez who wrongly believed the round had ended. Most observers also felt the score on his ballot, based on the action in the ring, was too close.

A victory over a fading Joe Frazier was one thing. Few boxing observers believed Ali could defeat George Foreman, however. Two months after Ali-Frazier II, Foreman demolished Ken Norton in two rounds in Caracas, Venezuela. Thus, Foreman had crushed the two men who had defeated Ali. When Ali signed to fight Foreman that autumn in Kinshasa, Zaire, he was a 3:1 underdog. Both Foreman and Ali were promised $5 million purses guaranteed by the Zairian government. (The fact that Zaire was a brutal dictatorship in 1974, whose leader, Mobutu Sese Seko, had introduced Gestapo-like secret police to Africa, did not seem to bother anyone in the boxing community.) In previewing the fight, Howard Cosell—a staunch supporter of Ali for more than a decade—figured Foreman would send Ali into ignominious retirement with a kayo loss.

Nevertheless, in one of boxing's great upsets, Ali knocked out Foreman in the eighth round to win the world heavyweight title for the second time, equaling the feat of Floyd Patterson. The way in which Ali defeated Foreman made his victory all the more stunning. After boxing and moving during the first round, which was what everyone expected, Ali retreated to the ropes for most of the next seven rounds and allowed Foreman to flail away at him. It seemed like a foolhardy strategy against someone who possessed the punching power that Foreman did, but Ali blocked the majority of Foreman's blows and calculated that the champion would exhaust himself in the humid conditions. By late in round eight, Foreman had spent his energy. A flurry of shots from Ali sent Foreman to the canvas where he failed to beat referee Zach Clayton's count. If it had not already been established, the legend of Muhammad Ali became permanently etched into sports history with his "rope-a-dope" victory in Zaire. Perhaps he was The Greatest, as he had been claiming for a decade.

Of course a rubber match with Frazier was necessary. It came on October 1, 1975, in the Philippines. Even though Ali had said he would retire when he beat Foreman—not if, but when—he reneged on his promise and kept active. Challengers Chuck Wepner, Ron Lyle and Joe Bugner all fell in 1975 without too much resistance before Ali-Frazier III occurred. When it finally came, it was perhaps a better contest than their first encounter in 1971.

Ali-Frazier III—quickly dubbed by fawning reporters as "the Thrilla in Manila"—completed the trilogy perfectly. In their first meeting, Frazier was the defending champion. In their second bout neither man held the title. Ali was the titleholder in the final installment. The bout produced 14 rounds of brutal give and take before Frazier's chief second, Eddie Futch, surrendered with one round to go as Frazier could no longer see well enough to continue. Ali was too exhausted to even rise from his stool to accept congratulations. It had been a war—a tremendously sapping and entertaining brawl that weakened the two men forever.

"I still reign supreme," Ali managed to tell reporters after the taxing contest. "I told you I was the greatest. Didn't I tell you I was superior?" Later a more pensive Ali stated, "What you saw tonight was something next to death. I almost quit after the tenth round. But I am the champion—and champions don't quit." Ali then added, "Joe Frazier is the toughest man in the world. He is the greatest champion of all-time—outside of me."[44]

Both men should have retired after Manila, but neither fighter did. Eight months after losing to Ali, Frazier endured one more ruthless pounding from George Foreman in an ill-advised comeback attempt in 1976. Five years later, at age 37, he tried again, fighting to a majority draw with a journeyman pugilist named Jumbo Cummings in Chicago. Frazier retired with a record of 32-4-1. His only losses came against Foreman and Ali (two apiece). Coincidentally, Frazier's final bout occurred just nine days before Ali's last fight.

In the 1980s, Frazier managed his son, Marvis, in his professional boxing career. Father and son appeared together on the June 1, 1981, cover of *Sports Illustrated* alongside the caption "A Chip Off the Old Champ." That was a bit of a stretch. Marvis compiled a 19-2 record as a pro. Unfortunately, Smokin' Joe Frazier's son is most often remembered for two defeats. Both were spectacular one-round losses—one to Larry Holmes in a 1983 world heavyweight title bout, and one to soon-to-be champion Mike Tyson in 1986. The latter bout lasted just 30 brutal seconds.

Ali continued to defend his world heavyweight crown beyond 1975, but he looked utterly dismal on a couple of occasions. Two of his decision wins—in an exciting third bout versus Ken Norton and snoozer versus light-hitting

Jimmy Young—were blatant gifts from the judges. Ali was finally dethroned as world champion on February 15, 1978, by 1976 Olympic gold medalist Leon Spinks, a man who had fought fewer than ten bouts as a professional. On September 15, 1978, Ali won his last pro fight by beating Spinks on a decision before an adoring packed house at the vast Louisiana Superdome in New Orleans. That victory made him the three-time linear world heavyweight champion. He retired shortly thereafter. Somehow with the passage of time, Muhammad Ali, the counterculture icon, had been transformed into an all-American hero. Joe Frazier was in attendance that memorable night as a paid performer: He sang the national anthem before the main event!

But the allure of the ring and its seven-figure paydays and public attention tempted Ali again. At a specially constructed outdoor arena at Caesars Palace in Las Vegas, Ali was battered ceaselessly and methodically by new champion Larry Holmes on October 2, 1980. The bout is painful to watch for anyone who remembered Muhammad Ali in his glory days. The 38-year-old Ali lost every round badly. For the only time in his professional career, Ali lost a bout by technical knockout when Angelo Dundee mercifully would not permit him to come out for the 11th round—much like Eddie Futch would not let Joe Frazier continue in Manila five years before. In calling the fight, Howard Cosell lamented that the great Ali could not escape the laws of physiology and that even he could not be "forever young."

Yet that one-sided shellacking did not finally persuade Ali to quit. It took a decision win by Trevor Berbick over the 39-year-old ex-champion in the Bahamas on December 11, 1981, to finally send Ali into a sensible retirement with a record of 56–5. Three of those losses came when Ali was long past his prime. One can only speculate how much the last two losses of his career affected his long-term health. As early as 1977 Ali's speech was slowing. By 1984, at age 42, Ali, now a beloved national figure, had been diagnosed with Parkinson's syndrome. Within a short time, Ali—who had once been invited to lecture on poetry at Oxford—lost the ability to verbally communicate swiftly. He became a prisoner within his own body. The last 32 years of his life saw him descend more and more into helplessness.

Ali and Frazier had something of a mercurial relationship from 1971 onward. At times Frazier seemed to be on friendly terms with Ali, only to suddenly criticize him for the cruel insults he had been subjected to in the past. He especially resented Ali frequently referring to him as a "gorilla." Ali would issue occasional public apologies for having stepped beyond the boundaries of good taste, but Frazier was often dissatisfied with them because he was only getting the message second-hand. To many people's amazement, Joe Frazier was the final surprise guest on the British *This is Your Life* program that honored Muhammad Ali in late 1978. He made the trip to London, spoke highly of Ali, and the two old rivals embraced warmly. Ali was thrilled and

March 8, 1971—Muhammad Ali vs. Joe Frazier

shocked simultaneously. "How did you get Joe Frazier over here?" he marveled over and over.

Joe Frazier passed away before Ali did. He died under hospice care at age 67 on November 7, 2011. Most of Frazier's ring earnings had disappeared through a series of mismanaged investments, financial naivete, and unchecked generosity. Toward the end of his life he was living in a small apartment in Philadelphia above a gym he operated. He had suffered from high blood pressure and diabetes for many years, but liver cancer was the official cause of Frazier's death. "The world has lost a great champion. I will always remember Joe with respect and admiration,"[45] said Ali in a prepared statement upon hearing the news. He attended the private funeral of the man he often called his greatest adversary.

Journalist Richard Goldstein wrote of the deceased champion, "Frazier could never match Ali's charisma or his gift for the provocative quote. He was essentially a man devoted to a brutal craft, willing to give countless hours to his spartan training-camp routine and unsparing of his body inside the ring."[46]

Ali himself retreated more and more into seclusion with each passing year. He would still make occasional appearances on television shows and at public events, but it was sad for his longtime fans to see him age ungracefully. Nevertheless, he still received high honors. At the 1996 Summer Olympics in Atlanta, Ali, shaking from the effects of his disease, dramatically lit the torch at the opening ceremony and was specially honored during halftime of the men's gold-medal basketball game. (He was given a new gold medal to replace the one from 1960 that had been mislaid.) In 2000 he was voted Athlete of the Century in Great Britain in a national poll conducted by the BBC. In a field of five nominees, Ali received more votes than the other four finalists combined. He was awarded the Presidential Medal of Freedom by George W. Bush in November 2005. His last noteworthy public appearance was at the 2012 London Olympics where he was seen at the Opening ceremonies. The 70-year-old former champion did not look well at all. Some British bookmakers were offering odds that he would light the torch again as he had done 16 years earlier, but he did not. He was too frail.

When Muhammad Ali's life came to an end at age 74 on June 3, 2016, as a result of septic shock following a respiratory illness, it was headline news for days. His passing was the most trended topic in social media, proving that Ali had transcended generations. Obituary writers had difficulty summing up what Ali had meant to boxing, to sports in general, and to the world. Britain's newspaper *The Guardian* described the late champion thusly: "Muhammad Ali, who has died aged 74, was acclaimed by many as the greatest world heavyweight boxing champion the world has ever seen. He was certainly the most charismatic boxer. His courage inside and outside the ring and his verbal taunting of opponents were legendary, as were his commitment to justice and his efforts for the sick and underprivileged."

Although Ali had resided in Arizona during his final years, he was still most associated with the town where he was born. Greg Fischer, Louisville's mayor, accurately stated, "Muhammad Ali belongs to the world, but he only has one hometown."[47] There was an enormous public memorial service for him in Louisville, but his interment at Cave Hill Cemetery was private. Old ring foes George Chuvalo, Larry Holmes and George Foreman served as honorary pallbearers.

When Joe Frazier died in 2011, his obituary in the *New York Times* featured a large action photograph. It was, of course, a classic image of Frazier walking away from the groggy Muhammad Ali after decking him in the final round of their epic March 8, 1971, bout at Madison Square Garden. The *Times*' piece not only summed up Frazier's life, it also captured what made the Ali-Frazier rivalry so meaningful and memorable:

> The Ali-Frazier battles played out at a time when the heavyweight boxing champion was far more celebrated than he is today, a figure who could stand alone in the spotlight a decade before an alphabet soup of boxing sanctioning bodies arose, making it difficult for the average fan to figure out just who held what title.
>
> Ali versus Frazier was a study in contrasts. Ali: tall and handsome, a wit given to spouting poetry, a magnetic figure who drew adulation and denigration alike, the one for his prowess and outsize personality, the other for his antiwar views and Black Power embrace of Islam. Frazier: a bull-like man of few words with a blue-collar image and a glowering visage who in so many ways could be on an equal footing with his rival only in the ring.
>
> Ali proclaimed, "I am the greatest" and he preened how he could "float like a butterfly, sting like a bee." Frazier had no inclination for oratorical bravado. "Work is the only meanin' I've ever known," he told *Playboy* in 1973. "Like the man in the song says, I just gotta keep on keepin' on."

Afterword

As was mentioned in the introduction to this book, the glory days of heavyweight boxing—and professional prize fighting in general—seem to be a thing of the past. The world heavyweight championship has not had much luster attached to it in the past 25 years. This reality was in evidence on May 24, 2018, when President Donald Trump formally posthumously pardoned Jack Johnson for his Mann Act conviction in 1912. When the chief-executive signed the document that addressed this century-old injustice, WBC world heavyweight champion Deontay Wilder was present for the ceremony as an invited guest. Despite President Trump praising the accomplishments of the reigning champion (specifically citing his perfect 40–0 ring record), Wilder could have walked out of the White House, circulated among Washington's tourists and, chances are, would have been utterly anonymous. For a world heavyweight champion, that prospect would have been unthinkable 40 years ago. The long-dead Jack Johnson was getting far more media coverage that month than the present heavyweight champ.

I have come to the conclusion that boxing was at its zenith when top-flight fighters attained celebrity status simply by being top-flight fighters. When boxing was huge, the sport and the world heavyweight championship title made them celebrities in their day and beyond. That is no longer the case. It is now the fighters who have to make the fans care about the titles they hold or are trying to win. Few are successful.

In researching this book, it never ceased to amaze me how much pre-fight publicity used to be generated before a major bout; often several weeks' worth of hype filled the sports sections of daily newspapers in anticipation of a heavyweight title clash. In days of yore, the public was once engrossed by the minutiae that James J. Jeffries was drinking only distilled water as he prepared to face Jack Johnson, and that Georges Carpentier arrived in America to face Jack Dempsey accompanied by a wardrobe of 75 silk shirts, and that Rocky Marciano had sparred precisely 99 rounds in training to ready himself to face Jersey Joe Walcott. Esoteric details such as these about the combatants served to fuel the public's excitement about an upcoming championship fight. The world heavyweight title was that important to casual boxing fans of yesteryear!

I suspect prizefighters were a different breed then—not as distanced from the public as professional athletes seem to be in the 21st century. Once, when my paternal grandfather made a rare visit to New York City, he made a point to go to Jack Dempsey's eatery for lunch. He casually inquired if the old champ was on the premises. Within a minute the famous Manassa Mauler was sharing a table with him and generously reliving his old ring exploits. I possess a letter penned by Max Schmeling to the father of a man who worked alongside my father. Written in German, the translation shows that Schmeling was more than happy—almost eager—to answer a letter sent to him by a boxing fan in Canada more than 40 years after he had last stepped into a ring.

Perhaps those two anecdotes indicate nothing. Perhaps they mean a lot. Will Deontay Wilder—whose nickname is "the Bronze Bomber"—be answering international fan mail 40 years from now? Will his name be famous enough to attract people to a business establishment long after he has hung up his boxing gloves? Only time will tell, but I have my doubts. I do know for certain that on the morning of Tuesday, March 9, 1971, my first-grade teacher made a point of telling her class that Joe Frazier had beaten Cassius Clay in the big fight at Madison Square Garden the night before and was still the heavyweight champion of the world. How often does the result of a prize fight in the 21st century garner such interest? It's a rhetorical question. No answer is required.

Chapter Notes

Introduction

1. Mel Heimer. *The Long Count*, Atheneum Books, New York, 1969, p. 118.

July 4, 1910

1. Ken Burns. *Unforgivable Blackness: The Rise and Fall of Jack Johnson*, PBS documentary, 2005.
2. *Ibid.*
3. *Ibid.*
4. Bert Sugar. *100 Years of Boxing*, Galley Press, New York, 1982, p. 58.
5. "Has Trailed Jeff for Several Years," *Milwaukee Sentinel*, July 4, 1910, p. 2.
6. Ken Burns. *Unforgivable Blackness: The Rise and Fall of Jack Johnson*, PBS documentary, 2005.
7. Bert Sugar. *100 Years of Boxing*, Galley Press, New York, 1982, p. 65.
8. Ken Burns. *Unforgivable Blackness: The Rise and Fall of Jack Johnson*, PBS documentary, 2005.
9. "New Champion Heavyweight of the World a Colored Man," *Milwaukee Journal*, December 26, 1908, p. 8.
10. Bert Sugar. *100 Years of Boxing*, Galley Press, New York, 1982, p. 66.
11. Ken Burns. *Unforgivable Blackness: The Rise and Fall of Jack Johnson*, PBS documentary, 2005.
12. Christopher Klein. *Strong Boy: The Life and Times of John L. Sullivan, America's First Sports Hero*, Lyons Press, Guilford, CT, 2015, p. 268.
13. "New Champion Heavyweight of the World a Colored Man," *Milwaukee Journal*, December 26, 1908, p. 8.
14. *Ibid.*
15. Bert Sugar. *100 Years of Boxing*, Galley Press, New York, 1982, p. 70.
16. *Ibid.*, p. 71.
17. "Has Trailed Jeff for Several Years," *Milwaukee Sentinel*, July 4, 1910, p. 2.
18. "Fortune Offered for Heavyweight," *Milwaukee Journal*, December 2, 1909, p. 8.
19. *Ibid.*
20. "Pugdom Not Scared by Mr. Gillette," *Pittsburgh Press*, June 16, 1910, p. 1.
21. *Ibid.*
22. *Ibid.*
23. *Ibid.*
24. "Reno Is Definitely Chosen as Scene for Big Fight," *Milwaukee Journal*, June 22, 1910, p. 9.
25. "Rickard Wants Personal Assurances from Dickerson," *Milwaukee Journal*, June 23, 1910, p. 13.
26. Bert Sugar. *100 Years of Boxing*, Galley Press, New York, 1982, p. 70.
27. "The Fighters Are Now at Their Training Quarters," *Milwaukee Journal*, June 25, 1910, p. 9.
28. "Crowd Sees Jeff in Hard Workout," *Milwaukee Sentinel*, June 30, 1910, p. 3.
29. "All Ready for Battle of Century," *Milwaukee Sentinel*, July 4, 1910, p. 1.
30. Jeffries and Johnson Are Ready for the Fateful Gong," *Milwaukee Sentinel*, July 4, 1910, p. 2.
31. *Ibid.*
32. *Ibid.*
33. *Ibid.*
34. "Jeff Prepares for Hard Punishment," *Milwaukee Journal*, July 2, 1910, p. 1.
35. *Ibid.*
36. *Ibid.*
37. Christopher Klein. *Strong Boy: The*

Life and Times of John L. Sullivan, America's First Sports Hero, Lyons Press, Guilford, CT, 2015, p. 268.
  38. "Jeffries-Johnson Battle by Rounds," *Milwaukee Journal*, July 5, 1910, p. 9.
  39. Ibid.
  40. Ibid.
  41. Christopher Klein. *Strong Boy: The Life and Times of John L. Sullivan, America's First Sports Hero*, Lyons Press, Guilford, CT, 2015, p. 273.
  42. Ibid.
  43. "Jeffries-Johnson Battle by Rounds," *Milwaukee Journal*, July 5, 1910, p. 9.
  44. Ibid.
  45. Ibid.
  46. Ibid.
  47. Ibid.
  48. Ibid.
  49. Ibid.
  50. "Johnson on Way East," *Boston Evening Transcript*, July, 5, 1910, p. 5.
  51. Ibid.
  52. Ibid.
  53. Ibid.
  54. "Reno Is Rapidly Returning to Its Usual Way of Living," *Milwaukee Journal*, July 5, 1910, p. 9.
  55. Ibid.
  56. "A Lesson for Jim," *Milwaukee Journal*, July 5, 1910, p. 9.
  57. "Reno Is Rapidly Returning to Its Usual Way of Living," *Milwaukee Journal*, July 5, 1910, p. 9.
  58. Ibid.
  59. "Wife Claims Battered Jeffries from Trainers; Races Riot as Johnson and Wife Banquet," *Toledo News-Bee*, July 5, 1910, p. 1.
  60. "Stop Fight Pictures Is Countrywide Cry," *Ithica Chronicle*, July 7, 1910, p. 1.
  61. Ken Burns. *Unforgivable Blackness: The Rise and Fall of Jack Johnson*, PBS documentary, 2005.

July 2, 1921

  1. Thomas Brennan. *The Million Dollar Man: Jack Dempsey*, Regent Press, USA, 2017, p. 24.
  2. Ibid., p. 83.
  3. Ibid., p. 116.
  4. Bert Sugar. *The Great Fights*, Gallery Books, New York, 1981, p. 53.
  5. Joseph W. Grigg. "England's Heavyweights Are 1-Round Heroes," *Milwaukee Journal*, December 5, 1919, p. II-14.
  6. "Rickard Is Not After Big Bout," *Milwaukee Journal*, December 5, 1919, p. II-14.
  7. "Jack Dempsey vs. Billy Miske (3rd Meeting)," Boxrec.com., Notes.
  8. Hype Igoe. "Champion Is Paid $55,000 for Abbreviated Workout," *Milwaukee Journal*, September 7, 1920, p. 18.
  9. "Jack Dempsey Begins Training Grind for Bout with Georges Carpentier," *Pittsburgh Press*, May 15, 1921, Sports Section p. 8.
  10. Ibid.
  11. John S. Radosta. "George Carpentier, Boxer, Dies in Paris," *New York Times* online archives, October 29, 1975.
  12. "Jack Dempsey Start East for Training," *Milwaukee Journal*, April 11, 1921, p. 12.
  13. "French Idol Is on Hand," *Pittsburgh Press*, May 16, 1921, p. 18.
  14. "French Challenger Is Confident of a Victory Over Jack Dempsey," *Meriden Morning Record*, p. 2.
  15. Jack Dempsey. "Champion Not Telling Much of His Plans," *Pittsburgh Press*, June 25, 1921, p. 10.
  16. Ibid.
  17. "Dempsey Calm as Bout Draws Near," *Milwaukee Sentinel*, July 1, 1921, p. 11.
  18. Bert Sugar. *The Great Fights*, Gallery Books, New York, 1981, p. 53.
  19. Ibid.
  20. "Asks Governor to Stop Fight," *Milwaukee Sentinel*, July 1, 1921, p. 11.
  21. Raymond G. Carroll. "Almost Everyone You Ever Heard About Was There," *Milwaukee Journal*, July 3, 1921.
  22. Ibid.
  23. "Rickard Cleaned About $550,000 on Saturday's Fight," *Meriden Morning Record*, July 4, 1921, p. 1.
  24. Thomas Brennan. *The Million Dollar Man: Jack Dempsey*, Regent Press, USA, 2017, p. 147.
  25. "Rickard Cleaned About $550,000 on Saturday's Fight," *Meriden Morning Record*, July 4, 1921, p. 1.
  26. Georges Carpentier. "Honestly Believe Better Man Won—Carpentier," *Milwaukee Journal*, July 3, 1921, Section III p. 1.
  27. Thomas Brennan. *The Million Dollar Man: Jack Dempsey*, Regent Press, USA, 2017, p. 150.

28. John S. Radosta. "George Carpentier, Boxer, Dies in Paris," *New York Times* online archives, October 29, 1975.
29. John Robertson. "Dempsey-Carpentier Drew 92,000 Fight Fans in '21," *Kitchener-Waterloo Record* online archives, July 4, 1998.
30. Bert Sugar. *The Great Fights*, Gallery Books, New York, 1981, p. 53.
31. Joseph J. O'Neill. "Sympathy All with Georges at Ten Count," *Milwaukee Journal*, July 3, 1921, p. 1.
32. H. L. Mencken. "Clean Fight If Not Beautiful, View of Artist," *Milwaukee Journal*, July 3, 1921, p. 1.
33. "Jack's Mother Says She Is Real Champion," *Milwaukee Journal*, July 3, 1921, p. 1.
34. "'Hurry Home,' Wife Cables to Georges," *Milwaukee Journal*, July 3, 1921, p. 1.
35. Thomas Brennan. *The Million Dollar Man: Jack Dempsey*, Regent Press, USA, 2017, pp. 151–152.
36. Red Smith. "Jack Dempsey, 87, Is Dead; Boxing Champion of the 1920s," *New York Times* online archives, June 1, 1983.
37. *Ibid.*
38. *Ibid.*
39. *Ibid.*
40. Shirley Povich. "Ex-Boxing Champ Dempsey Dies at 87," *Washington Post* online archives, June 1, 1983.
41. *Ibid.*

June 22, 1938

1. "Max Schmeling, German Boxer, Is Dead at 99," *New York Times* online archives, February 4, 2005.
2. "Joe Louis," biographical television documentary series, USA, circa 1985.
3. Ron Fimrite. "Send in the Clown," *Sports Illustrated*'s online archives, March 20, 1978.
4. "I Was Out, Says Maxie," *Pittsburgh Press*, September 25, 1935, p. 21.
5. John Robertson, "Controversy Followed Heavyweight Boxer Sharkey," *Kitchener-Waterloo Record* online archives, December 26, 1996.
6. "Max Schmeling, German Boxer, Is Dead at 99," *New York Times* online archives, February 4, 2005.
7. John Robertson, "Controversy Followed Heavyweight Boxer Sharkey," *Kitchener-Waterloo Record* online archives, December 26, 1996.
8. *Ibid.*
9. Ronald McIntyre. "Bout Recognized by Boxing Heads as Title Affair," *Milwaukee Sentinel*, June 14, 1930, p. 13.
10. Yale Merrill, "Maxie Proves Right to Heavyweight Title," *Pittsburgh Press*, July 5, 1931, Sports Section p. 1.
11. "Sharkey 'Victory' Rouses Storm; Fans Ask Probe," *Pittsburgh Press*, June 22, 1932, p. 4.
12. *Ibid.*, p. 1.
13. *Ibid.*, p. 4.
14. *Ibid.*, p. 4.
15. Stuart Cameron. "Max Battles Primo to End," *Pittsburgh Press*, June 15, 1934, p. 48.
16. Chester L. Smith. "Baer Toppled from Throne by Braddock," *Pittsburgh, Press*, June 14, 1935, p. 1.
17. Eddie Brietz. "Max Schmeling Beats Joe Louis by Knockout in the 12th Round," *Calgary Daily Herald*, June 20, 1936, p. 4.
18. Eddie Brietz. "Louis in Fog from Fourth to Bout End," *Calgary Daily Herald*, June 20, 1936, p. 4.
19. Alan Gould. "Jacobs and Garden Dicker for Title Bout," *Milwaukee Journal*, June 21, 1938, p. 1.
20. Eddie Brietz. "Max Schmeling Beats Joe Louis by Knockout in the 12th Round," *Calgary Daily Herald*, June 20, 1936, p. 4.
21. "Max Schmeling, German Boxer, Is Dead at 99," *New York Times* online archives, February 4, 2005.
22. "Max's Wife Is Surprised Over His Win," *Calgary Daily Herald*, June 20, 1936, p. 6.
23. *Ibid.*
24. "Victor Over Louis Plans to Take Rest, *Regina Leader-Post*, June 20, 1936, p. 1.
25. *Ibid.*
26. Ed Baker. "Short Shots on Sports," *Ottawa Citizen*, June 23, 1937, p. 10.
27. Eddie Brietz, "Braddock Is Not Through with the Ring," *Ottawa Citizen*, June 23, 1937, p. 10.
28. William Weekes. "Set for Schmeling, Says New Champion," *Ottawa Citizen*, June 23, 1937, p. 10.
29. Ed Baker. "Short Shots on Sports," *Ottawa Citizen*, June 23, 1937, p. 10.
30. *Ibid.*
31. Tommy Farr. *Thus Farr*, W. H. Allen & Co Pic., London, England, 1989, p. 92.

32. Henry McLemore. "Other Champions Agree Louis Didn't Look So Hot," *Milwaukee Journal*, August 31, 1937, p. 2.
33. Ibid.
34. Ibid.
35. Ibid.
36. Joe Williams. "Louis Still Sucker for Right-Hand Punch," *Pittsburgh Press*, February 24, 1938, p. 25.
37. R.G. Lynch. "Joe Louis Knocks Out Harry Thomas in Fifth," *Milwaukee Journal*, April 2, 1938, p. 6.
38. "Louis by Knockout—Braddock's Opinion," *Pittsburgh Press*, June 13, 1938, p. 20.
39. "Tommy Burns Selects Louis Over Schmeling," *Calgary Daily Herald*, June 18, 1938, p. 7.
40. "Louis Names Second Round If Schmeling Will Mix It," *Pittsburgh Press*, June 14, 1938, p. 24.
41. Alan Gould. "Champion Favored to Defeat German in Return Battle," *Montreal Gazette*, June 22, 1938, p. 14.
42. Marc. T. McHail. "Casual Close-Ups," *Montreal Gazette*, June 22, 1938, p. 14.
43. Ronald McIntyre. "Between You and Me," *Milwaukee Sentinel*, June 22, 1938, p. 11.
44. "Nazi Organ Complains of Stories on Battle," *Montreal Gazette*, June 22, 1938, p. 14.
45. "Art Donovan, Jr., Hall of Famer from an American Sporting Dynasty, Dies at 89," *The Guardian* online archives, August 6, 2013.
46. Newsreel of Louis-Schmeling fight; Arthur Donovan's referee's instructions.
47. "The Fight of the Century: Louis vs. Schmeling," National Public Radio: The Sounds of American Culture Series, npr.org., November 25, 2006.
48. Gayle Talbot. "Revenge Sweet as Louis Scores One-Round K.O.," *Regina Leader-Post*, June 23, 1938, p. 12.
49. "Schmeling Suffers an Internal Injury," *Milwaukee Journal*, June 23, 1938, p. 6.
50. R.G. Lynch, "Maybe I'm Wrong," *Milwaukee Journal*, June 24, 1938, p. 6.
51. R.G. Lynch, "Louis Knocks Out Schmeling in First," *Milwaukee Journal*, June 23, 1938, p. 6.
52. Chris Mead. "Triumphs and Trials," *Sports Illustrated*'s online archives, September 23, 1985.
53. Jeff Moshier. "Playing Square," *St. Petersburg Evening Independent*, June 25, 1938, p. 8.
54. Bob Considine as quoted by Howard Cosell. Retrospective on life of Joe Louis, *ABC's Wide World of Sports*, April 18, 1981.
55. Henry McLemore. "Louis Finishes Max Schmeling in Two Minutes and Four Seconds," *The Bend Bulletin*, June 23, 1938, Section 2, p.1.
56. Gayle Talbot. "Hard Right to Max's Kidney Gives Joe Revenge," *Kentucky New Era*, June 23, 1938, p. 5.
57. "Harlem Celebrates Joe Louis' Victory Over Max Schmeling," *Calgary Daily Herald*, June 23, 1938, p. 6.
58. "Tear Gas Quells Riots by Cleveland Negroes," *Montreal Gazette*, June 23, 1938, p. 14.
59. Mark Murphy. "Indiana Avenue Goes Wild," *Toledo News-Bee*, p. 1.
60. "World War II Graves: Schmeling, Maximilian," ww2gravestone.com.
61. "Max Schmeling (obituary)," *The Guardian* online archives, February 5, 2005.
62. Sam Lacy. "It Was THE Champion Who Died on Sunday in Las Vegas," *Baltimore Afro-American*, April 14, 1981, p. 20.
63. Ibid.
64. Howard Cosell. Retrospective on Life of Joe Louis, *ABC's Wide World of Sports*, April 18, 1981.
65. Sam Lacy. "It Was THE Champion Who Died on Sunday in Las Vegas," *Baltimore Afro-American*, April 14, 1981, p. 20.
66. Ibid.
67. Ibid.
68. Ronald Reagan. "Statement on the Death of Former World Heavyweight Boxing Champion Joe Louis," The American Presidency Project, University of California, April 13, 1981.
69. Jesse Jackson. Retrospective on life of Joe Louis, *ABC's Wide World of Sports*, April 18, 1981.

September 23, 1952

1. W.C. Heinz. "Something About Rocky Marciano," *The Ring*, June 1950, p. 8.
2. Ibid., p. 9.
3. John Jarrett. *Rocky Marciano: The Brockton Blockbuster*, Pitch Publishing, Durrington, UK, 2018, chapter 1.
4. Ibid.
5. "Young Boxer Is Carried from Ring," *Schenectady Gazette*, December 31, 1949, p. 18.

6. "Vingo Relives Tragic Fight," *Rome News-Tribune*, February 28, 1971, p. 6-C.
7. Betting Bruiser. "The Blemishes of Rocky Marciano's 49–0 Record," mmaoddsbreaker.com.
8. "First Defeat for LaStarza," *Regina Leader-Post*, March 25, 1950, p. 18.
9. *Ibid.*
10. Nat Fleischer. "Marciano Next Champion; Recalls Young Dempsey," *The Ring*, October 1952, p. 4.
11. "How Many Rounds Will It Take?" *Pittsburgh Press*, December 5, 1947, p. 41.
12. "Bomber Admits He Has Slipped," *Pittsburgh Press*, December 6, 1947, p. 6.
13. "Walcott Regrets Being Cautious," *Pittsburgh Press*, December 6, 1947, p. 6.
14. Michael Carbert. "Dec. 5, 1947: Louis-Walcott I," thefightcity.com, December 5, 2017.
15. Edwin Beachler. "Walcott Walking on Clouds After Win Over Charles," *Pittsburgh Press*, July 19, 1951, p. 1.
16. *Ibid.*
17. "Couldn't Lift Pappy's Title, Fight So Close—McTiernan," *Pittsburgh Press*, June 6, 1952, p. 1.
18. Chester L. Smith. "Walcott Deserved Victory," *Pittsburgh Press*, June 6, 1952, p. 33.
19. *Ibid.*
20. *Ibid.*
21. "Couldn't Lift Pappy's Title, Fight So Close—McTiernan," *Pittsburgh Press*, June 6, 1952, p. 1
22. Roy McHugh. "Charles' Conservative Style Helps Champion to Unanimous Decision," *Pittsburgh Press*, June 6, 1952, p. 33.
23. "Joe Louis Picks Walcott by Kayo," *Pittsburgh Press*, September 16, 1952, p. 30.
24. "Marciano Boss Fires Ultimatum," *Pittsburgh Press*, September 17, 1952, p. 31.
25. "Walcott Chases Sparring Partner," *Pittsburgh Press*, September 20, 1952, p. 6.
26. "Writers Pick Marciano to Win Title from Walcott," *Pittsburgh Press*, September 20, 1952, p. 19.
27. "Crowd Mobs Drive-In," *Calgary Herald*, September 24, 1952, p. 26.
28. Nat Fleischer. "The Story with a Punch," *The Ring*, December 1952, p. 37.
29. Jack Cuddy. "Walcott Changes Retirement Plans—Will Fight Marciano Again," *Pittsburgh Press*, September 24, 1952, p. 34.
30. "Right to Chin Set Walcott Up for Finish," *Pittsburgh Press*, September 24, 1952, p. 35.
31. Oscar Fraley. "Jersey Joe Bowed to Shackles of Time," *Newburgh News*, September 24, 1952, p. 24.
32. Nat Fleischer. "The Story with a Punch," *The Ring*, December 1952, p. 4.
33. *Ibid.*
34. *Ibid.*
35. *Ibid.*
36. *Ibid.*
37. Jack Cuddy. "Walcott Changes Retirement Plans—Will Fight Marciano Again," *Pittsburgh Press*, September 24, 1952, p. 34.
38. John Douesnard. "Sports Parade," *Granby Leader-Mail*, September 25, 1952, p. 11.
39. Roy McHugh. "Marciano Holds Title Dumping Challenger in Easy First Round," *Pittsburgh Press*, May 16, 1953, p. 6.
40. *Ibid.*
41. *Ibid.*
42. "Rocky Marciano vs. Jersey Joe Walcott (2nd meeting)" BoxRec.com, Notes.
43. "Marciano Knew Walcott Hurt," *Calgary Herald*, May 16, 1953, p. 31.
44. "Rocky Marciano Keeps Title with First-Round Knockout," *Calgary Herald*, May 16, 1953, p. 31.
45. *Ibid.*
46. "Rocky Says He May Quit Ring," *Pittsburgh Post-Gazette*, September 22, 1955, p. 20.
47. *Ibid.*
48. "Rocky Retires Unbeaten in 49 Pro Fights," *Pittsburgh Post-Gazette*, April 28, 1956, p. 14.
49. "Plane Crash Kills Rocky on Eve of 46th Birthday," *Calgary Herald*, September 2, 1969, 16.
50. Gary Lucken. "The Death of Rocky Marciano—An Avoidable Tragedy," Boxingmonthly.com, August 31, 2017.
51. "Never Beaten, Marciano Loses Life in Plane Crash," *Montreal Gazette*, September 2, 1969, p. 26.
52. "Everything About Him Was Good, Say Louis," *Montreal Gazette*, September 2, 1969, p. 26.
53. "Rocky Marciano," ESPN Sports Century television documentary.
54. "Thousands Mourn Rocky Marciano," *Altus Times-Democrat*, September 2, 1969, p. 5.
55. "Clay Watches His Downfall," *Pittsburgh Press*, January 21, 1970, Section II, p. 6.
56. Roy McHugh. "A Rocky Night for

Clay in Computerland," *Pittsburgh Press*, January 21, 1970, Section II, p. 6.
  57. "Clay Watches His Downfall," *Pittsburgh Press*, January 21, 1970, Section II, p. 6.
  58. Roy McHugh. "Unlikely Champion," *Pittsburgh Press*, September 2, 1969, p. 36.

March 8, 1971

  1. George Vecsey. *Frazier/Ali*, Scholastic Book Services, New York, 1972, p. 13.
  2. Will Deorge. "Powell Falls in Three for Clay," *Pittsburgh Press*, January 25, 1963, p. 20.
  3. Jack Dempsey's mystery guest appearance on *What's My Line?*, CBS Television, July 11, 1965.
  4. Bob Orkand. "I Ain't Got No Quarrel with Them Vietcong," *New York Times* online archives, June 27, 2017.
  5. Joe Frazier. *Smokin' Joe: The Autobiography*, Macmillan, 1996, New York, p. 9.
  6. "'Beaten by Miracle'—Quarry," *Pittsburgh Press*, October 27, 1970, p. 34.
  7. *Ibid.*
  8. Roy McHugh. "Ali as Prophetic—and Masterful—as Ever," *Pittsburgh Press*, October 27, 1970, p. 34.
  9. Roy McHugh. "Ali Misses His Stop, Finally Finishes Oscar in 15," *Pittsburgh Press*, December 8, 1970, p. 50.
  10. Dan Daniel. "Frazier-Clay Title Fight Set Up by Ali's KO of Ringo," *The Ring*, March 1971, p. 19.
  11. *Ibid.*
  12. Roy McHugh. "Ali Misses His Stop, Finally Finishes Oscar in 15," *Pittsburgh Press*, December 8, 1970, p. 50.
  13. "Joe Frazier Unimpressed," *Pittsburgh Press*, December 8, 1970, p. 50.
  14. "Ring Camera Clicks," *The Ring*, August 1971, p. 22.
  15. Simon Burnton. "Muhammad Ali on Joe Frazier: That's One Helluva Man and God Bless Him," *The Guardian* online archives, November 8, 2011.
  16. *Ali: Skill, Brains and Guts*, 1975 video documentary.
  17. Simon Burnton. "Muhammad Ali on Joe Frazier: That's One Helluva Man and God Bless Him," *The Guardian* online archives, November 8, 2011.
  18. "Crowd-Watching Rivalled Ali-Frazier Fight," *Calgary Herald*, March 9, 1971, p. 1.
  19. Will Grimsley. "Ringside at Garden: A Happening in NYC," *Schenectady Gazette*, March 9, 1971, p. 19.
  20. *Ibid.*
  21. *Ibid.*
  22. Larry Hug. "Good vs. the Evil," *St. Petersburg Evening Independent*, March 9, 1971, p. 1-C.
  23. *Ibid.*
  24. *Ibid.*
  25. *Ibid.*
  26. *Ibid.*
  27. *Ibid.*
  28. Bob Chick, "Could Closed-Circuit Disease Spread?" *St. Petersburg Evening Independent*, March 9, 1971, p. 1-C.
  29. David Wiessler. "Fight Packs Big Punch Around the World," *Pittsburgh Press*, March 9, 1971, p. 2.
  30. Gerald Eskenazi. "Don Dunphy, 90, Distinctive Fight Broadcaster," *New York Times* online archives, July 24, 1998.
  31. *Ibid.*
  32. *Ibid.*
  33. Roy McHugh. "Fall of a King," *Pittsburgh Press*, March 9, 1971, p. 34.
  34. *Ibid.*
  35. *Ibid.*
  36. Dan Daniel. "Tough Joe's Win Decisive, Many Questioned Unanswered," *The Ring*, May 1971, p. 8.
  37. "Ali Mauled as Frazier Keeps Title," *Schenectady Gazette*, March 9, 1971, p. 1.
  38. Dan Daniel. "Tough Joe's Win Decisive, Many Questioned Unanswered," *The Ring*, May 1971, p. 8.
  39. Jim Coleman, "There's a Fist Down Cassius's Throat," *Calgary Herald*, March 9, 1971, p. 11.
  40. Dan Daniel. "Tough Joe's Win Decisive, Many Questioned Unanswered," *The Ring*, May 1971, p. 8.
  41. *Ibid.*
  42. "We'll Be Back…," *St. Petersburg Independent*, March 9, 1971, p. 1-C.
  43. "…Surprised Him," *St. Petersburg Independent*, March 9, 1971, p. 1-C.
  44. "Champ Ali Wins 'Thrilla in Manila,'" *Pittsburgh Press*, October 1, 1975, p. 57.
  45. Richard Goldstein. "Joe Frazier, Ex-Heavyweight Champ, Dies at 67," *New York Times* online archives, November 7, 2011.
  46. *Ibid.*
  47. Bruce Schreiner et al. "Ali: Citizen of the World," *The Columbian* (online version), June 4, 2016.

Bibliography

Books

Arnold, Peter. *All-Time Greats of Boxing*. London: Bison Books, 1987.
Aycock, Colleen, and Mark Scott. *Tex Rickard: Boxing's Greatest Promoter*. Jefferson, NC: McFarland, 2012.
Brennan, Thomas. *The Million Dollar Man: Jack Dempsey*. Regent Press, 2017.
Carter, Jimmy. *Why Not the Best?* New York: Bantam Books, 1975.
Cavanaugh, Jack. *Tunney*. New York: Ballantine Books, 2006.
Collins, Nigel (editor). *The 2000 Boxing Almanac and Book of Facts*. Fort Washington, NY: London Publishing Co., 2000.
Cooper, Henry. *The Great Heavyweights*. London, 1978.
Cosell, Howard. *Cosell*. New York: Pocket Books, 1973.
Dempsey, Jack. *Dempsey*. New York: Harper and Row, 1977.
Farr, Tommy. *Thus Farr*. London: W. H. Allen & Co., 1989.
Frazier, Joe. *Smokin' Joe: The Autobiography*. New York: Macmillan, 1996.
Gilmore, Al-Tony. *Bad Nigger! The National Impact of Jack Johnson,* Port Washington, NY: Kennikat Press, 1975.
Goldman, Herbert G. (editor). *1986–87 Ring Record Book & Boxing Encyclopedia*. The Ring Publishing Corp., 1987.
Hauser, Thomas. *Muhammad Ali: His Life and Times*. New York: Simon & Schuster, 1991.
Heimer, Mel. *The Long Count*. New York: Atheneum Books, 1969.
Jarrett, John. *Rocky Marciano: The Brockton Blockbuster*. Durrington, UK: Pitch Publishing, 2018.
Klein, Christopher. *Strong Boy: The Life and Times of John L. Sullivan, America's First Sports Hero*. Guilford, CT: Lyons Press, 2015.
Louis, Joe. *My Life Story*. New York: Duell, Sloan and Pearce, 1947.
Mora, Manuel A. *Stanley Ketchel: A Life of Triumph and Prophecy*. Bloomington, IN: Author House, 2010.
Roberts, Randy. *Jack Dempsey: The Manassa Mauler*. Baton Rouge: Louisiana State University Press, 1979.
Sugar, Bert. *The Great Fights*. New York: Gallery Books, 1981.
Sugar, Bert. *100 Years of Boxing*. New York: Galley Press, 1982.
Vecsey, George. *Frazier-Ali*. New York: Scholastic Book Services, 1972.
Waltzer, Jim. *The Battle of the Century: Dempsey, Carpentier, and the Birth of Modern Promotion*. Santa Barbara, CA: Praeger, 2011.
Wells, Jeff. *Boxing Day*. New York: HarperCollins, 1998.

Newspaper Archives

Altus Times-Democrat
Arizona Journal-Miner
Bakersfield Californian
Baltimore Afro-American
Bangor Daily News
The Bend Bulletin
Boston Evening Transcript
Butler Times
Calgary Herald
Cambridge Weekly Republican Press
Cleveland Press
The Columbian
Detroit Free Press
Duluth Daily Star
Edmonton Journal
Galt Evening Reporter
Granby Leader-Mail
The Guardian
Ithaca Chronicle
Kentucky New Era
Lewiston Morning Tribune
Los Angeles Times
Meriden Morning Record
Milwaukee Journal
Milwaukee Sentinel
Montreal Gazette
New York Daily News
New York Herald
New York Herald Tribune
New York Times
New York World
Newark Sunday Call
Newburgh News
Ottawa Citizen
Paris Excelsior
Paterson Press
Philadelphia Ledger
Pittsburgh Post-Gazette
Pittsburgh Press
Rome News-Tribune
St. Albans Messenger
St. Petersburg Evening Independent
St. Petersburg Times
San Francisco Chronicle
Saskatoon Daily Phoenix
Schenectady Gazette
Times of London
Toledo Blade
Toledo News-Bee
Washington Post
Wichita Gazette

Periodicals

KO Magazine
Life
New York Times Magazine
Playboy
The Ring
The Sporting News
Sports Illustrated

Video Documentaries

Ali–Frazier: The Fight
Ali: Skill, Brains & Guts
Jack Johnson
Joe Louis: America's Hero Betrayed
The Legendary Champions
Rocky Marciano: ESPN Sports Century
Unforgivable Blackness: The Rise and Fall of Jack Johnson

Index

ABC's Wide World of Sports (television show) 164, 193
Abrams, Al 173
Addie, Johnny 192
Aidala, Artie 193
Alger, Horatio 109
Ali, Rahaman 183–184
Allen, Neil 168
Alston-Frazier, Dolly 175
Arcel, Ray 147
Armstrong, Henry 176
Assad, General Hafez 165
Astor, Vincent 73
Attell, Abe 30

Baer, Max 102–103, 108–109, 112, 117, 119–120, 125, 140
Baker, Bob 159
Baker, Ed 113, 114
Balthasar, Max 37
Barbour, Warren 57–58
Baroudi, Sam 145
Barrow, Lillie 101–102, 128
Barrow, Munroe 101
Baxter, Portus 36
Becker, Boris 131
Beckett, Joe 64, 65
Belz, Glenn 160–161
Benitez, Manuel 134
Bentham, Teddy 178
Benvenuti, Nino 168
Berbick, Trevor 132, 198
Berger, Sam 36
Berger, Victor 43
Bivins, Jimmy 145
Blackburn, Jack (Chappie) 117
Bocchicchio, Felix 148, 153, 155
Bonavena, Oscar 177, 179–180, 181, 182
Bowes-Lyon, Cecilia Nina 124

Braddock, James J. 103, 108–109, 112–114, 115, 117, 119, 126, 141, 162
Brennan, Bill 67–68, 75
Brennan, Dr. Robert 125
Brietz, Eddie 111
Briggs, Shannon 1
Brooklyn Dodgers 149
Brooks, Pat 101
Brown, Bill 124
Brown, Drew (Bundini) 193, 195
Browne, Lucas 1
Bugner, Joe 197
Bull, Lillian 50
Burman, Red 128
Burns, Tommy 11–15
Bush, George W. 199

Café de Champion (Jack Johnson's saloon) 16
Campbell, Frankie 108
Carbert, Michael 144–145
Carey, Michael 107
Carnegie, Andrew 21
Carnera, Primo 102, 107–108, 109
Carpenter, Harry 170
Carpentier, Georgette 90
Carpentier, Jacqueline 94
Carroll, Raymond G. 81
Carter, Jimmy 122
Cassidy, Robert 165
Cates, Maxine 61
CBS Late Night (television show) 164
The Challenge of Chance (movie) 55
Chaplin, Charlie 81
Charles, Ezzard 97, 130, 145–148, 158
Chicago Cubs 136
Chick, Bob 186
Choynski, Joe 7, 24
Chuvalo, George 174, 177, 200

211

Cinderella Man (movie) 109
Clay, Cassius, Sr. 166
Clay, Odessa 166
Clayton, Zack 147, 153, 196
Clement, H.B. 41
Cobb, Ty 91
Cockell, Don 158
Cohan, George M. 81
Coleman, Jim 193
Condon, John F.X. 143
Conn, Billy 128–129, 143
Conn, Mark 180
Considine, Bob 126
Cooney, Gerry 2
Cooper, Henry 137–138, 169–171, 174
Copelin, George 54
Corbett, James J. 7, 9, 10, 27, 33, 34, 37, 39–40, 116–117
Corbett, Tom 27–28
Cosell, Howard 133, 172, 174, 175, 193, 196, 198
Crafts, Dr. Wilbur F. 80
Cram, Mark 165
Crosby, Bing 184
Crowe, Russell 109
Crowley, Jimmy 105
Cuddy, Jack 154
Curley, Jack 45
Cummings, Jumbo 197

Daggert, Charley 151–154
Daniel, Dan 179, 181, 191, 193
Daniels, Terry 195
Dawson, James 105
DeGaulle, Charles 97
Dempsey, Bernie 53–54
Dempsey, Hannah 133
Dempsey, Hyrum 53, 57
Dempsey, Mary Cilia 53, 89
Dempsey, Nonpareil Jack 54
Descamps, François 76
Dickerson, Denver S. 22–23
Dixon, George 8
Donovan, Art 121
Donovan, Arthur 115, 120–121, 122–124, 133
Donovan, (Professor) Mike 120
Douesnard, John 156
Douglas, Buster 108
Downey, Hardy 54
Dryburgh, Dave 126
Dundee, Angelo 170, 172, 188, 191, 198
Dundee, Chris 162
Dunphy, Don 186–192

Durant, John 105
Durham, Yancey (Yank) 177, 187

Edward VII, King 11–12
Edwards, Edward Irving 80
Eilander, Henry 160
Ellis, Jimmy 175, 177
Ellis, Steve 173
Epperson, Lee 137
Erenberg, Lewis 121
Ertle, J. Harry 84–87, 91
Eustace, Jim 128

Faris, Barry 49, 80, 82, 84
Farr, Tommy 115–116, 120
Farrell, C.P. 28
Farrell, Frank 160
Farrell, Henry L. 67, 68, 72
Felix, Barney 173
Ferdinand, Archduke Franz 47
Finch, Bruce 37
Finnegan, Jack 10
Firpo, Luis 96
Fischer, Greg 200
Fisher, Bud 76
Fitzsimmons, Bob 10, 116, 154
Flanagan, Tom 24
Fleischer, Nat 5–6, 50, 105, 135, 140, 154–155, 175, 177–178
Florio, Dan 148–149
Flynn, (Fireman) Jim 45–46
Folley, Zora 174, 178
Forbes, Frank 143
Ford, Henry 81
Foreman, George 195–197, 200
Fornoff, Fred 46
Foster, Bob 181
Fraley, Oscar 154
Frazier, Marvis 197
Frazier, Rubin 175
Frelinghuysen, Joseph S. 89
Futch, Eddie 177, 187, 197, 198

Gallico, Paul 20
Gans, Joe 8, 20
Gaynor, William Jay 43
Gibbons, Tommy 96
Gillett, James 21–22
Gilson, Hubert Clark 89
Glarner, André 92
Gleason, James 5, 20
Goebbels, Josef 111–112, 119
Goldman, Charley 137
Goldstein, Richard 199

Goldstein, Ruby 130, 143–144
Gorgeous George (wrestler) 168
Goss, Woody 177
Gould, Alan 111, 118
Gowdy, Curt 144
The Great Fights (book) 60
Griffin, Hank 10
Grimsley, Will 183
Grody, Ray 165

Hague, Frank 72
Hall, Frank 28
Hancock, One Punch 54
Hand, Jack 135
Harding, Florence 90
Harding, Warren 81, 89–90
Hart, Marvin 10–11, 21, 23
Harting, George F. 32
Haye, David 1
Heeney, Tom 104
Hefner, Hugh 183
Heifetz, Jascha 102
Heimer, Mel 76
Heinz, W.C. 135
Herman, Pete 128
Heuser, Adolf 130
Hines, Ann 183
Hitler, Adolf 130
Hoffer, Richard 51
Holmes, Larry 2, 11, 132, 197, 198, 200
Huber, Hans 176
Hug, Larry 185–186
Hull, Chuck 132
Humphreys, Joe 84
Hunsaker, Tunney 168

Igoe, Herbert (Hype) 66–67
International Boxing Federation 2
International Reform Bureau 80, 89
I've Got a Secret (television program) 172

Jackson, Hurricane 159
Jackson, Jesse 134
Jackson, Peter 54
Jackson (Shoeless) Joe 91
Jacobs, Joe 105, 107, 115
Jacobs, Mike 112, 120–121
James, David 195
Jeannette, Joe 73
Jeffries, the Rev. Alexis C. 40
Jeffries, Freida 27, 50
Jeffries, Jack 8
The Jerry Lewis Show (television program) 172

Johnson, (Battling) Jim 46
Johnson, Henry 6
Johnson, Irene 50
Johnson (Tiny) Tina 6, 41–42
Jolson, Al 81
Jones, Doug 169, 177
Jones, Elzia B. 128
Jones, Jersey 184
Jones, Soldier 82
Jordan, Billy 31
Journee, Paul 73

Kaufman, Al 21
Kearns, Jack (Doc) 57, 58, 59, 61, 64, 75, 77, 85–86, 91, 93, 116, 140
Kenty, Hilmer 133
Ketchel, Stanley 17, 21, 28
Ketchel, Steve 112
Kilrain, Jake 30
Koppett, Leonard 172
Kracken, Jack 102

Lacy, Sam 133
Ladino, Lupe 182
Lancaster, Burt 183, 188–191
Lane, Tommy 51
Langford, Sam 21, 30
Lardner, John 86
Lardner, Ring 52
LaStarza, Roland 139, 149, 158
Lauder, Polly 104–105
Layne, Rex 139
Lenglen, Suzanne 81
Leonard, Benny 116
Leonard, Sugar Ray 37
Levine, Jackie 138
Levinsky, Battling 63, 73
Levinsky, King 125
Levy, Sam 50
Lewis, Jerry 171–172
Lewis, Whitey 147
Liakhovich, Siarhei 1
Liberace 172
Lindsay, John V. 183
Liston, Charles (Sonny) 59, 158, 169, 171–173, 184
Little, George 24
Little, Tommy 170, 171
Lloyd, Harold 165–166
Loeb, William 194–195
London, Brian 174
London, Jack 15, 19, 39
The Long Count (book) 76
LoScalzo, Joe 169

Index

Lyle, Ron 197
Lynch, R.G. 116, 125

Machen, Eddie 177
Machon, Max 123
Maddox, Lester 178
Madison Square Garden Corporation 107
Mailer, Norman 181–182
Mann, Nathan 116
Marchegiano, Mary Anne 161
Marchegiano, Pierino 135
Marciano, Barbara 161
Marciano, Rocco Kevin 161
Martin, Lt. Gus 89
Martin, Joe 167
Maskaev, Oleg 1
Mathis, Buster 176, 177
Matthews, Harry 140, 149
Mauriello, Tami 129
McAlinden, Dan 183–184
McCarthy, Clem 122, 123–124
McHugh, Roy 157, 163, 164, 178–179, 180
McIntosh, Hugh 13, 14, 19
McIntyre, Ronald 119
McLaughlin, Victor 17
McLemore, Henry 115, 125, 126
McTiernan, Buck 146
Mencken, H.L. 52, 88–89
Mercante, Arthur 187–193, 195
Merchant, Larry 177
Merrill, Yale 106
Metzner, K. 124
Mickelson, Paul 118
Mildenburger, Karl 131, 174
Miler, Johnny 102
Miller, Nathan L. 68–69
Miller, Pete 147
The Million Dollar Gate (book) 59
Les Miserables (movie) 150
Miske, Billy 65–67, 68, 83
Mitchell, Edgar 183
Mitchell, Richie 59–60
Mogard, Don 137
Monroe, Marty 143
Moore, Archie 149, 158, 162, 188–191
Moran, Frank 47, 55, 63, 70
Moshier, Jeff 126
Muhammad, Elijah 173
Muldoon, William 107
Mullan, Harry 105
"Mutt and Jeff" (comic strip) 76

Nardiello, Dr. Vincent 138
Nelson, Francis 26

Nelson, Oscar Matthew (Battling) 20, 21
Nichols, Joe 147
Nieman, Leroy 182
Nixon, Richard 149
Norris, Jim 150
Norton, Brian 81
Norton, Ken 195, 196, 197

O'Brien, Philadelphia Jack 30, 37
O'Grady, Sean 133
O'Keefe, Ronnie 167
Ondra, Anny 111–112, 118, 131
O'Neill, Joseph J. 88
Orbach, Barak Y. 16–17

Paar, Jack 171–172
Pacheco, Ferdie 173
Paget, Debra 150
Parker, Dan 121
Pastor, Bob 128
Patterson, Floyd 158, 159, 168, 169, 172, 173, 174, 196
Paychek, Johnny 128
Pecord, Ollie 57, 58
Perez, Tony 178, 196
Peter, Samuel 1
Petti, Brian C. 132
Phair, George E. 42
Philadelphia Phillies 149
Picciuto, Pasqualina 135
Pietrzykowski, Zbigniew 167–168
Pope Benedict XV 91
Povich, Shirley 98–99, 137
Powell, Charlie 169

Quarry, Jerry 175, 177, 178–179, 182

Ransom, Reverdy C. 5
Reagan, Ronald 134
Recht, Bill 193
Renault, Jack 75
Rendon, Mario 164
Rennie, Michael 150
Reynolds, Bernie 140
Rice, Grantland 60–61
Rickard, George Lewis (Tex) 19–20, 22, 23, 25–26, 29, 32, 35, 36, 44, 51, 56, 57, 65, 69, 71, 72, 76–78, 83, 84, 85, 91, 93, 94, 112
Robinson, Jackie 51
Rocap, William H. 59
Rochi, Antonine 43
Rockefeller, John D. 81
Roosa, Stuart 183

Index

Roosevelt, Franklin Delano 101, 117
Roosevelt, Theodore 120
Root, Jack 10, 23, 50
Rose, Murray 159
Roxborough, John 111
Ruiz, John 1
Runyon, Damon 88
Ryan, Elizabeth 81

Samuels, Jeff 196
Sanders, Colonel Harland 183
Sanders, Corrie 1–2
Savold, Lee 140
Scharre, C.R. 154
Scott, Fred L. 50
Seko, Mobutu Sese 196
Sesto, Ernie 169
Sharkey, Jack 105, 106–108, 109, 112, 133, 162
Sharkey, Tom 31
Shepard, Alan 183
Sikora, Frank 156
Simms, William Phillips 46
Sinatra, Frank 132, 183
Smith, Billy 148–149
Smith, Chester L. 109, 147
Smith, Ed (Gunboat) 107
Smith, J.O. 83
Smith, Red 60, 96–97, 98, 99
Smith, Tim 51
Spinks, Leon 198
Squires, Bill 11
Stallone, Sylvester 49
Stander, Ron 195
Stiyerne, Bermane 1
Stribling, Young (W.L.) 106
Sugar, Bert 1, 9, 13, 15, 16, 60, 79
Sullivan, John L. 1, 7, 8, 10, 13, 15, 17, 28, 30, 33, 39, 41, 60, 155
The Super Fight: Marciano vs. Ali (movie) 161–164
Swarts, Colleen 160

Taft, William Howard 25
Talbot, Gayle 122, 126
Taylor, Herman 150
This Is Your Life (television show) 167, 171, 199
Thomas, Harry 116

Tilden, Bill 81
Tomorrow's Champions (television show) 167
The Tonight Show (television show) 172
Tortorich, Dominick 65
Trotter, Marva 103
Trump, Donald 49, 183, 201
Tunney, Gene 2, 82, 96, 99, 100, 103, 104–105, 109, 113, 117, 120, 145, 147, 151, 155, 157, 191
Turnbull, A.R. 43
Turner, Nelson 41
Tyson, Mike 2, 108, 197

Uzcudun, Paulino 105

Valdes, Nino 159
Valentino, Rudolph 74
Vanderbilt, William H. 73
Vingo, Carmine 138–139, 149, 161
Vogt, Richard 130

Walcott, (Original) Joe 141
Walker, James J. 107
Warren, Earl 50
Washington, Booker T. 16
Waters, Bob 172
Watson, Jack 139
The Way It Was (television show) 144
Weill, Al 137, 139, 148, 152
Weiss, Seymour 150
Wells, Bombardier Billy 62
Welsh, Jack 48
Wepner, Chuck 197
White, Maj. Andrew 83, 87
White, Charles 25–26
Wilder, Deontay 1, 201, 202
Willard, Jess 47–49, 55–59, 65, 70, 71, 80, 91, 96, 98, 173, 195
Williams, Cleveland 174
Williams, Joe 116
Williams, Larry 75
Wolgast, Ad 21
World Boxing Association 2, 81
World Boxing Council 2
World Boxing Organization 2

Yemelyanov, Vadim 176
Young, Jimmy 197–198

www.ingramcontent.com/pod-product-compliance
Ingram Content Group UK Ltd.
Pitfield, Milton Keynes, MK11 3LW, UK
UKHW041958140426
5217IPUK00015B/856